cdy

Evalyn a.

THE GERMAN IMAGE
OF GOETHE

Oxford University Press, Amen House, London E.C.4

GLASGOW   NEW YORK   TORONTO   MELBOURNE   WELLINGTON
BOMBAY   CALCUTTA   MADRAS   KARACHI   KUALA LUMPUR
CAPE TOWN   IBADAN   NAIROBI   ACCRA

THE
GERMAN IMAGE
OF GOETHE

BY

WOLFGANG LEPPMANN

OXFORD
AT THE CLARENDON PRESS
1961

'The European poet must not only be one who holds a certain position in history: his work must continue to give delight and benefit to successive generations. . . . The history of what has been written *about* the work of such a man will be a part of the history of the European mind.'

T. S. ELIOT, *Goethe as the Sage*

PRINTED IN GREAT BRITAIN
AT THE UNIVERSITY PRESS, OXFORD
BY VIVIAN RIDLER
PRINTER TO THE UNIVERSITY

PREFATORY NOTE

No modern author on Goethe can possibly acknowledge, within the few lines traditionally reserved for that purpose, the debt he owes to his predecessors. If any of their works had to be singled out, they would be Victor Hehn's *Goethe und das Publikum* (1887), Albert Ludwig's *Schiller und die deutsche Nachwelt* (1909), Stuart Atkins's *The Testament of Werther in Poetry and Drama* (1949), Reinhold Buchwald's *Goethezeit und Gegenwart* (1949), Eduard Castle's *Goethe in den Wendepunkten zweier Jahrhunderte* (1950), and Heinz Kindermann's *Das Goethebild des XX. Jahrhunderts* (1952). Among the reference works which have been consulted, J. Zeitler's *Goethe-Handbuch* (1916–18, presently being reissued by A. Zastrau) and H. Pyritz's *Goethe-Bibliographie* (1955–   ) have proved to be invaluable. Any direct indebtedness to these and other scholars has been suitably indicated.

Goethe's works are cited from the *Gedenkausgabe der Werke, Briefe und Gespräche* (Artemis-Verlag); passages not included in that edition are from the *Sophien-* or *Weimarausgabe*.

Translations are mine unless otherwise acknowledged.

W. L.

March 1960

ACKNOWLEDGEMENTS

IN the preparation of this study, valuable technical information has been furnished by Arnold Elston (University of California), Hermann Boeschenstein (University of Toronto), and Walter Silz (Columbia University). It is a pleasure to express my gratitude to these scholars, and to my wife, who has borne the burden of proofreading with a devotion above the call of marital duty.

I am indebted to the University of Oregon and to the Modern Language Association of America for grants received while engaged in this work, and to the editors of *PMLA* and *Modern Language Quarterly* for permission to reprint, in amended form, articles which first appeared in these publications.

W. L.

CONTENTS

INTRODUCTION

GREAT literary reputations are like kaleidoscopes: their basic elements are constant, but the pattern in which they are arranged is capable of infinite variations. Vergil, honoured in the Middle Ages like no other Latin poet, has been much deflated by later generations, who were less concerned with what he had foretold about the future than with what he had written about the past. Dante was a convinced monarchist; in some periods of history he was blamed for this, and his own city had exiled him partly for that very reason. But the Italian monarchists of the nineteenth century who unified the country blessed him for it and made him their literary standard bearer. Shakespeare's bawdiness was as much taken for granted by his contemporaries as it is by us; to the Puritans it was an outrage. There is no enduring literary reputation which has not had similar ups and downs. It is the purpose of this study to trace such fluctuations in the German view of Goethe.

Why Goethe? Why the *German* view of Goethe?

The modern German has developed an uncanny sensitivity to the transitoriness of values which were once thought permanent. Perhaps this is an accident of history. Perhaps it is the result of two lost wars, of inflation and depression, destruction and partition, experienced by a people of a strongly speculative cast of mind. At any rate, one cannot quite imagine an American or English critic looking at, say, *Hamlet*, in terms like these: 'Goethe's *Faust*, read before the War [of 1914] and after, was no longer the same. What earlier had been the continuing vitality of an established tradition, was afterwards the history of a past epoch' (Fritz Klatt). Still less can one imagine Ernest Hemingway, or for that matter André Malraux, making observations like the following: 'Just looked through the Goncourts' Diaries. Strange are the changes in reader and book which this war [1939–45] brings about: I cannot help feeling that countless works of literature will be unable to cross the intellectual borders it has established. These are almost unnoticed areas of devastation. Thus do moths wreak their

damage in locked closets. . . . Boredom will reduce the number
of books much more tellingly than any censor' (Ernst Jünger).
Nor were remarks of this nature suggested only by the cata-
clysmic events of the recent past. Some sixty-five years ago the
literary historian Otto Harnack, in recalling Goethe's statement
'Classical is what I call healthy', wondered if it should not be
amended, for the literary public of the 1890's, to 'Classical is
what we call tedious'. These men have obviously wrestled with
a problem which concerns readers everywhere, but is perhaps
more acutely felt in Germany and Austria than in other
countries: what do the classics still mean to us? In regard to
Goethe, this question has been intermittently asked ever since
before his death. His fame has survived nonetheless, and the
answers which successive generations have given to that question tell us something about the nature and meaning of all
literature.

Furthermore, Goethe's fame has been subjected to more
manipulation than that of other classical authors. Great as it
is and deserves to be, it did not merely *happen*. It was also *made*:
purposely formulated and spread. On the positive side, this is
exemplified by the painstaking, selfless, and anything but
haphazard scholarly work of the German Goethe Society, of
the Vienna Goethe Club, and of similar bodies of unimpeachable integrity. On the negative side, we shall come face to
face with the managerial, the 'business' side of its survival, and
with the efforts of propagandists of various ideologies to claim
Goethe as a spiritual ancestor.

If Goethe thus seems an appropriate subject for an investigation of this kind, he at the same time transcends its boundaries
because his reputation is not limited to literature. The image
which the Germans have formed of this poet who gave his
name to a street in Teheran, to a bone in the human skull, to a
literary society in Japan, to a mineral, and for all practical
purposes to a system of government—it was he who created
the Weimar with which the Republic of 1919 claimed a kinship—cannot be drawn in terms of literary history alone. His
influence clearly has dimensions which have no counterpart
in that of other authors. It is inextricably bound up with the
development of modern Germany, and much German history
will accordingly be found in these pages.

Even without these extra dimensions, Goethe enjoys some distinct advantages, in regard to the survival of his fame and influence, over the other indisputably 'classical' authors of Western literature. He was so famous among his contemporaries that the story of his life became common knowledge to millions of them; he lived so recently that this knowledge has come down to us essentially intact; and he lived so long that he himself was able to add to it, in autobiographical writings and in commenting on what others said about him. Thus we have not one but two avenues leading to him: his works, and the story of his life, which is known to us in such detail as to let him emerge as a distinct human being even if none of the works had been preserved. In this, Goethe was more fortunate than Homer, who lived so long ago that his very existence is often denied, or Shakespeare, so obscure in life that even the authorship of part or all of 'his' works is still occasionally disputed.

It is one of the characteristics of a classical author that he forces later generations to read his works and to formulate their own attitude to them. Goethe began to do this not after death but early in life. Unlike Vergil or Dante, Cervantes or Calderón, Shakespeare or Milton, Corneille or Racine, or any other writer recognized as 'classical', Goethe had the good fortune of being so recognized in his early twenties. This enabled him to take a hand in the shaping not only of the contemporary, but of the posthumous image which his people had of him. He has made ample but discreet use of this opportunity. It is well to remember that the German image of Goethe goes back in many instances to—Goethe's image of Goethe. His statements about his own works fill nine stout volumes. No other classical author has so amply commented on his own production. And because he became a classical author so early in life, this production has been handed down to us more completely and more faithfully than has been the case with merely posthumous classics. With Goethe, the reader is, on the whole, free to examine the works without doubts as to their authenticity. In this Goethe was more fortunate than Euripides or Cervantes, whose respective claims to *Rhesus* or *La tía fingida* may never be settled.

However, Goethe was significant not only in his work. A

great poet of whom a friend could say, as Schiller did of Goethe, that he is 'even more beloved and admired as a man than he is as a writer', is not just another author whose life story we happen to know. The tenor and achievement of his life, not the biographical facts, have made Goethe not only a classical writer, but a 'classical man' as well; and again he was so recognized early in his career. With the man as with the writer, almost every expression of admiration is balanced, in the history of his reputation, by one of criticism. But once he had become known, Goethe the Personality (or 'entelechy', as he might have preferred) could no more be passed over in silence than could Goethe the Writer. Admiration as well as criticism became more intense when a second facet of his being was discovered: not only its intrinsic worth, but its extraordinary fitness for life. It is precisely this mastery of life, from the most abstract philosophical tenets to the most superficial skills of 'Lifemanship', which is most stressed by the Germans of today—as it was the part of his personality which was most condemned by certain earlier generations, who might have forgiven Goethe his literary pre-eminence if Divine Providence had not seen fit to endow him with an uncommon degree of worldly success as well. Whether Goethe's life was a happy one we do not know; he does not seem to have considered it so, at least when he looked back on it in old age. But there is no doubt that it was an outwardly successful life. In this Goethe was more fortunate than Cervantes and Shakespeare who had their brushes with the law, Ovid and Dante who died in exile, Goldsmith and Rilke who were beset by poverty, Schiller and Keats who were felled, in mid-career, by sickness. Essentially untouched, despite the occasional illness, by these and many other hazards of human existence, Goethe lived his long life as fully as ever a man did—not as serenely as was once thought, but still by any common measurement very successfully indeed. Among the world's great artists, only Horace and Rubens seem to have 'done so well'. Here again, our estimate of Goethe goes back, in many instances, to Goethe himself. No other classical author has so amply commented on his own life. Concern with one's posthumous reputation is a human trait by no means restricted to writers, but few have carried this concern as far as Goethe did as an old man, when he asked his friends to return to him the letters he had written half a century before.

Plain luck, too, favoured him in his reputation, as it had favoured him in life. Even some of the most insignificant details in his life story are of a nature which does not allow one to forget them easily. For example, any number of writers, in the long and sometimes bibulous history of literary endeavour, must have had wine cellars. But the sale of the Goethes' cellar was more than a business transaction: it is woven into the texture of world history not only because the wine belonged to the poet and his mother, but because it was bought by two merchants of whom one was connected with the philosopher Hegel, the other with Thomas Jefferson. As far as Goethe's biography is concerned, this surely is the most inconsequential of details. We can get a perfectly good idea of the man without knowing who bought his wine. Yet there is something very typical of Goethe in the frequency of such coincidences in his life, compared with the obscurity which surrounds the lives of many of his contemporaries. Mozart, too, was famous; but we do not know his grave to this day.

Thus fame came to him early, and it rested securely on the recognition of his excellence on two planes, as author and as man. To the combination of these factors, and to sheer luck, Goethe owes one final distinction which interests us here: the survival of his physical image. Of all the assets of early fame, this is the last one to bear fruit. It is an especially useful asset in our age, where even literary information is increasingly conveyed through pictures, by means of illustrated popular editions, photographic essays, motion pictures, television. Through innumerable reproductions, from toothpaste advertisements to art books, we have become positively saturated with certain faces; and in Germany, Goethe's is one of these. Once more he stands apart from the other great literary figures of the past, whose surviving portraits are, for the most part, few in number and indifferent in quality. During his long life Goethe sat for so many artists that every detail of his appearence has come down to us. It would be hard to exaggerate the importance of this for the continued vitality of his influence. In the mind of a great many readers, physical attributes and defects form a first characteristic feature distinguishing one artist from all others. The schoolboy (and it is as such that most of us first meet the classics) may not remember immediately which symphony is called the Pastoral, or whether Ajax ever did get back to Greece; but once told, he will not forget that Beethoven was deaf, and Homer supposedly blind. By the same token Goethe's appearance—especially his eyes, so 'extraordinarily dark, piercing and brilliant' (Thackeray)—has exerted an eerie fascination on later Germans. When Thomas Mann wanted to castigate Gerhart Hauptmann for letting himself be taken in by Hitler, he did not call him a Fascist. Still less did he criticize his works. He was much subtler and upbraided Hauptmann (who prided himself on his Goethe-likeness) for consenting to have an interview with Hitler, during which the *Führer* could peer right into his eyes, which were 'small and pale, really quite un-Goethean'.

A great reputation cannot be established or maintained in a vacuum. It requires a person capable of being endowed with it, and a public which bestows (or withholds) it. We are not interested here in what would have happened if Goethe had lost the manuscript of *Faust*, or whether Caruso would still have been a great singer if he had lived on a desert island with only the waves to hear him. Conjectures of this nature are entirely valid, and have long intrigued writers and artists; some two hundred years ago, Goethe's friend Wieland declared that even if no one were to read a certain work of his, he would still feel rewarded in the knowledge that the Muses had been witness to his labours. However, at bottom these conjectures are exercises in logic, not literary problems. Nor are we concerned with Goethe as he appears to us now, after 150 years of scholarly investigation. This is neither a biography nor a commentary. At the risk of proceeding 'aspectually' (C. P. Magill), only such facets of Goethe's life and work are here treated as have significantly affected, at given periods, the image which the German people have had of him. During his lifetime the scientific works, *Der westöstliche Divan* and even *Faust*, did so to only a small extent; they are no more than mentioned in the first chapter, where some lesser works are discussed which at the time elicited far greater public response. The ironical fate of *Faust*—that this work in which

Goethe so unequivocally satirized academic pedantry, should itself have become the object of some of the grossest pedantry ever perpetrated in the name of scholarship—did not become apparent until long after its publication.

It is well to point out also that this book is in no way intended to be a *definitive* or *complete* history of the German image of Goethe. Just as the whole panorama of history changes as we daily move away from the past, the figure of Goethe, too, will never be permanently fixed in our minds. Not only does the quantity of material increase every year, in discoveries which must be added to our total knowledge of Goethe; even the qualitative interpretation of discoveries made long ago changes with every generation. For the classical author is not, as much of the nineteenth century conveniently believed, a stable element in the intellectual universe. On the contrary: Goethe is classical precisely because he is so 'unstable' that he presents a different shape to every age. It is our task to record the more important of these shapes which he has assumed in the eyes of posterity, knowing full well that certain traditional ones will have to be left out, and that some new shapes may have materialized by the time these lines are read.

Seen in this light, the evolution of the German image of Goethe has two aspects: the discovery of Goethe by successive generations of the German public, and the manner in which significant sections of that public, in many cases leading individuals, have revealed themselves in their reaction to him. For the *Goethe-Erlebnis*, the discovery of Goethe, has until very recently been both a communal—one might almost say 'tribal' —event in the life of every German generation, and an experience which every literate German underwent individually. This discovery of Goethe, and the formulation of an attitude to him, is one of the few experiences which Beethoven shared with Marx, Bismarck with Freud, Nietzsche with Schweitzer.

The German *Goethe-Erlebnis* began with the poet's contemporary public, with the men and women who, from the 1770's on, first came in contact with his work and personality, commented on both, in so doing affected Goethe in his turn, and thus set up the process of give-and-take which a literary reputation essentially is. It will not end as long as German is read and spoken.

I

GOETHE AND THE PUBLIC
OF HIS TIME

B Y the end of the eighteenth century the German literary
public had ceased to be restricted to isolated social and
professional groups like universities, learned societies, and
aristocratic circles. These were the sections of eighteenth-
century society which one would imagine to have been most
intimately concerned with literary matters, as they were in
England and France. Their relative unimportance in Germany,
and their replacement by a new type of reading public, are
among the peculiarities of Goethe's historical situation.

The German universities flourished in that century, and
several new ones were established (Halle 1694, Göttingen
1737, Erlangen 1742). But they were dedicated, in the main, to
studies in the natural sciences and in moral philosophy. The
scant literary fare offered was either derivative, consisting of
translations from the classical languages and from French, or
pragmatic: exercises in German prose, correspondence, even
poetry. While German literature did not yet rate as an academic
subject (in Prussia the first chair was not established until
1848), there did exist professors of poetry and rhetoric. The most
famous of these was, of course, Johann Christoph Gottsched,
Germany's arbiter of literary taste whom Goethe visited as
a very young student in Leipzig. Gottsched's *Versuch einer
kritischen Dichtkunst für die Deutschen* (1730) marks perhaps the
deepest penetration of rationalistic method into the precincts
of literature. According to its author, writing was a skill which
could be acquired by almost anyone who took the trouble to
obey certain rules—particularly Gottsched's own, which among
other things specified that in order to write a good play one
first had to select a moral which the plot would serve to illustrate; or that in observing the three dramatic unities special
care must be taken to restrict the action to one place, because

the audience, too, remains sitting in one place during the performance. In thus reducing artistic creation to an entirely cerebral process, Gottsched dismissed as worthless much of the large and superior body of world literature based on values other than pragmatic common sense. From Homer to Klopstock, he censured all those who in their writings had allowed free rein to the imagination. There was no common ground on which men with this outlook could meet the generation of the Storm and Stress. Instead of heeding the good professor's advice about the dramatic unities, Goethe incorporated into his first play, *Götz von Berlichingen,* no less than fifty-six changes of scene.

A similar gulf separated the rising literary generation from the learned societies of the period. Some of these dated from the seventeenth century and were specifically dedicated to the purification of the German language and the raising of literary standards. They had at one time represented a first planned attempt to establish a homogeneous reading public in Germany. However, their creative phase had passed, and those that survived had become mere social clubs. Here also, new institutions arose alongside the older ones: the Royal Prussian Academy of Sciences, founded in 1700 largely at Leibnitz's instigation; the Palatinate Academy at Mannheim, endowed by Karl Theodor of Baden; the Bavarian Academy, established in 1759. Yet these organizations did little to encourage the writer, or to provide him with the nucleus of a public. Like the universities, they were onesidedly devoted to the natural sciences, and whenever possible employed—even imported—French rather than German scholars. A case in point is the Prussian Academy, whose work was entirely limited to mathematics, philosophy, and the sciences. Its president was the French mathematician Maupertuis; French, not German, replaced Latin as the language in which the academy's proceedings were read and recorded; it was only when d'Alembert turned down the job that Frederick the Great grudgingly appointed, as successor to Maupertuis, a German-speaking president (the mathematician Leonhard Euler).

One might expect that at least the various temporal and ecclesiastical courts, with the example of Augustan Rome and the Italian Renaissance before them, would show an active interest in contemporary German letters. After all, they had done so in the Middle High German period, and again, to some extent, in the Baroque. But their counterparts in the Age of Enlightenment were interested not so much in supporting German culture as they were in imitating, as far as and sometimes farther than their means would allow, the style of life exemplified by Louis XIV and his successors on the throne of France. To be sure, the majority of German princes were not as crude and thoughtless as they are represented, thinly disguised, in Lessing's *Emilia Galotti* and Schiller's *Kabale und Liebe*. Many of them, especially in the latter part of the century when the example of Frederick the Great and Maria Theresa began to be felt, became true benefactors of their people. More patriarchal and less grandiose than the kings of France, they were genuinely concerned, as enlightened sovereigns, with the welfare of their subjects. The judicial reforms which did away with trials for witchcraft, the partial abolition of serfdom, the introduction of more humane methods of education, and the advances made toward the emancipation of the Jews—these great social reforms (symbolized, in the German language area, by the names Cocceji, Karl Friedrich of Baden, Pestalozzi, and Moses Mendelssohn) are among the lasting gains of that period. Very little of this, however, directly affected the writer or his public. Despite the shining example of Anna Amalia of Weimar and her son Karl August, none of the princes included among their hobbies an interest in German literature, or even in the German language, which as late as 1783 was regularly spoken at only one court: that of Weimar.

Augustus the Strong, Elector of Saxony and one-time King of Poland, established the porcelain manufacture which has made the name of Meissen a household word throughout the world. Karl Friedrich of Baden, good physiocrat that he was, introduced from England the practice of crop rotation. Karl Eugen of Württemberg turned pedagogue and founded the Hohe Karlsschule rendered famous, or infamous, by Schiller. All these endeavours sprang from the rationalistic ideal of the perfectibility of Man, as citizen of states which were regarded not as natural organisms, but as delicately adjusted, well-lubricated machines. These activities and others like them were, in fact, adjustments and lubrications of the body politic. Their nature, at any rate, was too pragmatic, and their execution too arbitrary, to allow the authors of the time much participation in them. They were initiated not by the middle class and the intelligentsia whom they benefited, but by the princes themselves who needed a strong middle class for the economic, an articulate intelligentsia for the cultural and religious welfare of their lands. Thus the great artistic and economic achievement of Saxon porcelain manufacture is vitiated for us by the fact that the inventor of the process, Johann Friedrich Böttger, was virtually held prisoner in the old castle at Meissen—for fear that he might escape, as he previously had from Berlin, and take his skill with him to some competing court. Similarly the poet Christian Friedrich Schubart was imprisoned by the Duke of Württemberg, for a variety of minor misdemeanours, and held *incomunicado* for ten years. Having served the King of Prussia for twenty-five years and become almost blind in one eye, Leonhard Euler finally accepted an invitation to go to Moscow. Frederick dismissed him not with a pension or a knighthood, but with the laconic words 'I permit you to leave so that you may go to Russia'. Appointing the Frenchman Lagrange as Euler's successor, the King then congratulated himself on being able to replace 'a one-eyed mathematician by a two-eyed one'.

With these examples of princely ingratitude before them, many writers became wary and bitter whenever courtly patronage was extended to them. The poet and biologist Albrecht von Haller turned down an invitation to Berlin because he was 'too old to make an exhibition of himself'. Gotthold Ephraim Lessing was rejected for the post of Director of the Royal Library because he had quarrelled with the King's former favourite, Voltaire; later he observed that in enlightened Berlin freedom consisted solely of the opportunity to publish 'as many foolish attacks on religion as one might want to'. It is easy to understand why these men were bitter, and that those who did accept princely favours were often suspiciously regarded by the general public. Hence the seriousness of the accusation levelled against Goethe, from the 1770's on into the twentieth century, that in following Karl August's call to Weimar he had become a *Fürstendiener*, an abject servant of the princes.

Far from leading in the formation of a new reading public,

the German court circles actually represented one of the last elements of eighteenth-century society to be conquered by the new literature. Lessing's correspondence with the courts of Vienna and of Mannheim, Klopstock's call to Karlsruhe and Matthias Claudius's to Darmstadt, the invitations to Weimar accepted by Wieland, Goethe, and Herder: all these planned and completed moves were to some extent colonizing missions, and were often so regarded by both writers and readers. The progressive, tolerant Vienna of Joseph II especially was the object of high hopes on the part of German authors. It was with Joseph II in mind that Wieland wrote *Der goldne Spiegel oder die Könige von Scheschian*, the design of a truly humanitarian order of society, and Klopstock *Die deutsche Gelehrtenrepublik*, in which he projected a German Academy of Sciences which would unite the scholars of an otherwise divided nation. The indomitable Lessing went to Vienna in person, in connexion with a similar academy planned by the Emperor himself.

There is no doubt that Goethe's development and that of the other figures of German Classicism, and indeed the history of Germany herself, would have been very different if there had been a closer connexion between the seats of political and of cultural power in the eighteenth century—a connexion, for example, as productive as that which existed between the great princes and the leading artists of the Italian Renaissance. As it was, the two most seminal events in eighteenth-century Germany turned out to be the rise of Prussia to pre-eminence within the political system of Central Europe, and, concurrently but quite independently, the rise of German culture (language and literature, philosophy, educational theory, and music) to preeminence on the continent. In modern journalistic jargon, it was the rise of the 'two Germanies', of the twin symbols of Potsdam and Weimar.

In 1700 the Electorate of Brandenburg, whose capital Berlin was a town of some 50,000 inhabitants, consisted in the main of Brandenburg, Pomerania, and a non-contiguous portion of East Prussia. It was no more important than the Electorates of Saxony, Hanover, or Bavaria. By 1800 the population of Berlin had grown to almost 200,000, and the area of the former Electorate had doubled in size; as Kingdom of Prussia, it was now the equal of Austria, France, Russia, and England. Again, not one German author was active in 1700 whose name still lives; but by 1800 Lessing, Klopstock, Wieland, Herder, Goethe, and Schiller were famous in many lands. Yet the man chiefly responsible for the rise of Prussia, Frederick the Great, spoke and wrote French much better than German, invited Voltaire, not Klopstock or Lessing, to be his guest at Potsdam, and throughout his life admired French literature to the exclusion of all others. Instead of encouraging the German writers of his time he attacked them, in an essay written in French, whose title ends on that note of What-can-we-do-about-it? which was as dear to eighteenth-century Europe as it is to twentieth-century America: *De la littérature allemande; des défauts qu'on peut lui reprocher; quelles en sont les causes; et par quels moyens on peut les corriger* (1780). Lessing's name does not once occur in this treatise, and *Götz von Berlichingen*, the drama which had just made Goethe famous, was roundly condemned as a 'detestable imitation of those worthless English plays'.[1] It is indeed a measure of Goethe's stature that this attack did not cool his admiration for Frederick, whom he defended at the time and later eulogized in his autobiography.

The indifference of Germany's greatest eighteenth-century statesman toward her greatest poet is a symbolical expression of the fact that the classical phase of German literature developed in a political vacuum. With the exception of a few minor princes like Karl August, the powers of the day took no interest in it. At the same time there existed in Germany no feasible political alternative with which writers could identify themselves, as even foreign men of letters like Wordsworth and Schiller identified themselves with the early stages of the French Revolution. Thus it is not surprising that the authors of German Classicism have little in common with the type of *littérateur engagé* represented, in more harmonious civilizations, by the exiled Dante who placed his political enemies in Hell, by the soldier Cervantes who was prouder of having had a hand maimed in battle than of having written *Don Quijote*, or by the Shakespeare of 'This royal throne of kings, this scept'red isle...'. The only event in eighteenth-century German history which

---

[1] The reference is to Shakespeare. Like his mentor Voltaire, the King looked askance at these *mauvaises pièces*.

might have directly stimulated a nationally oriented literature, the Seven Years War, did so in only a few instances. Despite his admiration for Frederick's deeds, Goethe ended by feeling sorry for those who had to live in that 'pitiful' time, which provided a poet with so little inspiration that even Lessing, in *Minna von Barnhelm*, had 'nothing better to do than to get involved in the petty squabbles of Saxony and Prussia'.[1]

In comments such as these, and in his refusal to take up an unequivocally anti-French attitude during the Napoleonic Wars, Goethe laid himself open to the charge that he had no patriotic feelings. This charge was made by men—we shall meet them, in almost every generation since 1800—who forgot that the Storm and Stress period of the 1770's was, in a very real way, a frustrated German Revolution. It was channelled from the political into the literary field because that was the only one in which a spirited young German could express his protest against the disunited, impotent, apathetic, and convention-ridden society in which Werther foundered.

Thus the universities, learned societies, and ruling circles on the whole remained aloof from all but the most pragmatic contemporary German literature. Instead of being made up of scholars and noblemen, the reading public became increasingly identified with the middle classes.[2] More specifically, the literary public had become a society within Society, a group whose members were drawn to one another, across the lines which separated men by age, profession, and faith, precisely by the fact that they read the works of a particular author. Ever since the beginning of the century, literary magazines had begun to spread all over the country, and it was in large measure due to them that the women of Germany now developed an interest in contemporary writing. The great eighteenth-century hobby of establishing collections had benefited public and

---

[1] J. P. Eckermann, *Gespräche mit Goethe in den letzten Jahren seines Lebens* (hereafter cited as Eckermann), entry for 7 Feb. 1827.

[2] An example of this is furnished by the subscription list for the Göschen edition of Goethe's Works (1786–90), which shows a marked preponderance of the literate middle class: civil servants, teachers, writers, merchants, clergy (in that order), over the few princes and landowning nobles who pledged themselves to purchase the set. See M. Sommerfeld, *Goethe in Umwelt und Folgezeit* (Leiden, 1935), pp. 261–2.

private libraries as well as museums. The lending library was well on the way to becoming a familiar institution. Specific literary 'fan clubs' were being organized, like the Hainbund which formed around Klopstock and published its own *Musenalmanach*. Similar in structure and aims were the numerous Friendship Leagues of that sentimental period; Goethe's earliest extant letter, of 1764, is a plea for admission to one of these informal groups. Led by the firms of Cotta and Breitkopf, the publishing industry also grew rapidly. By its very nature it was a nationwide enterprise which transcended the bounds of princely mercantilism and embraced the entire German language area. Many attempts were also undertaken to set up a German National Theatre; one of the better known of these was the Hamburg experiment, in connexion with which Lessing wrote his *Hamburgische Dramaturgie*.

All these developments by way of broadening the literary public took place within the urban middle class, whose rise to power characterizes the social history of the eighteenth century. In Germany this group formed the financial and cultural mainstay of several flourishing cities. Unlike France, England, and Spain, the country was to lack, for another century, a political and intellectual metropolis to whose public an author could address himself, and which, once conquered as Shakespeare conquered the London stage and Molière that of Paris, would assure him of national fame and recognition. Germany, divided in this as in other respects, had several such cultural centres, each of which contributed its own characteristic feature to the great panorama of Enlightenment (as other cities were to do in the Romantic period, and indeed throughout the nineteenth century). With this in mind we can understand that when authors of nation-wide appeal finally did come forth in Goethe and his contemporaries, their reception varied greatly according to the pattern of cultural geography. Of particular interest to us are the newspapers and reviews in these cities, because it was in publications of this nature that the German reader first came across the name of Goethe.

One such centre was Hamburg, hardly touched by the devastations of the Thirty Years War and already Germany's foremost seaport, politically independent, ruled by a prosperous, level-headed merchant aristocracy; stoutly Protestant, and open, by virtue of its trade and geographical position, to influences from England. It was through Hamburg that the English periodical of the type of the *Tatler* and *Spectator* found its way into Germany. *Der Vernünftler*, founded in 1713 and soon followed by the weekly *Der Patriot*, was the first such publication of lasting effect: a critical journal devoted, by means of short, skilfully written personal essays, satires, news reports, book and theatre reviews, to the moral and aesthetic refinement of the upper *bourgeoisie* and of their ladies. The city boasted poets of its own, like B. H. Brockes and F. von Hagedorn, both highly regarded in their time. It also welcomed within its walls other illustrious men of letters like Leibnitz, Lessing, and above all Klopstock, who died in Hamburg in 1803. He had been Germany's most celebrated poet around the middle of the century. One of the great forerunners of Classicism, and the creator of a whole new German language in point of religious and lyric emotion, he had outlived himself and in old age turned bitter toward Goethe and Schiller. Equally hostile to Goethe was another local luminary, the redoubtable Pastor J. M. Goeze of St. Catherine's, a Lutheran of orthodox bent with whom Lessing tangled in a famous literary feud. As a thriving commercial centre, the city had many influential newspapers. Despite its formidable title, the *Staats- und gelehrte Zeitung des Hamburgischen unparteiischen Correspondenten* was Europe's most widely read paper at the beginning of the nineteenth century, with a circulation of 30,000. From the pages of this and other Hamburg journals, Goeze for many years hurled impassioned diatribes against Goethe.

Scarcely less important than Hamburg was Leipzig, already the centre of the German book trade, and the home of Gottsched, who despite his pedestrian theories did much to improve the taste of a reading and theatre-going public which was soon to be Goethe's. By translating many French classical dramas he enabled the people of Leipzig, which at the time had Germany's best stage, to acquire a more sophisticated notion of what a performance could offer. Until then, much of the theatrical fare had consisted of clownish farces; with his friend Caroline Neuber, Gottsched now abolished the bewigged Catos and high-heeled Lucretias of the contemporary stage, and insisted on classical garb for plays dealing with Greek and Roman subjects. He also greatly influenced a whole generation of critics, whose modes of thought and expression showed traces of Gottschedism for many years to come. As late as 1774 Goethe was credited with having 'constructed with much industry' a play.[1]

Several Leipzig poets collaborated on an influential review called, after its place of publication, *Bremer Beiträge*. This journal was not limited to upholding the tenets of middle-class morality, but free to publish works of no pragmatic application, such as the first three cantos of Klopstock's *Messias* (1748). The most famous among its contributors was the fabulist C. F. Gellert; like Gottsched, he was a professor of poetry, a writer, and a teacher of Goethe's at the University of Leipzig. He thus symbolized, with Gottsched, C. H. Schmidt, and others, an institution characteristic of German Rationalism: that of the Poet as Teacher. It was based on the belief that the writing of poetry can be learned (and, therefore, taught), and on the necessity of combining a paying profession with the economically uncertain literary work. It was, furthermore, an expression of the great value which that century attached to critical perspicuity as well as to genuine creativeness, even in a man like Lessing—no teacher, to be sure—who was amply gifted with both. The tradition of the author as *grand seigneur*, exemplified in modern Germany by men like Richard Wagner and Thomas Mann, had practically died out with the passing of the Baroque. Its revival at this time is not the least of the many achievements which must be credited to Goethe.

Leipzig's significance as fountain-head of French influence was by no means restricted to the arts. The city was, in all the shadings of the term, the 'Gay Paree' of the time, where both Lessing and Goethe acquired the social graces. Less worldly but just as important a centre was Zürich, where two Swiss patricians, J. J. Bodmer and J. J. Breitinger, had meanwhile begun to sing the praises of English (as against French) literature, in a review called *Discourse der Malern*. Bodmer, who had

---

[1] *Berlinische privilegirte Zeitung*, 14 Apr. 1774. Cited in J. W. Braun, *Goethe im Urtheile seiner Zeitgenossen* (Berlin, 1883–5, 3 vols.), i. 31. For the purpose of this study, the above anthology of Goethe criticism (hereafter cited as Braun) has been cross-checked with H. Blumenthal's *Zeitgenössische Rezensionen und Urteile über Goethe's 'Götz' und 'Werther'* (Berlin, 1935).

translated Milton's *Paradise Lost* and Pope's *Dunciad*, emphasized the value of the irrational and imaginative elements in poetry as forcibly as Gottsched had stressed the pragmatic and rational dimension. He also wrote dramas in imitation of Shakespeare, whose introduction to Germany suddenly gathered momentum around the middle of the century. It may be said that in 1740 Shakespeare's works in their true form were virtually unknown to the German public, while by 1775 they were admired by a substantial portion of that public as the greatest dramatic achievements of all time.

Berlin's intellectual growth during the eighteenth century did not keep pace with its great rise in political importance. Here, as elsewhere in Germany, the factors which favoured the one tended to retard the other. Nonetheless the city had an active theatre life, and it became, in due course, the scene of Goethe's 'world première': the performance of *Götz von Berlichingen* on 14 April 1774 (with a gipsy ballet added as a concession to local taste). The Prussian capital's best newspaper was the *Berlinische privilegirte Zeitung*, among whose early contributors had been Lessing. (It later became the *Vossische Zeitung*, which survived until 1934. During much of its long history it was the most respected German language daily in the world.) In the latter part of the eighteenth century, the paper closely mirrored the views of F. Nicolai, a book dealer and journalist who founded the *Allgemeine deutsche Bibliothek*, the fountain-head of a somewhat insipid brand of late Rationalism. Nicolai much resembled Gottsched, in his reformist zeal no less than in the stubbornness with which he defended opinions which were steadily becoming outmoded. It was in Berlin that Goethe found some of his most violent detractors among the Rationalists of the late eighteenth, and some of his most ardent admirers among the Romanticists of the early nineteenth century.

Aside from these main centres, several other cities had a large literary public which was kept informed by responsible editors and critics: Halle, the home of German Pietism and of a vigorous, newly founded university, the first to permit the use of German, rather than Latin or French, for lecturing; Goethe's own Frankfurt, with its *Frankfurter gelehrte Anzeigen* where the poet appeared in print as an author of reviews; Weimar, where Wieland, tutor to the princes Karl August and Konstantin, had launched *Der teutsche Merkur*; and several court cities with lively theatres, like Vienna, Karlsruhe, and Mannheim.

This, then, was the nature of the German literary public at the time of Goethe's youth. It was no longer recruited from isolated segments of the population, but embraced much of the middle class. It was an educated public, in the sense that it was familiar, in the original and through many translations, in print and on the stage, with the Greek and Roman classics and with the great literature of seventeenth- and eighteenth-century France. Lately it had also been introduced to Shakespeare, a process which had been formalized, as it were, in Wieland's translation during the 1760's, and in Lessing's, Herder's, and young Goethe's critical essays which came out in the period 1759 to 1773. It was an articulate public which had come to rely for its literary information on a number of reviews among whose contributors figured not only journalists and professors, but first-rate authors like Lessing, Wieland, Claudius —and eventually, Goethe and Schiller. A whole new form of prose writing, the essay, had been imported into Germany. The imitative phase of German literature was at an end, and the language itself, a contemptuously regarded dialect as late as 1730, had been refined and enriched until it had become a tool as forceful, pliable, and expressive as French or English. With the works of Klopstock, Wieland, Lessing, and Herder, German letters had regained, after two centuries, a quality and stature of their own. The stage was set for Goethe.

When Herder had read the *Geschichte Gottfriedens von Berlichingen mit der eisernen Hand. Dramatisirt,* he returned it to the author with the comment 'Shakespeare has spoilt you altogether!' Goethe took his mentor's criticism to heart, toned down and partly eliminated the most violent scenes, and in June 1773 published, anonymously, a somewhat more conservative version of the same play, with the title *Götz von Berlichingen.* It was for all practical purposes Goethe's first work to reach the public: the dramatized story of a one-armed robber knight who succeeds for a time in defending his independence against the central government, succumbs in the end through the treachery of a trusted friend, and dies brokenhearted as the quasi-innocent remnant of a bygone historical

epoch. Written in forceful prose, the play also offers a kaleido-
scopic view of German life in the time of Luther.

It was, in a way, unfortunate for Goethe that his first major
work should have been a dramatic one. More than any other
literary genre, the drama had become ossified with laws and
conventions reaching back to Aristotle. It did not take the
critics long to point out that Goethe had broken them all: 'The
unities of time, place, and action, indeed all dramatic rules
have here been set aside. If an author disregards that much, the
reader is entitled to be compensated by a great work. We doubt
that every reader will consider himself sufficiently compensated...'[1] Other early reviewers were more charitable, or,
perhaps, franker: 'The title "drama" frightened us at first
because it seemed to portend one of those dull, hybrid creations
[i.e. a run-of-the-mill contemporary drama]. We saw on the
very first pages that matters were going to proceed quite
wildly in this play. But we forgot our Aristotle and enjoyed
ourselves greatly.'[2]

From 'forgetting one's Aristotle' it is but one step to the
suspicion that the traditional dramatic rules were, perhaps,
inadequate after all; or at least that they did not apply to this
author, who seemed a law unto himself. Thus the first comment
on *Götz* in Wieland's *Der teutsche Merkur* stated that in regard
to this work,

> our critical Linnés [the Swedish biologist Linnaeus had just pub-
> lished his classification of fauna and flora] will be flabbergasted. They
> will wonder into which category it should be put, this play in which
> all three unities are mistreated in the cruellest fashion, a play that is
> neither comedy nor tragedy—and yet the most interesting monstro-
> sity, against which we would cheerfully exchange a hundred of our
> lachrymose comedies. . . . The author deserves profound gratitude on
> the part of all German patriots, who have long wished not that our
> poets would imitate the Greek drama as such, but that they would
> select their subjects as the Greeks selected theirs, and then develop
> them in the way the Greeks would have done.[3]

According to this reviewer, all the play's little defects dissolve
before the power of the dramatic dialogue and the author's
ability, which he shares with Shakespeare, to carry the reader

[1] Braun, i. 4.   [2] Ibid. 5.   [3] Ibid. 7–9.

along into 'violent sweeping emotions' by means of even the smallest, most insignificant details.

The reference to the Greeks and to Shakespeare was not accidental. Like any other beginning author, Goethe was at first judged comparatively: by the way he measured up not only against the poets of his time, those long forgotten creators of *comédies larmoyantes*, but against others who were already considered classical. The remarkable feature about the reception of *Götz* lies in the critics' unanimity in placing the young author— 'who is supposed to be Herr D. Göthe in Frankfurt am Main'— immediately at the side of Sophocles, Shakespeare, and Lessing (whose *Emilia Galotti* had appeared the year before). No less an authority than Wieland wrote that with *Götz*, Goethe showed that he could be another Shakespeare; and from the translator of Shakespeare's dramas, this was high praise indeed. Even where the comparison was ludicrous, as in the frequently advanced suggestion that Goethe should try to write in Lessing's manner, it rarely failed to be complimentary for the young author. The public's conviction that a literary titan had suddenly arisen in their midst was so widespread that no one believed that this play could be performed on the primitive stage of the time. Even after the première had been favourably reviewed in the *Berlinische privilegirte Zeitung*, Wieland still insisted that the author 'surely intended this play to be *read*'. With this in mind, and remembering Germany's long dependence on literary importations from abroad, one can understand Schubart's pride on hearing that 'our Goethe's masterpiece, *Götz von Berlichingen*, has been translated into English and will soon be performed in London. A German play in London, where Shakespeare first presented his tremendous creations! Who would have imagined it?'

Nothing in literary history is quite as indicative of a book's impact as is the reissue of a similar, older work in which the same topic is treated. Thus the historical knight's autobiography, after which Goethe had fashioned the outline and sequence of his plot, was reprinted in 1775, after collecting dust since its first publication in 1731. (After Goethe's next play, the much weaker *Clavigo*, Beaumarchais's *Mémoires* were also reissued in a new German edition.) The critical evaluation of *Götz*, at any rate, continued for many years. It gained in validity as it turned from discussing details (such as the absurd question, hotly debated for a time, as to which of the hero's hands had been of iron: the right, as in the play, or the left, as in the auto-biography?) to problems of greater import. The praise bestowed on the work still strikes a responsive chord in the modern reader. There is no doubt that the release of the dramatic vessel from the barnacles of aesthetic theory with which it had become encrusted, and its launching on the open seas of national history rather than the calm waters of boudoir intrigue, was a remarkable feat which resulted in a permanent gain for German literature. Less obvious to us, but feasible within the context of the times, was the critics' evaluation of the various characters in the play. Adelheid and Weislingen were instantly recognized as familiar types: the *femme fatale* and the *chevalier à la mode*. Götz himself, to be sure, was appreciated as a fine, upstanding German citizen; but his estate was felt to be too lowly—a mere knight on a stage hitherto occupied by the kings, queens, and princes of the French drama—and his language was considered to be lamentably crude.[1] A similar idiosyncracy of the period caused Maria to be praised above Elizabeth. Götz's wife is merely faithful and capable, but his sister's fate epitomized a predicament dear to eighteenth-century literature: that of the young lady of family who is gifted with a sensitive soul and yet has to make her way in an unfeeling world.

What must surely be the ultimate accolade for any historical dramatist came to Goethe in 1777, when a member of a family long famous in German history, a Baron von Riedesel, offered a prize of 20 ducats to any writer who would glorify that family in a play, as Goethe had immortalized the Berlichingens. The prize was to be awarded at the Leipzig Fair of 1778, and no less a man than Lessing was to be the judge. As far as is known, the offer found no takers.

If *Götz von Berlichingen* rendered Goethe famous in Germany, *Die Leiden des jungen Werthers* made him a European celebrity at the age of twenty-five. The publication of this novel in late 1774 marks the high point of Goethe's fame during his lifetime.

---

[1] A. Nollau has pointed out that the main objection on this account was not to the hero's famous challenge which has set generations of German schoolboys a-giggling, but to the Captain's epithet *Scheißkerle*, an inconceivable expression in the mouth of a powdered, perfumed, and beribboned eighteenth-century officer (*Das literarische Publikum des jungen Goethe* [Berlin, 1935], p. 45).

The history of this book, one of the great success stories of all literature, is so well known even today that we can, perhaps, limit ourselves here to a survey of only the most striking manifestations of the *Werther* craze. The work was reprinted many times, in legitimate and pirated editions; it was parodied, imitated, discussed in books and reviews, in all European countries throughout the remainder of the century. The clothes which Werther wore and in which he committed suicide—yellow vest and trousers, blue dress-coat, brown boots —swept the continent in a sartorial revolution to gladden a haberdasher's heart. There was, supposedly, a sharp increase in suicides committed out of unrequited love, or love otherwise incapable of fulfilment; at any rate, many suicides thus motivated were blamed on the author of *Werther*. The theological faculty of Leipzig University banned the book's sale, and the city fathers of Copenhagen its printing, because of its allegedly enervating effect on the young. Goethe himself tells us that the Bishop of Milan had his clergy buy up all bookstore copies in order to protect the lay public from this poison. The novel was translated into French 1775, into English 1779, and before long into all other civilized tongues; the French word *werthérisme* to this day denotes 'morbid sentimentality'.

The reasons for *Werther's* popularity are not difficult to find. The public, already familiar with Richardson's *Pamela* and Rousseau's *La Nouvelle Héloïse*, was here offered a contemporary German story of similar scope, written in a passionate language which bears all the marks of the author's own emotional involvement in his work, in epistolary form like its famous predecessors (although Goethe presented only one side of the correspondence, Werther's letters). It was a book in which sensitivity as an overriding personality trait, and a hopeless love affair as its characteristic expression, were portrayed as powerful and valuable far above the canons of calm reason. Out of the emotional starvation and the social and aesthetic straitjacket of their daily lives, men and women by the thousands fled into Werther's world of solitude and mystic communion with Nature. Escaping from the rationalistic thought system where the will was free, passion evil, and conflict impossible between the individual and his environment, they embraced Werther's unbridled passion and the thesis that

Man can be condemned to a strident disharmony between himself and the world at large. It was Napoleon who reproached Goethe for having added to his account of Werther's unhappy love for Lotte, the story of the social discomfitures which the hero suffers, as a commoner, in the aristocratic circles in which he moves in the novel's second part. But Napoleon was wrong in considering the book only a love story. Its impact on the contemporary reader was heightened precisely because it combines the appeal of a superbly written love story with the analysis of a quite specific sociological case history: that of a man for whom the fashionable prejudices of the time loom as tragic obstacles which cannot be overcome. Eighteenth-century Society was a very powerful entity; to belong to it meant much more than belonging to a particular social group means in our time. Conversely, exclusion from this entity was 'almost tantamount to suicide'.[1]

Unlike the public, whose applause was almost unanimous, the critics found themselves sharply divided on the merits of this book. One group praised it to the skies while a somewhat smaller one, made up of men with much literary prestige of their own, rejected it on grounds which have lost their cogency for us but were quite comprehensible at the time. Like many of their generation, Goethe's friends J. J. W. Heinse, J. G. Jacobi, C. F. D. Schubart, and others praised *Werther* not so much for its artistry as because it seemed to vindicate their own flamboyantly sentimental tastes. At any rate, when a cleverly done imitation came along in the shape of J. M. Miller's *Siegwart* (1777), this exceedingly tearful novel, too, was enthusiastically received, although it quite lacked *Werther*'s literary distinction. Typical of the reaction of these men, and altogether of what has been called 'lyrical' *Werther* criticism, are Schubart's words: 'Here I sit, with my heart melted away . . . with eyes that shed tears of delight, to tell you, dear reader, that I have—read? No, devoured!—*Die Leiden des jungen Werthers* by my dear Goethe. I am supposed to criticize, am I? . . . I'd rather be eternally poor, subsisting on roots and water, than not be able to sympathize with an author of such sensitivity'.[2]

Against effusions of this sort must be set the hostility of a man

---

[1] L. L. Schücking, *Die Soziologie der literarischen Geschmacksbildung* (2nd ed., Leipzig, 1931), p. 45.   [2] Braun, i. 64.

of Lessing's calibre, whom F. Jacobi quoted as saying that if Goethe 'ever comes to his senses, he will be no more than any ordinary person'. As a dramatist who never wrote a novel, Lessing perhaps resented the success of *Götz* more than that of *Werther*: with one drama Goethe had swept away the edifice of rules, and the pre-eminence in theatre writing, which the older man had spent a lifetime in creating. But it was the novel which made Lessing's cup of bitterness run over. He considered writing a drama *Werther der Bessere*, and in 1776 ostentatiously edited and published the philosophical essays of that K. W. Jerusalem whose suicide over an unhappy love affair had, as everyone knew, provided Goethe with the idea of letting his hero die in the same manner. In the preface to this edition Lessing went to great lengths to show that Jerusalem had been a calm and sensible young fellow, and that Goethe had been grossly unfair in 'borrowing' the circumstances of his death for the end of his own hotheaded hero.

Some of Lessing's dislike of *Werther* no doubt goes back to his resentment of the brash young man who had so effortlessly pushed him from his pedestal as Germany's leading dramatist. Nor were matters helped by the fact that he was told, when he had begun working on his *Faust*, that Goethe, too, was interested in that subject. Yet other and deeper causes existed as well. There is in *Werther* something so alien to the spirit of Rationalism that the work must have struck Lessing as a regrettable relapse into practices which he had done his best to eradicate, not to mention the element which was relatively new at the time, that of autobiographical catharsis: the author is plainly involved in the story he tells, and 'cleansed' by telling it. And even if one granted that the book contained much that was praiseworthy, had Goethe not taken liberties which in the works of lesser hands might become licences? Lessing felt exasperated by the Storm and Stress movement as a whole, and history has vindicated his judgement to some extent: with the exception of Goethe, Schiller, and, to a lesser degree, Lenz, none of its representatives has left works of sufficient stature to warrant the violence with which they had attacked the old literary order. There is much truth in F. Gundolf's observation that the others 'stormed and stressed because they wanted to, because it appealed to them', but that Goethe 'did so because he had to;

it did not appeal to him at all, he suffered from that in which his imitators cheerfully "splashed around"'—er litt unter dem worin seine Nachahmer vergnügt puddelten.[1] Be that as it may, the others who criticized *Werther* did not do so because it happened to be a love story. They, too, had written and continued to write stories and poems in which ardent shepherds pursued, in Arcadian groves, chaste and elusive nymphs. But in their daily lives they were steadfast citizens who did not dream of coveting other men's lady friends, as Goethe was known to have done in Wetzlar and Ehrenbreitstein, where he had 'lived' what later became the first part of his novel. Still less could they imagine shooting themselves over such unseemly trifles. To be sure, not all Rationalists were as prosaic as Gottsched had been; but even to Lessing and the Berlin group, literature continued in some measure to be a skill to be acquired, not the spontaneous human utterance as which Werther's spiritual godfathers, Hamann and Herder, had just defined it. Furthermore, most rationalistic writing was didactic. It incorporated if not always a clear message, then at least a 'moral' of some sort. But *Werther* bore no message and presented no moral, unless it was that suicide is the only way out of a hopeless situation. Goethe's apparent indifference to the moral and social problem of suicide was especially repugnant to some members of the clergy, among them Pastor Goeze, who thundered: 'Eternal God! who would have imagined, twenty years ago, that we would live to see the times when . . . there would be published, and praised in the newspapers, glorifications of suicide!'[2] His colleague J. R. Piderit called Goethe a murderer, and in a circular presented to the clergy of Hessen-Kassel asked: 'Show me the young man who can read such a disgraceful book without retaining in his soul a malignant abscess which will surely burst when the time comes! Is there no censorship to prevent the publication of such devil's bait?'[3]

It is with relief that one finds, in the emotionally charged reception accorded this novel by friend and foe alike, at least one critic, F. Nicolai, who refrained from name-calling and sat down instead to write a good parody, *Die Freuden des jungen Werthers*. Here the fatal pistol is loaded with chicken blood, and

---

[1] F. Gundolf, *Goethe* (13th ed., Berlin, 1930), p. 107.
[2] Braun, i. 103.   [3] Ibid. 89–90.

after pulling the trigger Werther is found spattered but unhurt. Of course he goes on to live to a ripe old age, by the side of his Lotte who presents him with a number of little Werthers. What was probably the most balanced contemporary review came from the pen of Goethe's friend J. H. Merck. Aware that many readers were asking themselves to what extent the poet had described actually existing conditions and living people, Merck admitted that many local and personal references had no doubt found their way into the novel. But he made a virtue out of what had been considered a defect, by holding *Werther* up as a warning to those who would write about persons and conditions not personally familiar to them. For how can anyone, he asked, convincingly describe heroes, knights, and fairies, whom surely no living man ever saw in the flesh, if he lacks eyes with which to see the poetry inherent in so many scenes of everyday life, as Goethe saw and rendered them in his novel? Merck, of course, knew Goethe well. He could therefore say that the author 'had probably endowed his hero partially with his own gifts'.[1]

One result of Goethe's sudden fame was the visits and invitations he now received from prominent men in many walks of life. The Swiss poet and phrenologist J. K. Lavater, the pedagogue J. B. Basedow, the publisher H. C. Boie of the *Göttinger Musenalmanach*, the great Klopstock himself stopped at the Goethe house in Frankfurt in order to see the new celebrity and to let themselves be captivated by his charm and by the works from which he read to them. Among these visitors was K. L. von Knebel, who had stopped over in Frankfurt with the young princes of Weimar, Karl August and Konstantin, whom he was about to chaperone on a trip to Paris. He suggested that Goethe might want to pay a courtesy call on the princes, who had heard much about him and wanted to meet the author of *Werther* in person. A few days later, in December 1774, Goethe made the fateful visit which eventually resulted in his lifelong friendship with Karl August, and his permanent residence in Weimar.

Goethe's move to Weimar in late 1775 thus was a direct outcome of the fame he had acquired with his first play and his first novel. But immense as this reputation was—at twenty-six he

[1] Braun, i. 213.

was acknowledged to be the greatest writer in the German language—it went by no means unchallenged. Added to the discomfiture which *Werther* had provoked in many a reader's mind was the general disapproval with which the drama *Clavigo* was greeted in 1774. Merck's harsh comment, that Goethe should not write any more 'nonsense'—Quark—like that because others could do this sort of thing just as well, is unjustified; perhaps it was suggested by the fact that the unpleasant figure of Carlos in the drama resembles no one as much as Merck himself. None the less the cool reception accorded this play is understandable enough. In *Götz* and *Werther* Goethe had just given expression to the deepest yearnings of the generation of the Storm and Stress. The new work represented not only a renunciation of the emotionalism of that period, but, even stylistically, a return to the more traditional theatre. *Clavigo* is a clearly outlined tragedy devoid of the picturesque, quasi-Romantic background, the secondary figures, and the local colour in which the author had gloried when he wrote *Götz*. Thanks in part to this economy of action and diction, *Clavigo* has remained to this day Goethe's most effective stage drama. But the public mood was not one of calm evaluation, and we have seen that in any event, the contemporary drama was as likely to be read as performed. Furthermore, the subject matter was foreign, and of all things, French—just after Lessing had broken the French theatre's domination of the German stage, and shared with Goethe in substituting for it, with *Minna von Barnhelm* and *Götz von Berlichingen*, a type of play solidly based on German history, customs, and modes of thought. Now the same Goethe, instead of writing another German drama, had taken Beaumarchais's *Fragment de mon voyage en l'Espagne*, and fashioned out of that pamphlet a tragedy which was part imitation, part invention, but in no way a 'German' work.

Nor did Goethe's reputation gain in wholesomeness by the publication of *Stella* (1776). The play's hero, Fernando, is an attractive but weak man who cannot decide whether to return to his wife, whom he deserted some years ago and now meets again by accident, or to remain with Stella, to whose arms he has just come back from the wars. The first version ended with a *ménage à trois*: Fernando was going to live with both women, in an enviable arrangement rendered improbable only by the fact that both ladies accept it. In the second version of 1805 Goethe, himself a husband and father by then, had Stella take poison and the hero, or scoundrel, shoot himself. The play's central problem is, of course, an old one in life and literature; it was treated in the medieval legend of the Count von Gleichen and in Lessing's *Miss Sara Sampson*; in real life the same situation is known to have tormented Jonathan Swift and Goethe's friend F. Jacobi. But this august literary ancestry did not endear *Stella* to the public, and the cathartic ending by way of double suicide was added thirty years too late. Coming hard upon the heels of *Werther*, this play shocked the public even more than the novel had done—for was this not a clear invitation to bigamy, an undermining of the sacred bond of matrimony, coming from the pen which had just glorified suicide? Such, at least, was the opinion of the critic Wittenberg, who mocked, in the earliest extant review of *Stella*, that Goethe,

that fertile mother, so often gives birth that her children do not have time to gain strength and sinews, but drag themselves around, with emaciated bodies which are nonetheless distended with flatulence and evil odours, before they disappear again from view. His *Götz von Berlichingen* had that fate, and his *Stella* is not likely to fare better. His novel, *Die Leiden des jungen Werther*, is a school for suicide; his *Stella*, a school for seduction and polygamy. A virtuous school, indeed![1]

These outspoken, if indelicate, remarks had no sooner been made than Pastor Goeze joined in the fray: 'In [Goethe's] moral code, that which the law calls malicious desertion and which Holy Writ condemns as fornication and adultery, presumably forms part of "Man's noble freedom". . . .'[2] But there were dissenting voices none the less. One critic of more valour than discretion went to some trouble to show that *Stella* was really Goethe's masterpiece, only to be set upon by Wittenberg, who insisted that the play was highly immoral, and for good measure called Goethe's hapless admirer a 'miserable peddler' and 'penny-pinching haberdasher'. Deadly insults, no doubt, in the commercial world of Hamburg, where this particular altercation took place! (Along with Berlin, Halle, and Leipzig, Hamburg

---

[1] Braun, i. 228–9.   [2] Ibid. 241.

had continued to be a citadel of Rationalism while the rest of
Germany was already fermenting with the yeast of the Storm
and Stress. Most of the leaders of that movement, among them
Goethe and Schiller, came from Central and South Germany.
Goethe's reputation began in the south-west and only slowly
spread to the north, where the traditional literature was more
firmly entrenched.)

For a variety of reasons which lie outside the scope of this
study, Goethe's introduction to England and the United States
was retarded for decades by the moral objections which had
been raised to his early works. One of these was *Stella*; a full
twenty-five years after its publication, a London reviewer had
this to say of an English performance of the play: 'This work is
very popular in Germany, a fact from which we may draw our
own conclusions as to the lax moral principles prevailing in that
country.' It is interesting to note a German journalist's reaction
to this comment, because it offers an indication of Goethe's
popular appeal around the year 1800. '*Stella*', this writer replied
to the report from London, 'cannot possibly have an adverse
effect on our morals, because this play, far from being popular,
has long been forgotten in Germany'.[1] By far the most urbane
comment on the work was that made by J. G. Pfranger, court
preacher at Meiningen in Saxony. Declaring that he had heard
so much about Goethe's sterling character that he simply could
not believe that the poet had meant the play to end on a note
of Sin Unrepentant, this gentleman proceeded to write a
sixth act, printed and paginated to look like a legitimate supplement to the drama, in which Fernando is imprisoned for his
misdeeds.

After Goethe's arrival in Weimar, the furore created by his
early works gradually died down. He published very little
during the next decade, and thus if nothing else, at least added
no fuel to the flames of controversy. The public's attention soon
shifted to the works of newer writers. Miller's *Siegwart* to some
extent replaced *Werther* as the epitome of the sentimental novel,
while Schiller, with *Die Räuber* and other early plays, carried on
the Storm and Stress at a time when Goethe had already lost
interest in it. The latter continued to write, of course, even after

[1] Ibid. iii. 8.

he had become a privy councillor, and eventually a minister, of the Duchy of Weimar. It is customary to consider Goethe's first decade in Weimar as a lean period in point of literary productivity, but the record does not altogether bear this out. The first part of *Wilhelm Meister* (i.e. the *Lehrjahre* in the original version, which was only discovered in 1910), the first two acts of *Torquato Tasso* (then still in prose), the first (prose) version of *Iphigenie*, a part of what later came to be called the *Urfaust*, the first version of *Egmont*, the *Elpenor* fragment, and many of the great lyric poems were created in that decade. However, at the time most of these works were known only to Goethe's intimates. Lavater, Herder, Merck, Jacobi, Barbara Schulthess, and other old friends given, or allowed to make for themselves, copies of one or several of them. They also freely circulated at the court of Weimar, where *Iphigenie* was performed as early as 1779. The public at large, however, knew little of these works, beyond the occasional rumour that Goethe was occupied with them. In their eyes he had for all practical purposes ceased to be a productive author. It is only natural under these circumstances that the 'press coverage' given Goethe in these years should show an abrupt drop in extent and intensity. If mentioned at all, he was treated as a celebrity. In terms of modern journalism it might be said that while news of him was formerly restricted to the Literary Supplement, he had now secured a foothold on the Social Page as well. This is borne out by a number of reports like the following: 'Goethe has just been named Privy Councillor in Weimar', or 'The Privy Councillor Goethe has been knighted', or, most indicative of all in the days before the pictorial section, 'Goethe's picture, engraved by Chodowiecki, is now for sale in Berlin.'[1]

A few days after making Goethe's acquaintance in Weimar, Wieland wrote that his soul was 'as full of Goethe as a dewdrop is full of the morning sun'—although this was the same young man who a few months before had satirized Wieland's somewhat saccharine concept of Greek mythology, in the farce *Götter, Helden und Wieland*. This example of the effect of Goethe's personality (in this case, on an older man who might well have

---

[1] Braun, iii, 288, 400, and 295, respectively.

been hostile and envious) could be multiplied many times. This is not the place to assess Goethe's relationship with Frau von Stein, the Duke Karl August, the Dowager Duchess Anna Amalia, or any other members of the social and intellectual *élite* of Weimar. Suffice it to say that the ups and downs of Goethe's literary reputation with the general public in no way affected the recognition, by a great majority of those who came in contact with him, that his personal qualities were quite as outstanding as his literary and administrative talents. His reputation as author had procured for him an invitation to pay a visit to Weimar; his human qualities caused the invitation to be made permanent.

In the eyes of some observers, the very fact of his instantaneous and unquestioned acceptance into Weimar put Goethe under a certain obligation. For example, it was known that the Duke, who had become a reigning prince when only eighteen, sowed more than his share of wild oats during the first few years of his rule. It was also common knowledge that he did much of his drinking, wenching, hunting, and practical joking in the company, and even with the encouragement, of Goethe, who, at twenty-six, was young enough himself. But Goethe was the older of the two, and a public figure in his own right, to whom thousands of young people looked up in veneration. As such, some thought, he should have endeavoured to restrain the impulsive prince, through the voice of reason and experience, instead of spurring him on to new excesses. It was Klopstock who took it upon himself to express these grievances, in the famous 'Friendly Letter' which he addressed to Goethe in early 1776. It was full of dire forebodings for the State of Sachsen-Weimar if the Duke were allowed to continue to lead a dissolute life. Goethe, who had lightly dismissed earlier warnings of this nature, reacted strongly to this letter, which came, after all, from one of Germany's foremost authors, of whom he had thought as a friend. 'Leave us alone with such letters in the future, my dear Klopstock', he replied, 'they do no good except to spoil one's mood for a couple of hours.' Before long, of course, the Storm and Stress period drew to a close, and this type of complaint died down. The Duke became older and more mature; in the end he turned out to be a model prince. Goethe outgrew the court favourite and developed into a statesman, and as such acquitted himself well in a variety of government positions.

Mention has already been made of the gulf which separated the rulers of eighteenth-century Germany from her authors. Now that one of the youngest and most promising of these rulers had called the country's greatest author to his court, hopes were aroused in many hearts that Goethe would 'promote' German literature at the court of Weimar, or at any others with which he might come in contact. It was known that Karl August took a lively interest in literary matters—his mother Anna Amalia and his tutor Wieland had seen to that—and many now expected Goethe to concentrate his energies on keeping alive this interest in his patron, and if possible, to make of the Duke a sort of latter-day Lorenzo de' Medici: a ruler whose prime historical significance lies in his support of the arts. This is, of course, precisely the light in which Karl August appears to us now. But contemporaries only saw that Goethe, who had just extolled freedom from social restraints in *Götz*, *Werther*, and *Stella*, suddenly put on the straightjacket of an administrative position at court. They had hoped that the prince would become like the poet, and saw to their dismay that the poet was daily becoming more like the prince. They did not know, and perhaps could not have known, that Goethe needed and welcomed the experience of occupying a responsible official position, and that this experience would eventually benefit even his poetic production. Nor did they realize that if he were to exert a lasting influence on the Duke, he would first have to gain not only the latter's friendship, but, more importantly especially in the case of a commoner, his respect. He had to show that he, Wolfgang Goethe, was a dependable, experienced man of affairs as well as a famous poet, a charming storyteller, and a good hunting companion. Again it was Klopstock who in his 'Friendly Letter' expressed the fear that in adopting the Duke's wild life, Goethe was jeopardizing the unique opportunity he had of bridging the gap between the intelligentsia and the ruling classes of Germany. 'The Germans have rightly complained', he wrote, 'that their princes will have nothing to do with their intellectuals. Now they make an honourable exception for the Duke of Weimar. But think of all the arguments with which you provide the other princes [for their continued indifference to the arts] if you persist in your present mode of life.' As we saw, Goethe did not long persist.

An accusation often levelled against Goethe in his later years was that he was cold-hearted, stiff, and indifferent to all but his own comfort. It began to be expressed after his return from Italy. By then he was determined to withdraw from most of his administrative duties and to devote himself entirely to his work in literature and in the natural sciences. The journey to Italy had cured him of much of the introspectiveness which had tortured him in earlier years, and not only enabled, but driven him to write a book like *Werther*. It had also obviated much of his former need to communicate his impressions to friends. It had shown him his limitations, for example in painting, in which he had dabbled for years without marked success, and the extent to which he had 'dried up' and turned ascetic in the last years at Weimar, when he worked on the bloodless schemes of the original *Iphigenie* and *Tasso*. From the Italian journey of 1786–8 dates the period of his classicism, which the general public and even most of Goethe's friends were only able to understand much later. For the time being, they only saw in him a man whose style of writing and whose whole manner of being had suddenly changed. He had withdrawn into himself, withdrawn from many former friends with whom he had now little left in common. Although he had largely given up his official duties, there continued to cling to him, to the end of his life, the formal, unbending manner of a senior civil servant. Even an intimate like Frau von Stein complained of his aloofness when he returned to Weimar, although in her case the disappointment was compounded by personal reasons.

Goethe's reputation has never altogether lost the dimension of reserve which it gained in those years. Henceforth he was, to a small but vociferous minority, a ceremonious ex-minister whose face had hardened into a mask and whose heart beat only for himself. When G. A. Bürger, the author of the famous ballad *Lenore* and a friend of Goethe's from the days of their youth, visited Weimar in 1789, he was so shocked by his cool reception that he wrote: 'I could not even get a glimpse of the artist behind the wooden minister.' Three years later Friedrich Schlegel wrote his brother August Wilhelm that '. . . *Werther,*

Götz, Faust, Iphigenie, and some lyrics represented the beginnings of a great poet; but a courtier has developed out of it all'. And when Heine visited Goethe in 1824, he, too, commented that he had recognized, in many traits, 'that Goethe to whom the beautification and preservation of his own existence . . . is of overriding importance'. Few of the contemporaries realized that Goethe's formal manner was, to a large extent, a protective device designed to keep away the many curious idlers who merely wanted to lay eyes on or shake hands with the Great Man. Those who divined this, and persevered in their quest for the man and poet without being discouraged by the reserved exterior, later came away charmed by the warmth and kindness with which they had been received. Schiller and Grillparzer had that experience, along with countless lesser men.

An author's relationship with his public is not one-sided but reciprocal. Except in very rare cases, he does not throw off his creations without caring whether they are read, or by whom. Before tracing Goethe's reputation during the last four decades of his life—very briefly, since most of the elements which went into the kaleidoscope of his particular image had been determined long before his death—a few words are in order about the poet's own attitude towards his public, during various stages of his career. Turning for a moment from the German image of Goethe to Goethe's image of the German public, we find that he took a sympathetic readership for granted when he wrote his earliest works, the anacreontic *Annette*-cycle of 1767 and the *Neue Lieder* of 1769. The rococo poet, member of as closely-knit a social group as ever there was, knew no feeling of distance between himself and the reader (and for that reason among others, liked to publish his work anonymously). The Storm and Stress, on the other hand, was a programmatic movement whose exponents wrote for their friends, for those who felt and 'emoted' as they did, and for the general public, as long as it was willing to let itself go and to judge the writer by his own standards rather than by those of rationalistic common sense. The Storm and Stress author addressed himself both to the mighty and exalted, the *Genies* and *Kerle* for whom he felt admiration, and to the lowly and afflicted with whom he felt kinship, to 'the beloved reader, whom I call "brother" from the bottom of my heart'.

The classical Goethe wrote for a select few. His ideal reader was the cultured man-of-the-world. He wanted to write nothing that 'men who lead . . . great and busy lives should and would not want to read'.[1] He no longer intended to sweep the reader along and to take him outside of himself, but to deepen and refine the sentiments of men and women who knew themselves and their limitations. In this vein, he asked in an epigram:

Was belohnet den Meister? Der zart antwortende Nachklang,
Und der reine Reflex aus der begegnenden Brust.

Such readers, however, were not always easy to find, and if Goethe did not exactly organize, he certainly took a hand in encouraging the formation of a public of this nature. His long and fruitful interest in the University of Jena, and altogether in higher education in the Duchy of Sachsen-Weimar, was no doubt partly motivated by such considerations, as were his varied activities on behalf of the Weimar court theatre, including the compilation of a set of rules for actors which he drew up and used in his theatre school. It is evident also that Goethe's own editorial activities, with Schiller on *Die Horen*, alone on *Die Propyläen*, and with Meyer on *Kunst und Altertum*, must be seen in this light.

The final stage in Goethe's attitude to the public was marked by the realization that only posterity would be able to judge and appreciate his works. Thus *Die Wahlverwandtschaften* was sent 'as a circular to my friends, so that they may remember me here and there', without any great expectation that a wider public would take to the novel. At the end of his life, the man who in his youth had swept the German public off its feet was forced to admit that as a whole, 'my works can never be popular. Anyone who thinks so, or works to that end, is mistaken. They have been written not for the masses, but only for individuals who are looking for similar things and walking along similar paths.'[2] As he began to see himself as a living historical phenomenon, Goethe believed that the *effect* of his works was their most important feature. The discovery that his books seemed to evoke no response from the younger generations was undoubtedly one of the bitterest disappointments of his life.

---

[1] Letter to Karl August, 17 Nov. 1787.   [2] Eckermann, 11 Oct. 1828.

A characteristic phase in Goethe's disenchantment with the public was his activity as theatre director and critic. This work is by definition selective and discriminatory; often it cannot fail to be controversial. Thus it is not surprising that the disenchantment should in part have been mutual, and that a whole complex of half-truths and rumours about the manner in which Goethe directed the Weimar theatre should have begun to circulate almost as soon as he had taken up the position. For example, A. von Kotzebue, a contemporary dramatist whose plays were performed much more often than Goethe's own, insisted that Goethe had a special seat built for himself, in the centre of the theatre pit, where he sat during performances and raised his arms whenever he wanted the public to applaud. One hesitates to think of Goethe in this Moses-like posture; however, the contemporary public's attitude might well have challenged a lesser man's autocratic tendencies. It was unfortunate for Goethe's reputation at the time that the most publicized incident of this nature should have taken place over a work which is, in truth, a very weak one. In 1802, Friedrich Schlegel's tragedy *Alarcos* was performed in Weimar, under Goethe's direction and in the author's presence. At the account of the King's death, the audience broke out in laughter:

> Entsetzt zu sterben, ist er so gestorben,
> Hat wütend sich in Angst den Tod erworben.[1]

It seems that at this point Goethe jumped up from his command post near the ramp, turned to face the audience, and with flaming eyes shouted 'Stop laughing!'—whereupon the audience did in fact fall silent, and the performance was resumed. In most contemporary reviews Goethe was severely taken to task for not letting people laugh at such nonsense. F. Schlegel's merits were great, but they were not those of a dramatist.

There is no point in exaggerating the importance of this incident, or of similar ones of the kind; nor should we deduce from this that Goethe was habitually a self-opinionated arbiter of taste. Goethe's action surely reflected no more than the proverbial theatre manager's temper, and his irritation with a public which had so very coolly received his own later works, and

---

[1] 'From fear of death the king expired, | In fury he thus death acquired', spoken by Ricardo near the play's end.

those of his friends such as the Schlegels. This frustration also explains his unusual action in regard to B. R. Abeken's review of *Die Wahlverwandtschaften*, one of the few favourable contemporary comments on this novel which is one of Goethe's finest works. To make certain that it would find a wide circulation, Goethe paid out of his own pocket to have the review reprinted and further distributed.

In retrospect, it may seem odd that Goethe's greatest failure as theatre manager should have aroused practically no comment at the time: his lack of artistic understanding, and even of human sympathy, for H. von Kleist. Like Beethoven, whom Goethe merely esteemed as a pianist and respected as a devoted artist, Kleist was one of the few among his contemporaries who were simply beyond Goethe's comprehension. Through his friend Adam Müller, Kleist had sent Goethe his *Amphytrion* and *Der zerbrochene Krug*, and somewhat later the tragedy *Penthesilea*, with a letter which is one of the most touching human documents in the German language, written, as the almost unknown young author put it, 'on the knees of my heart'. Goethe replied, coolly and condescendingly, that it always pained him to see gifted young dramatists write for a stage which was yet to come: *Hic Rhodus, hic salta!*

If Kleist had lived to see the second part of *Faust*, and to follow its stage history, he might have smiled at such *naïveté*. As it was, he reacted differently from Schiller, who had pursued Goethe even after having at first been rebuffed. Kleist was hurt, and his disappointment turned to hatred after *Der zerbrochene Krug* was performed in Weimar, in March 1808. Like the great Greek comedies, Kleist's work, too, was designed to be performed in one uninterrupted sequence. It is a delightfully earthy comedy, perhaps the best in German literature, and must be spoken and acted as such. Goethe, however, had so clumsily divided it into three acts that the curtain rose, and dialogue resumed, in precisely the same scene on which it had been lowered before the intermission. The effect must have been that of a motion picture stopped in order to splice the film. Furthermore, the style of delivery on which Goethe had insisted was the somewhat high-flown, impersonal one in which he himself had instructed the cast of the court theatre. It was appropriate enough for classical tragedy, but out of place in this realistic comedy. Kleist never forgave Goethe this wilful mutilation which resulted in a dismal flop on the stage; he wrote some cutting epigrams against him, and eventually went along his lonely way until his suicide in 1811.

Goethe's dislike of Kleist has been variously explained: as an outcome of Goethe's realization that his own personal and artistic discipline had been too laboriously gained to be now jeopardized on behalf of a faceless stranger; as actuated by a desire to 'test' Kleist (as Schiller and so many others had been tested) rather than to encourage him by immediate approval; as evidence of the uncanny prophylactic instinct which put Goethe on his guard against nervous, morbid, self-destructive personalities like Kleist, Lenz, or Beethoven. At any rate, one cannot but regret that the man who spared neither time nor effort to help dramatists like the Schlegels or Z. Werner, should not have seen that Kleist was a writer of quite a different order of magnitude. Yet it must also be remembered that Goethe was close to sixty when he first read Kleist, and that the latter is a very unusual author: immoderate and disharmonious, brutal in the concentrated power of his style, and uncompromising in the way in which he invests his characters with an emotional intensity which drives them to their doom; neither a Classicist nor a Romanticist, but a writer who must be read on his own terms or not at all. He has brought about a revolution in German letters, especially in the *Novelle*, much as Beethoven did in music. The contemporary of Lessing and Mozart can perhaps be excused for failing to do justice to men who even in our days are still being 'discovered', as Kleist currently is by the Existentialists.[1]

Goethe's age is frequently mentioned in connexion with another characteristic attitude of his which has deeply influenced the German people's image of him: his rejection of the political trends which dominated the second half of his lifetime. From the outbreak of the French Revolution to his death in 1832, Goethe found himself out of step with

---

[1] Although he was no Simon-pure Existentialist, Hofmannsthal expressed a commonly held view when he had his fictional Balzac ask, in the essay *Über Charaktere im Roman und im Drama*, 'Yes, who killed the soul of Heinrich von Kleist, who was it? Oh, I see him, the wizard of Weimar . . .'.

the social and political developments of the time. Unlike many of his fellow Germans, he detested the Revolution from its very beginning; and unlike an even greater proportion of his compatriots, he admired Napoleon to the very end. Goethe was a man of the eighteenth century, forty years old when the Bastille was stormed, to whom the French Revolution, that first modern mass movement, was not only reprehensible but incomprehensible. He was a realist in political matters, a man who had had much practical administrative experience of his own, and well knew that no programme is as neatly carried out as it might have been conceived. But although a realist, he was no Rationalist: he never subscribed to the notion that the conduct of human affairs can or should be based on the results of cerebral processes only. Goethe was a firm believer in organic evolution rather than in violent interference from without, in politics as in all other spheres of human endeavour. Far from being a reactionary, he realized earlier than most that the social structure of pre-revolutionary France had been subjected to intolerable stresses. Nor did he waver in his conviction that the corruption of the court at Versailles was primarily responsible for the train of events which began in 1789. Above all, he knew that the Revolution meant a turning point in the history of mankind, at a time when that realization was not at all common, and men were still dying so that it would *not* become a turning point. But from his middle twenties on, Goethe was a conservative in matters political. The attempts occasionally undertaken to claim him as spiritual ancestor of modern forms of social organization—whether made on behalf of Bismarck's *Reich* as by Herman Grimm, of Western Democracy as by Thomas Mann, of Nazi Germany as by Kurt Hildebrandt, or of the Marxist State as by Georg von Lukács—are ingenious but unconvincing. They are based on evidence (much of it in the form of aphorisms, of which Goethe gave forth many conflicting ones) which is contradicted by the great majority of his statements on politics, and all but nullified by his own actions in the political arena.

As a poet Goethe tried to cope with the Revolution in a number of works. They are among the weakest we have from his pen. From the list of his dramas, one would gladly see stricken *Der Gross-Kophta, Der Bürgergeneral, Die Aufgeregten,* and the fragmentary *Das Mädchen von Oberkirch*. Among the prose writings, the *Unterhaltungen deutscher Ausgewanderten, Die Kampagne in Frankreich*, and *Die Belagerung von Mainz* are equally unconvincing. Of all the works which to some degree deal with the Revolution and its effect on Germany, only the dramatic fragment *Die natürliche Tochter*, and the epics *Hermann und Dorothea* and *Reineke Fuchs* seem truly worthy of Goethe. His inability to do justice to the greatest historical event of his time springs from the fact that instead of looking it squarely in the eye, in the manner, for example, of Edmund Burke, Goethe contented himself with satirizing some of its more ludicrous and superficial expressions, especially among the Revolution's German exponents. These included some close personal friends, like the musician J. F. Reichardt and the scientist J. G. Forster.

To Goethe, the French Revolution and its consequences represented primarily a regrettable interference with Germany's cultural development, to which he himself had contributed so much. (At the same time, a word of caution is in order: he saw the Revolution as a contemporary, and it is idle to condemn his attitude from the vantage point of our time. Many years have to pass before the *causes* of such a world-shaking event can be neatly separated from its *symptoms*. Are we to blame Goethe for assigning the affair of the Diamond Necklace to the former category?) His attitude was unusual, and made him unpopular, not merely because he rejected the Revolution. A great number of other eminent men eventually came to regret their early enthusiasm. Klopstock, Wieland, and the historian Johannes von Müller in Germany, Wordsworth, Coleridge, and Southey in England, Alfieri and Pindemonte in Italy had all begun by welcoming the Revolution, and ended by condemning it. So had Schiller, the honorary *citoyen* of the French Republic. But Goethe courted the dislike of many by his premature hostility, his rejection out of hand. In the same way he later incurred the ire of many patriots not by his admiration for Napoleon, but by persisting in his approval of the Emperor long after the rest of his countrymen had begun to see in him their oppressor.

Napoleon granted Goethe an interview in October 1808, in Erfurt, and flattered him by a reference to *Werther*, which he had supposedly read seven times and even taken along to Egypt in

1799.[1] On dismissing his guest (according to some sources, on first receiving him), the Emperor is said to have cast an appreciative look at the poet and to have exclaimed to his retinue '*Voilà un homme!*'—'There's a man for you!'; a myth, perhaps, but an indicative one for the power of Goethe's personality. He invited the author to Paris and gave him the 'Legion of Honour'. And when he stopped in Weimar in 1813, alone, far ahead of the decimated *Grande Armée*, in order to change horses on his rapid return to Paris, he did not forget to inquire about the health of 'M. de Goethe'.

Napoleon, like many French rulers before him and since, was a past master at the art of cultural propaganda. Yet Goethe was not the man to be won over by flattery. He admired Napoleon not because the latter had read *Werther*, but because he had tamed the hated Revolution and because he symbolized, in his person as much as in his manifold and often constructive activities, the 'demonic' element in Man which had always fascinated Goethe. At the same time, there is little doubt that the Emperor's exquisite courtesy towards German men of letters (Wieland and Johannes von Müller had been similarly honoured during Napoleon's stay at Erfurt) added to the respect in which Goethe held him. It contrasted too sharply with the indifference shown by the German princes—especially, only a few years earlier, by Frederick the Great. If that ruler had chosen to ignore German authors and to surround himself with Frenchmen, how could a German writer remain indifferent to this French sovereign who bade fair to become a protector of German letters? Here again, one must guard against reading the future into the past. The admiration for Napoleon, so baffling to Anglo-Saxons, which men of the stature of Goethe, Hegel, Beethoven, Manzoni, and others exhibited at some time or the other in their lives must be judged not from the viewpoint of nineteenth-century Liberalism or twentieth-century Democracy, but from that of the eighteenth-century Absolutism under which these men had been raised. The far-sighted, rather

---

[1] One of the most impressive indications of Goethe's stature is the fact that great men have often selected works of his when they were faced, or imagined themselves to be faced, with the prospect of lengthy solitude: Napoleon (*Werther*), Lenin in his Siberian exile (*Faust*), and Bismarck (who disliked much of Goethe but admitted that 'with 7 or 8 of the 40 volumes, I should gladly spend some time on a deserted island').

tolerant, and tremendously intelligent Emperor surely had little in common with the petty local tyrant of Bourbon, Hapsburg, Papal, or lesser derivation.

When the German states finally rose up against Napoleon, under the leadership of Austria and Prussia and in alliance with Russia, England, and Sweden, Goethe stood aside and did nothing to encourage his fellow countrymen. His attitude is epitomized in the famous words 'Go ahead and rattle your chains! This man [Napoleon] is too big for you.' Instead of exhorting his people to throw off the foreign yoke, he busied himself with his studies, especially those of Persian poetry which later resulted in *Der westöstliche Divan* (1819). His refusal to take sides was the more resented as it strongly contrasted with the actions taken by many other German writers. Eichendorff, de la Motte-Fouqué, Körner, and many others took up arms; Arndt fought Napoleon as a propagandist, Jacob Grimm as a diplomat; two years before the uprising, Kleist had shot himself largely out of despondency over Prussia's servitude to the French. Goethe, however, asked Karl August, himself a general in the Prussian Army, to release his son August from the volunteer corps which the young man had joined when it had been formed in Weimar. Knowing that Goethe needed a secretary, the Duke immediately granted the request. But the general public was disgusted at this show of what seemed rank nepotism.

The dead Schiller, not the living Goethe, was Germany's poetic voice in the Wars of Liberation. He had extolled freedom and patriotism in his poems, in his historical writings, and above all in the dramas which he had written between 1781 and his death in 1805. From the moment of their first publication, these works—*Die Räuber, Don Carlos, Wallenstein, Maria Stuart, Die Jungfrau von Orleans*, and *Wilhelm Tell*, to name only the most famous—had in any case been much more popular than Goethe's beautiful, but abstract and theatrically rather ineffective dramas of the same period: *Egmont, Iphigenie, Torquato Tasso*, and even the so-called *Fragment* of what eventually became *Faust*. Schiller's dramas, unlike those of the classical Goethe, described mighty deeds performed by great historical personages, and the aspirations of noble individuals and entire peoples for freedom and personal dignity. One of these works, *Wilhelm Tell*, has meanwhile become a universal symbol for the poetic rendition of these strivings. It remains to this day the national drama of Switzerland, and it is a measure of Schiller's gift for creating poetry which inspires (rather than pleasing, enlightening, or uplifting the reader, as so much of Goethe's does), that he could write this work without ever having set foot in the country where it takes place.

Thus Schiller's popularity with the broad masses had early surpassed Goethe's, even in the years when the two men worked side by side in the most complete harmony (1794–1805). When Schiller died, a nation-wide collection was taken up for his widow and children, and the universal sense of loss found expression in an incredible number of memorial poems, among them Goethe's *Epilog zu Schillers Glocke*. In the period 1805–13 when Germany was occupied by the French, Schiller's *Jungfrau* was far and away the most popular of all German dramas written in the classical manner, whether by Lessing, Goethe, or Schiller himself, because it celebrated the virtues of patriotism above all else.[1] We know, better than his contemporaries could have known, that Goethe was no less a 'good German' than Schiller; he has given more to German literature than anyone else before or since, and in his undemonstrative way he was a patriot in his political thinking as well. However, he had written nothing comparable to Schiller's dramas and poems when it came to exhorting young men to take up arms in defence of liberty. Nor, it might be added, had he much gift for doing so. When he complied with a request by the famous actor Iffland to write a play commemorating the King of Prussia's return to liberated Berlin, the resulting work, *Das Erwachen des Epimenides*, was top-heavy with allegory, and no more convincing than the anti-revolutionary plays had been.

Looking ahead for a moment, we might add that the patriotic spirit which engulfed Germany in the years 1813–15 turned out to be short-lived. With the Congress of Vienna, the European system of states returned, at least outwardly, to a fair approximation of what it had been before 1789. To be sure, the flames of nationalism continued to burn on the periphery of the European community, in Greece, in Poland, in the Spanish colonies; but they did not sweep over the main European nations until the second half of the century, when the vast

[1] See A. Ludwig, *Schiller und die deutsche Nachwelt* (Berlin, 1909), p. 44.

national hatreds and ambitions began to be accumulated which finally exploded in 1914. Along with the memory of the Napoleonic Wars, the memory of Goethe's ambivalent reaction to them receded with the passing of time. The full fury of nationalistic resentment did not materially affect the German image of Goethe until the decades following the July Revolution. Similarly delayed was the reaction of the liberal-democratic element to Goethe's disdain of the French Revolution and to his strong identification with Metternich's policies after 1815. The disapproval of many Roman Catholics of what they considered to have been Goethe's pagan outlook on life, also increased in acerbity when the German Catholics became a distinct intellectual and political power in the country. There existed nationalistic, liberal, and Catholic factions in the Germany of 1815; in the period's literary life, they can be said to be represented, respectively, by Arndt, Varnhagen von Ense, and Görres. However, it was only after Goethe's death that these groups became so articulate that their views formed an integral part of the poet's reputation. To most of his contemporaries, Goethe's relative political intransigence and religious indifference were, at bottom, an annoyance, a flaw in an otherwise overwhelming personality. In the eyes of German nationalists, Liberals, and Roman Catholics of the later nineteenth century—which brought in its wake another revolution, another Napoleon, and the *Kulturkampf*—the flaw had become a fatal defect which effectively shut Goethe off from many.

In embryonic form, these attitudes are found foreshadowed in the Romanticists' view of Goethe. The elements, both positive and negative, which they added to the German image of Goethe represent the last major contribution made to it during the poet's lifetime. So mercurial were the temperaments and opinions of these men that with some, Goethe ran the whole gamut of human emotions, from veneration to detestation, within a few years. When the early Romanticists—F. and A. W. von Schlegel, L. Tieck, F. von Hardenberg (Novalis), W. von Wackenroder, and the philosopher F. W. von Schelling—first became acquainted with Goethe, they declared him to be the greatest poet of the age. And for good reason. They themselves proclaimed the supremacy of the imagination in art as in life;

insisted that the subconscious (as expressed in dreams, super-
stitions, legends) was as fit a poetic topic as were less subjective
products of the mind; considered Nature a mysterious force
which deeply affects human life; believed in the moral and intellectual emancipation of woman; and found the German past
a deeply poetic, and much more congenial, era than the present.
Furthermore, most of them had begun their literary careers as
students and admirers of Greek art, literature, philosophy. In
all of this they found themselves at one with Goethe. Was not
Werther a Romantic, Werther who reacted like a barometer to
every phenomenon of Nature, whose imagination had fought so
valiantly against the harsh realities of life? And Götz von
Berlichingen and the Faust of the *Fragment*, each, in his way, a
symbol of the German past and of the revolt against mere
reason? And Fernando in *Stella*, with his 'emancipated' marriage? And Tasso, blown hither and yon by the excesses of his
imagination? And above all Wilhelm Meister, for ever seeking,
for ever listening to the voices within rather than to the advice
from without, described in a novel which was, like those which
the Romanticists themselves would write, interspersed with
lyrics, leisurely drifting towards an ill-defined destination? And
was not the creator of all these figures one of them, this Goethe
who scorned, as they did, both the Rationalists of Nicolai's ilk
and the superficial realism of a man like Kotzebue, Goethe who
had just written *Iphigenie*, this truly Greek work, a worthy sister
to Euripides's own heroine?

It was Caroline Michaelis, married first to A. W. Schlegel and
later to Schelling, who 'discovered' Goethe for this group of
early Romanticists. She guided the Schlegels to him, largely
through her enthusiasm for *Iphigenie*, which at the time of
publication (1787) had otherwise met with little enough understanding. In a series of reviews which he wrote of Goethe's works,
August Wilhelm was one of the few contemporary critics who
praised *Tasso*, and realized that in the *Fragment* of 1790 Goethe
had immeasurably enriched the *Faust* theme and created a work
without peer in the German language. Some years later other
reviews of his appeared in Schiller's *Die Horen*, including the
masterly essay on *Wilhelm Meister*, as well as one of the best
interpretations ever given of *Hermann und Dorothea*. From 1798
to 1800 the brothers joined forces in publishing *Das Athenäum* in

Berlin, an influential journal which accorded to Goethe some of the most extravagant praise ever heaped on a German author. Along with Dante and Shakespeare, he was called 'one of the great trinity of modern [i.e. post Graeco-Roman] poetry'; *Wilhelm Meister*, although one-sidedly seen as the story of a man whose life is dedicated to the pursuit of art, was solemnly designated as one of the greatest events of time, as important for the future as the French Revolution and Fichte's philosophy; *Hermann und Dorothea* was no less effusively praised.[1]

Somewhat later Friedrich reviewed the Cotta edition of Goethe's Works for another Romanticist journal, the *Heidelbergische Jahrbücher der Literatur*. He was among the first to realize that Goethe was not only a great dramatist and novelist, but also Germany's foremost lyric poet. (Previously, the lyrics had often been looked at individually, as they happened to have been published, and compared, in Rationalist fashion, with other treatments of the same topic.) Goethe, on his part, was no less favourably impressed with the two brothers. In his correspondence he had at first nothing but good to say of them; as we have seen, he had Friedrich's *Alarcos* performed at Weimar. August Wilhelm's tragedy *Ion* was also performed in the court theatre, and when it leaked out that a Weimar newspaper was going to review it unfavourably, Goethe did not hesitate to use his influence to prevent the publication of the review. He profited by August Wilhelm's advice in metrical matters and admired his translations of Calderón and Shakespeare: it was in the Schlegel translation that *Julius Caesar* was played in Weimer in 1803.

The only disturbing element in this relationship, which was often parodied at the time, by Kotzebue and others, as a mutual admiration society, was the divergence of opinions in regard to Schiller. He was then Goethe's closest collaborator; in spite, or perhaps because of this, the Romanticists soon detested him to a man. In their eyes Schiller was too often rhetorical rather than poetic, besides being devoid of irony and of a deeper feeling for Nature. Furthermore, his oft-reiterated belief that the will

---

[1] The central position which the Romanticists assigned to *Wilhelm Meister* and to *Die Wahlverwandtschaften* in their praise as well as condemnation of Goethe springs from their belief that the novel is one of the highest of all art forms, and the literary genre best suited to the needs of modern man. Hence, also, A. W. Schlegel's derivation of the term *romantisch* from the German *Roman*—novel.

rather than the unfettered play of imagination rules human
affairs, showed him to be in bondage to Kant's abstract, altogether anti-Romanticist system of ethics and aesthetics. The
dislike was cordially reciprocated: Schiller considered Goethe's
fondness for the Schlegels a 'disease',[1] and liked to refer to his
arch-enemy Caroline as 'Lady Beelzebub'. Schiller, of course,
wrote primarily for the theatre; the Romanticists' indifference
to the demands of the stage infuriated him quite as much as did
the apparent lack of moral principles in their work and conduct
of life. We are used to having differences of literary and critical
opinion discussed by poets and professors, in genteel, little-read
journals; it is, accordingly, not easy for us to visualize the
vehemence with which this battle between the Romanticists
and Schiller exploded. It was vicious infighting, a public spectacle before thousands of partisan readers of the various newspapers and magazines in which these protagonists aired their
views. Even the mild Schelling took part in this campaign: in
Die Philosophie der Kunst, the bible of Romanticist aesthetics,
Schiller is not even mentioned, although he was the greatest
living dramatist at the time, and known as such to all and sundry.
In the period of his greatest popularity with the great mass of the
German people, the Romanticists were fond of insinuating that
without Goethe, Schiller would not have amounted to anything.

However, it was not long before Goethe, too, was subjected
to attacks of this sort, made this time not by people like Goeze
who had no legitimate voice in literary matters, but by men and
women whose taste and judgement he had esteemed highly. The
break with the Schlegels came when they began to turn away
from Classicism and to emphasize more and more the subjective
facets of literature. Friedrich, especially, began to sing the praises
of medieval art, above all, painting, because it incorporated a
religious and even a patriotic dimension which was lacking in the
more objective art of the ancients and the classicists. This was,
of course, totally at variance with Goethe's views, as expressed in
Die Propyläen and elsewhere. Altogether the brothers' Roman
Catholic tendencies annoyed him because they were an expression not only of emotional needs but of aesthetic preferences.
The Schlegels, on their part, objected to the pagan attitude

[1] Letter to Körner, 5 July 1802.

which they detected in some of Goethe's works, and to his continued adherence to classical art, which he had just reiterated in the essay *Winckelmann und sein Jahrhundert* (1805). By the 1820's the relationship had turned to outright hostility, expressed less in public attacks on Goethe than in cutting remarks about him in the brothers' correspondence and writings.

The Schlegels' story is representative of the other early Romanticists as well. Wackenroder died before the change in his attitude had found much reflection in his work. Novalis had begun by calling Goethe, in a fragment in *Das Athenäum*, 'the true present-day representative of the poetic spirit on earth'. But only a year later he wrote to Tieck: 'Much as I have learned, and still do learn, from [*Wilhelm*] *Meister*, the book as a whole is, at bottom, odious . . . it is a *Candide* against poetry.' Tieck himself never let it come to an open break with Goethe, as whose successor he was regarded by some of the more esoteric of the contemporary critics. Only much later, when Goethe was long dead and Tieck himself an old man, did he give vent to his contempt of the man he had once venerated, and who in retrospect appeared to him 'capricious, stiff and wooden, subject to moods and conceits . . . privy councillorish'. Like most Romanticists, Tieck drew a sharp dividing line between the impulsive, 'crypto-Romanticist' Goethe before the Italian journey, and the Classicist poet against whom the above comment was directed. Aside from a few individuals on the periphery of this group, like Rahel Varnhagen von Ense or the philosopher H. Steffens, it was Schelling alone among the early Romanticists who did not end by turning against Goethe. Schelling's belief in the unity and continuity of organic and inorganic natural phenomena had struck a responsive chord in Goethe because it seemed to complement his own scientific work. Goethe was generous in acknowledging this, and had been instrumental in calling the philosopher to the University of Jena. (In line with the belated recognition which this phase of his production has received, Goethe's standing as a scientist will be taken up at a later stage in this study. Suffice it to say for the present that the German estimate of Goethe has undergone no greater change than in regard to his scientific achievements, which were once in large measure denied and seen in the light of an ill-chosen pastime. Nor does any other aspect of his work show a similar discrepancy between the poet's own evaluation of his achievement, and the very meagre recognition granted it by his age. The following remarks, from a contemporary review of Goethe's *Beiträge zur Optik*, are entirely typical:

> The author, whose *Versuch, die Metamorphose der Pflanzen zu erklären* has already shown the public that he can successfully walk paths other than those by which he formerly entered the temple of immortality, is here seen taking a different road again. This is the more unexpected as . . . optics happens to be a science so different from the occupations hitherto known to have engaged the great poet; a science in which even a sharp mind is of no avail, unless it is equipped with a sound knowledge of higher mathematics.[1])

Unlike the early Romanticists, who formed a fairly homogeneous group and as such began by admiring Goethe and ended by disliking him, the later Romanticists were individuals each of whom went his own way, in regard to Goethe as in most other respects. With the exception of Kleist (if, indeed, he belongs to this group at all), their feelings towards him did not blow hot and cold as had those of the earlier generation. Some, like Z. Werner and Bettina von Arnim, flattered and to some extent used him; others, like Achim von Arnim and the brothers Grimm, respected Goethe without letting themselves be much influenced by him; others again, like E. T. A. Hoffmann and J. von Eichendorff, had only superficial contacts with their great contemporary, and were altogether able to 'take him or leave him'. On the whole, the attitude of these men was one of familiarity; not disrespectful, but just a trifle condescending. It is nicely expressed in a letter by Wilhelm Grimm: ' "That is very nice", says Goethe, when he cannot think of anything else to say.'[2]

One of the great achievements of the later Romanticists was the discovery of the German past not only poetically (their predecessors had already done that) but scientifically: through the collection of folk songs and fairy tales and by means of philological studies. The most famous of the collections of lyric poetry, Arnim and Brentano's *Des Knaben Wunderhorn,* bore a dedication to 'His Excellency, the Privy Councillor von Goethe' (1808). It

---

[1] Braun, ii. 111–18.
[2] Cited as characteristic by Schüddekopf and Walzel, *Goethe und die Romantik* (Weimar, 1898, 2 vols.), ii. xv.

was fitting that it should do so, because Goethe whole-heartedly approved of such endeavours to compile and examine these literary relics of the German past. The Grimm brothers' collection of fairy tales, as well as Jacob's studies in the history and structure of the German language, also commanded his full support, as did Wilhelm and Jacob themselves, as trusted young friends. But Goethe would not have been the man he was if he had been content to sit back and bestow praise from on high. He made these interests his own and spent much time and thought in examining for himself the values to be found in the German past. Through his friend Sulpice Boisserée, a Cologne business man and art collector, Goethe even regained some interest, lost since his Storm and Stress days, in Gothic architecture and painting. Similar influences led him to reread, at that time, the *Edda* and the *Nibelungenlied*. But when the Romanticists' Teutonic leanings, fanned by the Wars against Napoleon, turned into a decided preference for the German Middle Ages over any other civilization the world had yet seen, Goethe's classicist orientation quickly reasserted itself. 'I have eaten at Homer's table and at that of the Nibelungs', he wrote Knebel in 1814, 'but I have found nothing more congenial to me than . . . the works of the Greek writers and sculptors.'

Other Romanticist tendencies which in Goethe's view soon became excesses, and led to a parting of the ways, were the younger generation's patriotic zeal, their growing identification with the Roman Church whether by conversion (F. Schlegel, Z. Werner) or by turning bigoted where formerly they had worn their faith lightly (C. Brentano, J. von Görres), and the glorification of the specifically religious and nationalistic aspects of German history which is evidenced in the great majority of their novels. It was largely in response to these challenges that Goethe, never a believer in the word's traditional sense, became somewhat belligerently Protestant in his old age, and at the same time formulated ever more concisely his classicist credo in aesthetics. Yet it would be wrong to assume that his attitude to Romanticism was primarily defensive. Many of his late works, from *Die Wahlverwandtschaften* to the second part of *Faust*, show that for all the strain in their relationship, Goethe and the Romanticists gave more to each other than perhaps either party cared to admit.

The Romanticists' great historical contribution to the German image of Goethe consisted of investing the poet with a permanent, critically defined literary reputation. In the drawing rooms of Berlin, Jena, and Heidelberg, in the lecture halls of half a dozen other centres, through their panegyrics and later through the very violence of their hostility, they established him once and for all as an author whose works were 'classics'. They assigned to him, in lectures and critical writings, a definitive place in world literature: not simply by praising him but by specifically comparing his production to that of the great literary figures of other times and other lands (and as a group, they knew world literature better than any previous or later school of critics). They were the first to point out the characteristic qualities of his writing and to examine the validity of his works for their own problems as well. They were the first, finally, to spread his fame abroad, not haphazardly, as we saw happened with *Werther* and *Stella*, but because a thorough knowledge of Goethe was as much a matter of course with them as an acquaintance with Homer, Dante, and Shakespeare. Through the books and translations of Mme de Staël, Benjamin Constant, and other Romanticist missionaries, the critical tenets of German Romanticism, including a recognition of Goethe's 'exemplariness' in many respects, eventually spread over the world.

The works which Goethe wrote during the last two decades of his life have had an incalculable influence on German thought: *Dichtung und Wahrheit*, *Der westöstliche Divan*, *Die Marienbader Elegie*, *Wilhelm Meisters Wanderjahre*, and the second part of *Faust*. However, their effect on the public was delayed for several decades while the German image of Goethe was in danger of being thrown out of focus by the pressure of new literary and social developments. There is little doubt that in the eyes of the general public, Goethe had outlived himself by the time Romanticism reached its fullest flowering. He had become a fixture on the German Parnassus, a much-quoted, little read, seldom understood author, known by name to all but appreciated by only a small band of devoted followers. We have seen already that he himself had by then given up all hope of effectively communicating with the general reader. He knew that the great mass of the German people did not read his works at all since he had turned away from the Storm and Stress. It is well to point out that in the opening years of the nineteenth century, the most popular German writers were A. von Kotzebue, who, impervious alike to Goethe's scorn and to the Schlegels' parodies, continued to be the country's favourite dramatist until his death in 1819; and A. Lafontaine, a prolific novelist who extracted rivers of tears from the eyes of his readers (among them, the King and Queen of Prussia—the royal taste having, if anything, deteriorated since the days of Frederick the Great). The seeds of inspiration, admiration, and imitation which Goethe had implanted in so many significant nineteenth-century figures, did not begin to sprout until after his death. With the exception of Beethoven and Schubert, his great musical interpreters belong to a later age. So do his great interpreters abroad: Carlyle, Emerson and Longfellow, Gérard de Nerval, and those who most fruitfully wrestled with him in the German language area: Grillparzer, Stifter, Hebbel, and Keller. Even the antagonists of his last years: Menzel, Gervinus, Börne, did not grow to full stature until after 1832.

If the ups and downs of the German image of Goethe during its first century were to be represented graphically, in profile, the resultant line would have to rise steeply to an early peak— *Götz* and *Werther* in the mid-1770's—and slowly go down again in measure as the Storm and Stress came to be expressed by other authors; it would briefly rise once more, with the publication of certain works which elicited at least a modicum of public interest: *Hermann und Dorothea* (1797), the first part of *Faust* (1808), *Die Wahlverwandtschaften* (1809). The line would then flatten out at a rather low level throughout much of the nineteenth century. On the same graph, a line representing the German estimate of Schiller would quickly reach a high point with *Die Räuber* (1781), intersect Goethe's line, dip now and then as the Romanticists' antipathy found echoes in the public mind, and continue to rise until by the middle of the century it would run along the top of the scale while Goethe's line would touch bottom. The lines would not intersect again until about 1875, when Goethe's reputation rose steeply and Schiller's went into a precipitous decline from which it has recovered only within the recent past.

These tergiversations were only to a small extent based on the results of literary criticism as the term is now understood. They were, rather, the result of developments in fields other than literature, which ceased to be considered as a more or less autonomous entity in German life when a number of social, political, and religious problems became more pressing. Specifically, we shall see that the German public weighed Goethe, and for many long years found him wanting, not only as an author, but primarily as a human being and a German citizen.

II

FROM METTERNICH TO MARX

WHEN Goethe died in March 1832, one of Germany's most influential reviews, the *Literaturblatt* of Stuttgart, made no mention whatever of his death. For reasons which we shall examine, the editor, Wolfgang Menzel, disliked Goethe so heartily that he could not bring himself to print the hated name even in an obituary. No doubt he could have been made to do so by his employers, the publishing house of Cotta, who owned the copyright to Goethe's works as well as the *Literaturblatt* (literary supplement to the daily *Morgenblatt*). But the name of Menzel carried so much weight at the time, and Goethe's public had by then become so limited, that the editor was only mildly rebuked for his intentional oversight.

Four years later a remarkable monument was unveiled in the same city of Stuttgart. The money for it had been raised in a country-wide subscription, and the famous Danish sculptor Thorwaldsen was commissioned to do the work. It was a statue, the first erected in any public place in Germany which commemorated neither a prince nor a general, but a civilian. The man thus honoured was Friedrich Schiller. In the same spirit the centenary of Schiller's birth in 1859 was celebrated amid scenes of public enthusiasm hitherto unknown in German history. It was as if the entire country had rallied, on the eve of its unification, to do homage to the great poet who had long ago sung of Germany's liberty and greatness. Yet ten years before, an equally memorable date had been passed over in near-silence: the hundredth anniversary of Goethe's birth.

In 1885 Victor Hugo died and was mourned by all France. This moved a respected German scholar to wonder aloud what public reaction would have been in Germany if Goethe had died that year, and the government had asked for funds to give the dead poet a state funeral, like Hugo's in France:

Richter [leader of the liberal Left] would talk about the tax-

oppressed poor, and some of his followers would ask what the de-
parted had ever done for Liberty; Windthorst [parliamentary chief
of the Catholic Centre Party] would . . . add that Goethe had been a
heathen who never cared about his own or his people's salvation, and
in the newspapers the Jews would publish wretched articles copied
from some encyclopedia or other. . . . This, I do believe, is what
would have happened if Goethe had died in the Germany of 1885.[1]

Such instances could be multiplied many times to show that the
years 1820–80 mark the lowest point that Goethe's reputation has
ever reached in Germany. This indifference to Goethe was due
not only to changes in literary taste but to a changed conception
of the value and function of literature as such. It sprang from
certain shifts which had taken place, since the French Revolution, in the country's social and intellectual complexion.

In Germany as elsewhere, the struggle against Napoleon had
forged into an uneasy alliance two fundamentally hostile forces:
that of Liberalism, actuated by the pressure for civil liberty and
national self-determination which had formed the very core of the
Revolution and was later perverted by Napoleon; and that of
Reaction, borne by the urge to restore the pre-revolutionary,
legitimist order of the continent. Despite the limited success of
the Revolution of 1848, the decades after 1815 are, in retrospect,
characterized by the emergence of Liberalism and Nationalism
as guiding principles of nineteenth-century European history.
In Germany this ideological struggle was complicated, and
altogether overshadowed in the period immediately after 1848,
by a third historical force: the drive for unification which culminated in the foundation of the German *Reich* in 1871.

With these forces at large, it soon became clear that the political awareness which the French Revolution had sparked in the
European middle class (except in England and Holland, where
that class had long borne political responsibility) could not
simply be extinguished by Metternich's command. German
political and intellectual life in particular was punctuated after
1815 by a long series of public crises, which forced even the
most retiring of bookworms to take cognizance of the world
about him—unless he preferred to submerge in the *Biedermeier*,

[1] V. Hehn, 'Goethe und das Publikum' (in *Gedanken über Goethe*, 6th ed., Berlin,
1906), p. 189.

that charming escapist fashion in painting and literature, as well as furniture and dress, whose stress on homespun virtues, on being 'cosy and comfy', soon stifled the initiative of its devotees.

For the first time since the Reformation there now arose in Germany a specifically political literature, not unworthy of standing by the side of what Britain and France had created in that field since the seventeenth century. Newspapers and magazines increased greatly in number: with the spreading of popular education and the growth of the railway system, the better ones among them were no longer parochial in outlook or limited in distribution. This in turn gave impetus to journalistic writing, especially in the form of the political essay and the editorial, which in nineteenth-century Europe were often works of some literary distinction. The pamphlet likewise was brought to a high degree of effectiveness: the *Communist Manifesto* is merely the most famous of a great many political programmes fathered by the German middle class. To gauge the impact of political passion on German letters, we need only compare men like Hugo or Zola with their German contemporaries Heine and Wagner. The former, in so far as they wrote *littérature engagée*, directly continued a tradition established by Voltaire and Rousseau, while the latter's involvement in the social and political problems of their time represents a very sharp break with the attitude of the older generation. The drama, the novel, the travel book, even the diary were now frequently adapted to political ends. Lyric poetry, too, was made to serve such purposes, especially where it could be used in patriotic song. The German poem most often set to music is not, as one might expect, one of Goethe's, Mörike's, or even Heine's: it is Nikolaus Becker's 'Sie sollen ihn nicht haben, den freien, deutschen Rhein', which has engaged the attention of over seventy composers.

It is as idle to lament as it would be to ignore the loss that has accrued to German culture through the energies which Uhland and Heine, Büchner and Storm, Laube and Wagner, along with many lesser contemporaries, expended in political rather than artistic endeavour. The loss was unavoidable because these men were stamped by a great communal trauma, by a set of soul- and conscience-searing tests—prison and exile, war and revolution, censorship and witch hunts—much as, *mutatis mutandis*, a generation of French intellectuals was stamped by the Dreyfus

Affair, and a generation of American writers by the Depression of the 1930's. This circumstance demands of us some idea not only of dates and facts, but of the 'mood', the temper of the times. It is easier to understand why some of these men lashed out at Goethe, or at what he represented in their eyes, if we recall some of the provocations to which writers and readers, not to mention teachers and students, were subjected during the Era of Metternich.

A large number of the volunteers who had joined the fight against Napoleon had been students. Like any generation of veterans, they had had the disillusioning experience of seeing the sterling motives with which they had taken up arms, replaced by the petty compromises of everyday politics. The young had fought and were now expected, by their elders who had made the peace, to step back quietly into the anonymity of civilian existence. And the men of 1815 had particularly good reasons for resentment: theirs had been a sterile sacrifice because the Congress of Vienna was so onesidedly interested in resurrecting the world of 1789. They had fought for a free, not a few of them for a united Germany. They had not fought to re-establish the Papal States, to aggrandize Prussia at the expense of Saxony, or to substitute for Napoleon's loose-meshed censorship the pusillanimous thought control of Metternich and Gentz. After their return to the university, many of these youthful veterans banded together in a type of fraternity, the *Burschenschaft*, which kept alive the ideals of comradeship, Christian self-sacrifice, and patriotic action. The earliest and most influential of these bodies was the *Burschenschaft* at Jena, which adopted the colours of the celebrated Lützow Free Corps in which many of its members had served.[1]

On 18 October 1817 some 500 *Burschenschafter* from Jena and elsewhere assembled at the Wartburg for a double celebration: the 300th anniversary of the Reformation (in 1517 Luther had nailed up his Ninety-Five Theses in nearby Wittenberg), and the anniversary of the Battle of Leipzig, in which Napoleon had been forced to withdraw from Germany (16–19 October 1813). The idea of combining the patriotic occasion with the religious had, in part, been Goethe's. As curator of the university's

[1] These colours, the black, red, and gold of the medieval empire, eventually became the flag of the Weimar Republic and of the present *Bundesrepublik*.

library and museums, he had advance knowledge of the celebration and wanted to avoid snubbing the Roman Catholic
students, who could not be expected to take part in a festival
celebrating only the Reformation. In the evening some students
started a bonfire to which they consigned, in imitation of
Luther's burning of the Papal Bull, a number of objects symbolic
of the hated reactionary régimes of the day: the swaggerstick of
an Austrian Army corporal, books by Kotzebue and other propagandists of the Holy Alliance, the corset-like tunic of a Prussian lancer.

The various German governments had been perturbed for
some time by the restlessness of the *Burschenschaften*. This *auto-
da-fé*, little more than a student prank, now furnished them with
a convenient pretext for a series of long contemplated steps.
Austria and Prussia protested to the Grand Duke of Weimar, in
whose territory the 'outrage' had taken place; the Czar distributed to all and sundry a memorandum on the dangers of a
German Revolution engendered by the universities' liberalism.
This agitation was in full swing when a feeble-minded *Burschenschafter*, the Jena theology student Karl Sand, assassinated Kotzebue as a Russian spy and enemy of all progress. The deed was
thought despicable, but the motive was widely appreciated; for
a while the public seriously considered Sand, who was allowed
to recover from his self-inflicted wounds before being executed,
as a latter-day Brutus or Tell. The resultant official measures
were codified in the so-called Karlsbad Resolutions of 1819,
which effectively paralysed German intellectual life for the
following two decades. All books of less than 320 pages had to
be approved by the censor; the universities were to be controlled by a so-called 'curator', who dismissed professors suspected of liberal tendencies and enforced the suppression of the
Burschenschaften; members of the latter were threatened with
dismissal from the university and exclusion from the civil service;
a central commission was set up in Mainz to inspect universities
in the various states, and to see to it, if necessary by force of arms,
that no German ruler weakened in the rigorous application of
these laws. The results were appalling. The poet Arndt was
suspended from his post at the University of Bonn; the philosopher Schleiermacher was forced to submit his sermons to
censorship; the pedagogue Jahn was imprisoned; a great many

gifted *Burschenschafter* were exiled, like Menzel, or imprisoned, like Laube. Many lesser victims were dealt with even more arbitrarily.

Goethe's attitude to these developments was that of a calm observer whose own opinions were moderate enough. Having earlier recommended caution to the hotheads at Jena, only to see his advice disregarded, he now considered himself 'entitled to passivity'.[1] He lamented the severity of the Karlsbad Resolutions, and congratulated himself on not having to take a hand in their application at Jena: he equally condemned the students' rashness which had precipitated the crisis, as well as the encouragement given them by some of the faculty. It need hardly be said that this position pleased neither party. Many *Burschenschafter* and Liberals came away thinking that Goethe, who had, after all, once been a revolutionary of sorts himself, was a man without much political conviction, interested only in his own comfort: a sort of weather-vane which fell in with the prevailing winds. In the eyes of those who upheld the established order he was suspect, despite the admiration shown for him by Metternich and Gentz, as the close friend of Karl August. That prince was for a time the only German ruler who implemented the constitution he had promised his subjects back in the exciting days of 1813; once they were securely ensconced again upon their thrones, the other princes had quickly forgotten their quondam magnanimity.

In some respects European writers were even more restricted under Metternich than they had been in the eighteenth century. Two (on the whole, repressive) governments now functioned side by side where formerly there had only been one. Metternich had anticipated, not as problem but as an established fact, the great political question of our own day: how a nation's sovereignty can be limited in favour of an international government. It was at his bidding that the armies of the Holy Alliance intervened in Spain, Poland, Italy; it was also at his bidding that its agents, such as Kotzebue, exercised, across the borders of nominally independent states, a form of thought control which also foreshadows the twentieth century. Terribly frightened by the spectre of another revolution, the princes of Europe banded together in a dynastic International long before there was talk of

[1] Letter to Zelter, 16 Dec. 1817.

a proletarian one. For that reason alone, the freedom granted
Voltaire or Rousseau by the naïve *ancien régime* had become inconceivable in the once-burned, twice-shy monarchies of 1815–
30. But if the policies of the Holy Alliance in cultural as in other
matters were essentially conservative, those of some German
princes were reactionary. In their distrust of literary and intellectual matters, some of these men were far pettier than the
central government in Vienna. This is borne out by two characteristic incidents which may serve to complete our rapid survey
of the temper of that period.

In its issues of 30 and 31 August 1826 the *Vossische Zeitung*
reported at some length on a joint celebration, held by a private
club in Berlin, of Hegel's and Goethe's birthdays (27 and 28
August, respectively). This prompted the King of Prussia, Frederick William III, to write out in his own hand an order to his
cabinet, to the effect that the editor be warned to restrict any
further announcements of this nature to a brief notice only. In
the sovereign's view, the space allotted to this news item had
been altogether too ample for the birthday of 'private individuals'; indeed, such thoroughness was deemed suitable only for
descriptions of 'a monarch's accession to the throne'. Without
putting too fine a point on it, we may safely assume that the
royal ire was aroused by the publicity given not to any two
private individuals, but specifically to Goethe and Hegel: two
national figures in their own right, utterly independent in mind
and demeanour, and, of all things, a poet and a philosopher. Nor
was the King alone in his obscurantist zeal. In what is perhaps
the oddest comment on that much-commented work, Goethe's
Faust, the Police Commissioner of the City of Königsberg some
years later declared that 'from the standpoint of public security',
it would have been better if the work had never been written
at all.

These interludes were merely grotesque, and in any case
remained unknown to the public because the relevant documents
lay buried for many years in the Prussian State Archives. However, another passage-at-arms between a German ruler and a
number of the country's intellectual leaders erupted into a full-
blown national scandal. When William IV died in 1837 he was
succeeded in England by Victoria, and in Hanover by her
uncle Ernest Augustus, Duke of Cumberland (due to the Salic

Law prevailing in Germany). Politically this was a welcome development because in terminating the personal union between the Kingdoms of England and Hanover it removed a major road-block from the path to German unity. In all other respects, however, King Ernest Augustus's reign was an unmitigated disaster. He was an extreme reactionary, so reprehensible in the conduct of both public and private affairs that a British newspaper charged him with having committed every conceivable crime with the exception of suicide. This man had no sooner become King than he abrogated the Hanoverian constitution of 1833, released all civil servants from the oath they had taken to uphold it, and restored the far more restrictive constitution of 1819. Thus he almost literally 'turned back the clock', in so blatant a fashion that even Metternich was aghast. Seven well-known professors at the University of Göttingen thereupon declared that as public servants of the Kingdom of Hanover they would continue to consider themselves bound by their oath, and that as teachers they had a special obligation to uphold the sanctity of their word and to set an example to the young. The King instantly dismissed these men from their posts, giving three of them—the historians F. C. Dahlmann and G. G. Gervinus, and Goethe's friend Jacob Grimm—72 hours in which to leave the country. Public opinion throughout Germany was outraged, and the Seven from Göttingen were received with open arms elsewhere; but the edict remained in force even after protests had been registered with the German Federal Diet at Frankfurt. Despite the feelings aroused in the literary public by these and similar events, the nation as a whole did not seethe with unrest because this or that professor was dismissed, or one or the other book censored. Discouraging as these trespasses on intellectual and academic freedom were, they formed only one strand in a tissue of prohibitions which was steadily drawn tighter right up to the eve of 1848. In fact, nothing so clearly indicates the extent of the restrictions under which all Germans, not only those with literary interests, laboured in the civic sphere of life, as do the demands made by the revolutionaries of that year: aside from several other rights which in many Anglo-Saxon communities had long become traditonal, the German Liberals demanded freedom of the press, citizen militias, trial by jury, and universal suffrage.

With the gift for imagery which was his in prose as in poetry, Heinrich Heine thus defined, in *Die Romantische Schule*, the hostility with which Goethe was regarded by many at the time of his death:

The new poets who made their début during the rule of Emperor Goethe... resemble a stand of young trees, whose size becomes apparent only now that the century-old oak has fallen whose branches towered above them all. There was no lack of opposition ... to the great tree Goethe. Men of the most divergent opinions joined in attacking him. The Old Believers, the Orthodox, resented the fact that the tree lacked a niche with a saint's picture, indeed that the naked Dryads of pagan antiquity practised their witchcraft there. Like St. Boniface, they would willingly have felled the magic oak with a consecrated axe. The New Believers, the Liberals, were no less resentful because they could not use this tree for a freedom pole, least of all for a barricade. Truly, it was too tall to put a red cockade on its top and dance the Carmagnole around it.

In so far as the men of Heine's generation attacked Goethe on moral and aesthetic grounds, as pagan, salacious, or effeminate, they merely reiterated objections which had been raised ever since the publication of *Werther*. However, the recovery of both Protestantism and Roman Catholicism from the onslaughts of the rationalists, and the general quickening of Germany's religious pulse during the Wars of Liberation, led to a great intensification of these criticisms. Rome's growing intransigence towards the liberal, materialistic, and scientific tendencies of the age, which culminated in the promulgation of the Doctrine of Papal Infallibility in 1871, is, of course, a well-known historical development which affected all of nineteenth-century Europe. In Germany this Roman Catholic struggle for self-assertion was intensified when much of the Rhineland became Prussian in 1815, including such Catholic strongholds as Köln, Aachen, Trier, and Koblenz. This, in turn, led to a closer identification between temporal and spiritual power in a much enlarged Prussia whose state religion was Protestant. In Schleiermacher, Protestantism had found a particularly vigorous spokesman, an effective writer, philosopher, and preacher, a man without any great aesthetic sensitivity who none the less exemplified a parallel, or alternate, way to the full moral and spiritual development of Man advocated by the Classicists. The foundation of the

Prussian Bible Society in 1814, and of the Society for the Propagation of the Christian Faith among the Jews in 1825, are expressions of this reinvigorated Protestantism in both the Lutheran
and the Reformed Church; so, of course, was the fateful Wartburg
Festival of 1817. When Heine wrote his picturesque lines, the
most articulate of the Protestant Goethe critics was the ex-
Burschenschafter E. W. Hengstenberg, a Lutheran professor of
Old Testament Exegesis, and editor of the influential *Evange-
lische Kirchenzeitung*. Hengstenberg's ire was aroused by the discrepancy he found, especially in *Die Wahlverwandtschaften* and in
Goethe's correspondence with Schiller (published 1828–9),
between the Classicists' literary and their moral standards.
Warning his readers against letting themselves be lured away
from the straight and narrow path by Goethe's dazzling poetic
gifts, he attacked the 'illusion' that art, and for that matter all
aesthetic values as defined by Schiller, can ever be considered
separately from religious doctrine. On much the same grounds,
the late Romanticists of the ultramontane faction condemned
Goethe in the pages of J. von Görres's *Historisch-politische Blätter*.

Even before Goethe died, the attacks from the orthodox Protestant quarter had gained in momentum with the publication
of two hostile works. In 1823 an anonymously published pamphlet appeared under the title *Goethe als Mensch und Schriftsteller*.
It was basically the translation of a Puritan attack on Goethe in
The Edinburgh Review of June 1816, in itself a compendium of
slogans about the need for moral uprightness in literature, and
the lamentable lack thereof in Goethe's works. The translators—
Köchy and Vogler, alias 'Glover'—added a prologue and an
epilogue, both, to be sure, of astounding nastiness. Infinitely
more artful in form, however, were the so-called 'Pseudo-
Travels'. This purported to be the long-announced continuation
of *Wilhelm Meisters Lehrjahre*; however, the author turned out to
be not Goethe but the Protestant clergyman J. F. Pustkuchen,
who in 1821 published *Wilhelm Meisters Wanderjahre*. (Goethe's
own sequel to the *Lehrjahre*, under the same title of *Wilhelm
Meisters Wanderjahre*, was not published, in its entirety, until
1829.) In the same manner in which Goethe's Wilhelm, in the
Lehrjahre, holds judgement over Shakespeare, Pustkuchen's
hero here examines Goethe . . . whose works attract the spineless Wilhelm since 'in order to understand them, he needed

neither a positive faith nor any great enthusiasm, both of which
would have been required to do justice to Schiller, Klopstock,
or Herder'. Goethe had praised Shakespeare through the mouth
of his Wilhelm; Pustkuchen condemns Goethe through *his*
Wilhelm, as devoid of any moral conviction, a mere virtuoso of
literary form, a gifted lightweight whose very success portends
the rise of a decadent, Godless period. With various additions,
Pustkuchen's parody was reprinted in 1824 and 1828, in a
running battle with Goethe who during the same period published various instalments of his own novel.[1]

More serious and lasting than these moralistic pinpricks, and
infinitely more damaging to Goethe's reputation to this day,
were the attacks made on him on political grounds. The most
important, and by far the most articulate, of those who now
insisted that literature must assume an ethical and a social
function, and who proceeded to examine in that light Goethe
and the entire period dominated by him, were the writers
usually grouped together under the heading of Young Germany:
Heine, Börne, Gutzkow, Laube, Mundt, Wienbarg. For our
purposes we may safely add to their number Menzel and Gervinus; although the former ended by subverting, the latter by
disregarding the Young Germans, they are important as authors
of two of the century's most important Histories of German
Literature, in which they formulated an evaluation of Goethe
which is very close to that of the group as a whole. Disparate as
the Young Germans were in gifts, achievements, and fame, and
without much personal cohesion as a group, they yet had in
common a literary programme and even a literary fate: the
German Federal Diet banned their works as 'anti-Christian,
blasphemous, trampling underfoot all notions of decency, shame,
and propriety'.[2]

According to the Young Germans, the writer's foremost task

---

[1] During this altercation, many men of integrity disregarded their own reservations about Goethe and joined in condemning Pustkuchen (Achim von Arnim,
Varnhagen von Ense, Tieck, Immermann). A belated but forceful defender of
Goethe's was Karl Marx, who as a student at the University of Berlin wrote a
number of epigrams against Pustkuchen (1836–7). It is curious to reflect that the
founder of Communism, whose name is sacrosanct in one half of the world and
anathema in the other, should have calibrated his critical guns on this long-
forgotten country parson.

[2] In the words of the proposal submitted to the Diet by the Austrian representative. The ban lasted from 1835 to 1842.

lay not in the cultivation of his personality but in the instruction and guidance of the literary public—the entire literary public, not the small circle of highly cultivated readers to whom the Classicists and Romanticists had addressed themselves. Furthermore, the Young German author took part in the life about him and wrote 'realistically', *en homme engagé*, endeavouring to mirror in his works the political and social tendencies of his time. Thus the present, rather than the classical or medieval past glorified by the Classicists and Romanticists, was considered the proper subject for literature. Within this present, life as it is lived with the senses and the soul was of more concern to the writer than the cerebral constructions of the Rationalists, or of the contemporary philosophers of Hegelian or other persuasion. Religion, likewise, was an emotional matter for the Young Germans; not doctrine but living faith, whose literary expression was to be kept free of abstractions.

It is readily evident that the tendencies of the age with which the Young Germans wanted writers to identify themselves were precisely those for which Goethe had had the least sympathy: the patriotic struggle against the French, and the agitation for a united Germany of a strongly liberal, if not altogether democratic complexion. Menzel was not alone in wishing that Goethe had made himself Germany's spiritual leader against Napoleon, instead of 'working hand in hand with the external enemy', as he put it, and being 'our evil genius who made us forget . . . religion, fatherland, and honour, who led us to mirror ourselves like Narcissus . . . while the chains and daggers were being forged behind our backs . . . in a word: who turned us into weaklings just when we most needed to be heroes'.[1] Furthermore, Goethe, not content with keeping himself aloof from the Wars of Liberation, had supposedly lacked the courage, in fact the interest, to intervene on the side of progress in the years after 1815. Thus Börne found him lacking in this respect in comparison to Dante, Alfieri, Montesquieu, Voltaire, Rousseau, Swift, Byron, Thomas Moore, and others who had at one time or the other taken up the defence of the poor and downtrodden. This lack of patriotism and of a social conscience, the Young Germans explained, was partly due to certain moral defects in

[1] *Literaturblatt*, 9 Sept. 1835 (reprinted in M. Holzmann, *Aus dem Lager der Goethe-gegner* [Berlin, 1904], p. 75).

Goethe, such as his servility, his egotism, and his unmanliness. In the atmosphere prevailing at the time, the most telling of these accusations was the first, which to Börne was epitomized in the following entry in Goethe's diary: 'Then I had the unexpected good fortune of receiving worshipfully—zu verehren—in my home and garden Their Imperial Highnesses The Grand Duke Nicholas and The Grand Duchess Alexandra. ... Her Imperial Highness The Grand Duchess deigned to allow me to write a few reverent poetic lines in her delicately, yet magnificently bound album.'[1]

However, the Young Germans' most serious reservations about Goethe had little to do with his moral character, or even with the morality of the characters he had created. Menzel, to be sure, throughout his life condemned Goethe from the sophomoric viewpoint of a *Burschenschafter* bubbling over with Christian righteousness and patriotic fervour;[2] but the others quickly realized that their great contemporary was neither deficient in probity nor, as Menzel, Pustkuchen, and Glover had also charged, lacking in poetic gifts. On the contrary: the Young Germans were constantly and painfully aware of the disproportion between his towering achievement and their own, somewhat meagre production. Their occasional attempts to belittle Goethe (demoting him, in the parlance of the day, from a 'genius' to a 'talent') no doubt partly sprang from the feeling of inadequacy frequent among those who follow in the footsteps of a great man. In part it was also a by-product of their egalitarian boosting of 'the people'—as readers, as political entity, as bearer of progress, even as arbiter of taste—at the expense of the gifted individual. Common to them all was the realization that Goethe's death marked the end of a period in German history, a period whose values, for all their glory, had little relevance to the age

---

[1] From the *Tag- und Jahreshefte* for 1821. In his *Briefe aus Paris*, Börne commented: 'This he wrote in his seventy-first year. What youthful power!' (appendix to *Brief* No. 51).

[2] The depth and taste of Menzel's criticism may be judged from his famous comment on *Faust*: 'If Faust deserves to be saved after seducing and deserting Gretchen, then any pig rolling around in a flower bed deserves to be made a gardener' (*Literaturblatt*, 6 May 1833).

Menzel's *Die deutsche Literatur*, introduced into the United States by his friend K. Follen, may have contributed to the low esteem in which Goethe was held by many nineteenth-century Americans. Follen became professor of German at Harvard in 1830, and was Longfellow's predecessor in that position.

whose battles they were now fighting. In calling that period the 'Kunstperiode', Heine merely expressed what was felt to have been one of the characteristic features of Goethe's time, when the arts were largely cultivated for their own sake and for the enjoyment and instruction of a select circle. This period of 'pure' literature, they argued, must now be followed by the 'applied' literature of those who wrote in the service of various social and political causes. Although in other respects his attitude to Goethe underwent many changes, Heine does not seem to have wavered in his paradoxical belief that Goethe was the greatest author who had yet written in German, but that despite, or because of, his great achievement, he had ended by standing in the way of political as well as literary progress. Gervinus carried this argument even further by insisting that the mature Goethe had little to say to the young generation not because he lacked greatness, but because the very nature of literature had changed. What mattered now—in the 1830's, that is—was not the aesthetic but the historical value of a literary work, especially the ties which bind it to the people from whose soil it sprang. For Gervinus, the measure of a poet's stature was not the beauty or originality of his work, but the extent to which this work is a living influence in the nation's daily political life. In his *Geschichte der poetischen Nationalliteratur der Deutschen,* he praised Dante and Shakespeare for their profound concern with their country's political fate, and ranked Schiller above the classical Goethe for much the same reason. It does not seem to have occurred to him that even from the limited viewpoint of national prestige, Goethe had rendered a signal service by raising his country, through its language and literature, to a leading position in European life. In his treatise *Über Goethes Briefwechsel* he expounded, along with much petty criticism of Goethe as a person, the historian's limited view that Goethe would have been as great a poet as Schiller if he, too, had studied history with a view to enriching his poetic output; 'as it was', Gervinus regretfully concluded, 'he preferred to cultivate all of his interests and to develop the whole man, which is bound to remain a half-finished task'.

We have seen something of the trials which beset the Young Germans in the civic as well as the literary sphere. The purely human element must not be exaggerated, but it would have been odd indeed if Börne in the Frankfurt ghetto, Laube in a Berlin gaol, Heine in his Parisian exile, or Gervinus on his flight from Göttingen had been able to look dispassionately on Goethe. He not only towered above them all in gifts, but was (wrongly but inevitably) represented to them, by all who had known him in his last years, as a formal, maddeningly calm Olympian, a seemingly permanent literary institution, His Excellency the Privy Councillor who was far removed from human strife. It has been pointed out that the novels of Stendhal and de Musset describe not only the atmosphere of Restoration France, but that of Metternich's Germany as well, with its dissatisfied, restless bright young men who found no outlet for their talents and ambitions.[1] With what envy must these men have looked on Goethe, who for all they knew had been able to develop freely all the gifts and inclinations that lay in him, who had never been in a ghetto or a gaol, in exile or in flight!

It is greatly to their credit that the Young Germans at least tried to do justice to him. In his *Ästhetische Feldzüge* Wienbarg attempted to explain Goethe's indifference towards politics on the basis of his individuality and of his position at the court of Weimar. Before turning Goethephobe in his old age, Gutzkow wrote a lengthy essay, *Goethe im Wendepunkt zweier Jahrhunderte* (1836), in which he specifically refuted certain criticisms often levelled against the poet: for example, that he was really a very limited person who never understood such things as music or abstract philosophy (according to Gutzkow, self-limitation is a prerequisite of genius), or that he had rejected a nationally oriented literature in favour of an indiscriminately cosmopolitan one (false, in Gutzkow's view; Goethe's concept of the coming age of world literature, far from precluding an appreciation of national literatures, furnishes writers with a wider public). Even in this early work Gutzkow was by no means an unconditional admirer of Goethe's; yet in acknowledging the wide gap between German Classicism and his own generation, he also insisted that contemporary writing must begin where Goethe left off at the opening of the nineteenth century, and that the latter's works will remain a critical standard for all future German writers. A similar defence was undertaken by Laube, who in his *Geschichte der deutschen Literatur* and *Reisenovellen* also had reservations about

---

[1] R. Buchwald, *Goethezeit und Gegenwart* (Stuttgart, 1949), p. 150.

Goethe, as cold and by nature incapable of enthusiasm, but who did not for a moment deny the poet his eminent position in German letters. Along with Heine and Gutzkow, Laube blamed the artless idolatry of Goethe's partisans for the vehemence of Menzel's and Gervinus's attacks. This contempt for Goethe's early apologists and biographers is one of several characteristic attitudes which the Young Germans shared with the early Marxists, who in the 1840's developed their own theory about the phenomenon of Goethe.

This theory was first formulated in a book review which Friedrich Engels wrote for Marx's *Deutsche Brüsseler Zeitung*, in November and December 1847. The book in question was *Goethe vom menschlichen Standpunkte*, by the philosopher Karl Grün.[1] By dint of stressing Goethe's administrative work on behalf of Weimar's schools, roads, and industries, Grün had made of the poet a forerunner of the contemporary social philosophers Proudhon and Feuerbach, a humanitarian minister intent on reforming the working and living conditions of the population entrusted to him. In Engels's view, this stress on the human element has resulted in the picture of a philistine do-gooder, of an ineffectually kind-hearted man devoid of any hint of demonic striving. Engels's objection was not that Grün had erred in seeing in Goethe the embodiment of a type of German petty bourgeois. He had said himself that 'Goethe and Hegel were, each in his own fashion, Olympian gods. Yet they never quite got rid of the German Philistine's pigtail.'[2] However, he considered this a onesided evaluation because it made no allowance for the tragic element in Goethe's life. This tragic element, in the Marxist view, lay in the discrepancy between Goethe's gifts and the lack of opportunity to exercise them properly:

There is a continuous struggle in him between the superbly gifted poet surfeited with his miserable surroundings, and the circumspect scion of a patrician Frankfurt family. . . . Even Goethe was incapable of overcoming the German misery;[3] on the contrary, it overcame

[1] Engels's review was to be part of a work entitled *Deutscher Sozialismus in Versen und Prosa*. With the exception of the articles printed in Marx's paper, the work was not published until the 1930's, when it was issued by the Moscow Marx-Engels Institute.

[2] 'Ludwig Feuerbach und der Ausgang der klassischen deutschen Philosophie' (in Marx–Engels, *Über Kunst und Literatur* [Moscow, 1949], p. 215.)

[3] The French word *misère* is a term frequently used in early Marxist literature.

him, and this victory of the German misery over the country's
greatest poet is the best proof that the misery could not be cleaned up
"from inside" [i.e. presumably through the cultivation of the individual which was Goethe's own aim]. . . . His temperament, his gifts,
the whole direction of his mind led him to an active, "practical" life;
and the practical life he found was miserable. Goethe was always in a
dilemma: that of living in a sphere of life which he could not help
despising, and yet of being bound to this sphere as to the only one
in which he could exist. . . .'[1]

This struggle was responsible for the ambivalence which Engels
saw in Goethe's attitude to his social and political surroundings,
to the 'German misery'. He sometimes fought it as in *Götz* and
Faust, or escaped from it altogether as in *Iphigenie* and the other
works of Classicism. At other times, however, he meekly adapted
himself to it, as in the playlets and occasional poetry written for
the court, or even defended it as in the anti-revolutionary
writings.

This represents, to be sure, a somewhat arbitrary view of
Goethe's historical position; nor is there much evidence that the
poet himself regarded his life in these terms. It is, however,
interesting not only as proof of the serious thought given to
Goethe by the founders of Marxism, but because it represents
substantially the earliest postulation of a tragic side to the
existence of this man, who until well into the twentieth century
was generally considered to have been one of the most fortunate
of mortals. The pages which Marx and Engels devoted to
Goethe reached only a minute fraction of the public of their
time, and exerted no appreciable influence on the nineteenth-
century's view of the poet. It remained for the literary historian
Franz Mehring to restate in more forceful terms this concept of
Goethe as victim rather than master of his circumstances, and to
buttress it with the general Marxist theory of historical causality
by explaining not only Goethe, but the entire classical age of
German literature exclusively in terms of the economic situation
of the middle classes:

It is foolish to imagine that in the second half of the 18th century, a
great many talented men of letters simply happened to come along in
Germany, by a lucky coincidence or through the inscrutable will of

[1] Marx–Engels, op. cit., pp. 216–17.

Providence. It was, rather, the economic growth which took place at the time which gave a strong impetus to the German middle classes; but as these classes were none the less too weak to make a bid for political power, as they did in France, they created for themselves an idealized literary image of a bourgeois society.[1]

However, these lines were written a good many years later. For the period presently under investigation, we must, for once, follow in Engels's footsteps, and examine the Goethe biographies which were then being published.

[1] F. Mehring, *Deutsche Geschichte vom Ausgange des Mittelalters* (2nd ed., Berlin, 1947), p. 138.

III

EARLY BIOGRAPHY

FEW men of letters have been as deeply aware of their own historical position as Goethe was of his. To the extent that he left several autobiographical works as well as diaries, letters, and much other carefully gathered source material, Goethe himself can be called the initiator of a minor but important subdivision of German literature: the Goethe biography. In writing *Dichtung und Wahrheit*, in publishing his correspondence with Schiller, in encouraging his first biographers: in a word, by not leaving the formulation of his posthumous fame to blind chance, Goethe merely acted in accord with the conviction he expressed in one of the last letters we have by his hand: 'I am bound to confess that in old age, life becomes for me more and more a matter of history. It is all the same to me whether something takes place in the distant past and in far-away lands, or quite close in space and time. In fact, I am growing more and more historical in my own eyes. . . .'

Even with the help which the poet provided for his biographers, many years had to pass before anything like an adequate account of his life could be written. The very length of this life, the tremendous scope of his interests (which never failed to turn from curiosity into active investigation), the fact that so many relevant documents lay hidden in archives for years, and the concentration of his immediate posterity on political rather than literary or aesthetic problems all combined to render the first biographical attempts little more than gropings in the dark. Such was the nature of the books published in Goethe's lifetime, by Schubarth, Zauper, Eckermann, Varnhagen von Ense, and Nicolovius, as well as of the works by Falk and Riemer which came out later. None of these fragmentary early biographies achieved a clear picture of Goethe's personality and production. On the contrary, they did much harm because they fairly dripped with idolatry and repelled all but the most insensitive of readers. We can understand some of the Young Germans' surfeit with Goethe if we read in Nicolovius's book that he quoted only favourable reviews—against the poet's own advice—because Goethe is 'above criticism'. We can understand it even better if we read Eckermann's claim, in his *Beiträge zur Poesie mit besonderer Hinweisung auf Goethe*, that if the poet had taken the Lord's place in creating the world, the birds would have turned out just as feathered and the trees just as green, which moved Heine to observe that Goethe might indeed have done better than the Lord, in creating an improved Eckermann, also feathered and green!

Johann Peter Eckermann, of course, soon redeemed himself with another book, no less encomiastic but infinitely more valuable than the early work satirized by Heine. His *Gespräche mit Goethe in den letzten Jahren seines Lebens* (1836, with later additions) were no more intended as biography than Bettina von Arnim's *Goethes Briefwechsel mit einem Kinde* (1835), or the compilations which Karl Friedrich Zelter made of his correspondence, or those which Friedrich von Müller made of his conversations with the poet. Yet without these early collections of material, none of the biographies which were eventually forthcoming would have been reasonably complete. The value of Eckermann's book lies in the fact that it was published with the poet's approval, and thus represents a dependable documentation of those of his ideas and opinions which Goethe wanted to have preserved for posterity. It is true that Eckermann's boundless veneration of the Great Man, his air of breathlessly hanging on Goethe's lips, has constituted a challenge to lesser wits than Heine's.[1] Nor can it be denied that the work contains some unfortunate lapses of taste, such as the author's revolting examination of the dead Goethe's body. However, the fact remains that without this book, Goethe's last years would in many ways have remained as enigmatic to posterity as they appeared to his contemporaries. By showing us the poet in the daily routine of his life, Eckermann has afforded us a glance at the human being behind the ministerial mask. His utter self-denial and 'apostolically simple' way of life in the service of an immeasurably greater man,[2] his uncanny ability to feel his way into Goethe's

[1] Hebbel compared Eckermann with Adam, inert unless the god Goethe, in whose image he has been fashioned, breathes life into him (letter to Elise Lensing, 13 Sept. 1837).

[2] E. Beutler, 'Johann Peter Eckermann' (in *Essays um Goethe*, Wiesbaden, 1947-8, 2 vols.), ii. 285.

modes of thought and even speech, and his acute gift of observation have rightly gained for him a measure of literary immortality. His book has withstood the critical assaults of over a century, during which time much material has come to light which shows that his account of Goethe's thoughts and conversations, while somewhat stylized, is essentially truthful.

This cannot be said of Bettina von Arnim's wildly imaginative book. However, *Goethes Briefwechsel mit einem Kinde* was written with an infectious enthusiasm which made it a valuable counterweight to the Goethephobia of the 1830's. By the end of his life Goethe himself had become very cool towards the young authoress, whose 'importunities' he had had to 'repel'.[1] Nevertheless her book bears, in a way, a higher sanction than the formal seal of approval bestowed on Eckermann's. It uncovers a much earlier stratum of the poet's life than do the *Gespräche mit Goethe*, and Goethe himself had to some extent relied on Bettina when he wanted to recapture the atmosphere of his youth for *Dichtung und Wahrheit*. It remains the most valuable literary monument of the group of Berlin Society ladies—Bettina, Henriette Herz, Rahel Varnhagen, in their younger years Caroline and Dorothea Schlegel—in whose drawing-rooms two generations of Romanticists had been introduced to Goethe.

Eight years after Bettina's book the first account of Goethe was published which has proved to be a work of enduring value: Carl Gustav Carus's *Goethe, zu dessen näherem Verständnis*. The author, a medical man who eventually became personal physician to the King of Saxony, was a dilettante in the best sense of the word: musical, highly literate, a gifted amateur painter. Goethe shared with him an 'organic' way of looking at Nature in that both endeavoured to deduce, from the infinite variety of phenomena in the physical world, certain laws which form the basis of all life. Carus was one of the last representatives of the Classicist and Romanticist period in the history of German science, and one of the forerunners of modern psychology. As such, he viewed the human mind not as something to be defined, measured, and dissected into its component parts, as does the empirical researcher, but as an organic whole subject to laws of its own. Along with Goethe and Schelling, and their somewhat more experimentally inclined contemporaries A. von

---

[1] *Tagebücher*, entry for 7 Aug. 1830.

Humboldt and J. Müller, Carus never lost sight of this totality even in the most specialized research. In the final instance, Nature was to him, as to Goethe, a phenomenon actuated not by material but by divine or at least spiritual forces. When Carus wrote his books on Goethe,[1] this school of natural philosophy had arrived at the end of its influence. Its speculative tendencies, mildly satirized in A. von Humboldt's observation that its adherents liked to study chemistry without getting their hands wet, were about to be replaced by the pragmatism of the later nineteenth century, when researchers were loath to grant philosophers any share whatever in the definition and evaluation of science.

Carus looks at Goethe as he would have looked at any other 'significant organic phenomenon—a plant, a palm tree, an eagle, a lion', trying to show 'what he has become, and how he could become just that', instead of pointing out what Goethe did *not* become, 'that he did not turn out to be a great mathematician or lawyer or painter'.[2] Considering his subject in this manner, as *Gestalt* above all, Carus necessarily stresses attributes which are not always conceived of as relevant to poetic achievement. Foremost among these is Goethe's scientific talent, to which Carus devotes an enlightening chapter. Much is also made of the poet's physical constitution, not as a chance gift of Providence but as an essential part of an existence which Carus calls 'well-born', from the old German form of address, *Wohlgeboren*. Goethe was well-born not only socially but because he was endowed with a perfect balance between physical and intellectual powers. He thus represents an archetypal version of a healthy man: not because he was a stranger to bodily or emotional crises, but because he was capable of almost complete recovery and regeneration after an affliction had run its course. Mental hygiene, no less than physical prophylaxis and quarantine, enabled him not only to survive but altogether to throw off the shocks of life. In the chapter on 'Goethe's Personality', Carus makes special mention of Swift and Byron as examples of writers whose physical shortcomings conditioned the outlook on life which characterizes their works. Much of Goethe's strength, on the other hand, lay in the jealousy with which he guarded what

[1] Apart from the work here discussed, these are *Briefe über Goethes Faust* (1835) and *Goethe, dessen Bedeutung für unsere und die kommende Zeit* (1863).

[2] *Goethe, zu dessen näherem Verständnis* (ed. by Merian-Genast, Zürich, 1948), pp. 175–6.

he himself had called 'the lines of fortification' of his existence.[1]
In the poet's refusal to engage in personal polemics, in the only
half-conscious preservation of his independence towards women,
even in his reluctance to leave Weimar when he could have
played an outwardly much more brilliant role in Berlin or
Vienna—in all these peculiarities of Goethe's Carus sees signs of
his 'Lebenskunst', his masterful handling of his own life. 'Lebenskunst' is the perfection of one's personality to the utmost extent,
through the (largely instinctual) faculty of developing all the
potentialities afforded one at birth and by the circumstances of
one's life. In this connexion Carus was the first biographer to
remark that Goethe was fortunate not only in the standard
meaning of the term, in that he was spared poverty, disease,
and obscurity, but even more because he found, when he most
needed them for his growth, antagonists who acted as 'irritants':
Behrisch, Merck, Herder, even Karl August and Schiller: men
of very different type and calibre who liked him, fought him,
and 'kept him on his toes'.

These observations are as valid today as they were when first
made. The modern scholar, to be sure, possesses infinitely more
factual information on Goethe than was available to Carus.
But the hand of specialization has lain heavily on Goethe
scholarship, and Carus's book has had to be rediscovered much
later and newly appreciated as one of the best over-all evaluations ever made of the poet. (Practically unnoticed when it was
first published, this biography has only very slowly made its way
until it was reprinted in 1948, in no less than three different
editions, more than a century after it first saw the light of day.)[2]

Less convincing than the remarks summarized above is the
author's predilection for phrenology as a key to human nature,
and his claim that a liking for Goethe is indicative of a person's
intrinsic worth. He makes much of Goethe's cranial measure-
ments and gravely asserts that Schiller's forehead, broad rather
than high, indicates that he was fond of philosophical speculation, a pastime alien to high- but narrow-domed men such as

---

[1] Letter to Zelter, 31 Jan. 1830.

[2] So deep was the oblivion to which Carus was once consigned that he is not
mentioned at all in H. Maync's *Geschichte der deutschen Goethe-Biographie* (Leipzig,
1914). Even J. Zeitler's *Goethe-Handbuch* (Stuttgart, 1916–18, 3 vols.) dismisses him
in seven lines. No doubt the reissue of this work by A. Zastrau (Stuttgart, 1955—)
will make amends for this.

Napoleon or Goethe. Elsewhere he writes that 'nothing so shows a man's views and character ... as does the way in which he sees Goethe'. This is, of course, a presumptuous kind of nonsense if applied beyond the sphere of literary preferences. For all that, it was an idea soon taken up by others, and encapsuled, by the novelist Berthold Auerbach, in the adjective 'ready for Goethe' —goethereif—as denoting an exalted state of spiritual and emotional grace. Crying in the wilderness as he did, Carus can surely be forgiven for thus imputing to Goethe's work a moral dimension which is normally only claimed for the Bible. Nor would the modern reader unreservedly agree that Goethe was the quintessence of all that is German, with his 'deep, receptive soul', his 'striving for universality and depth', and his 'tenacity and active cosmopolitanism'.

Brilliant as this book is, it still represents a compendium of thoughts on Goethe rather than a proper biography. It is a morsel for the connoisseur, and has remained so to this day; it is no food for the layman. To a lesser degree this applies as well to another book written in that period, *Göthe und seine Werke* by Karl Rosenkranz (1847). Its author, to be sure, tries to do justice to the whole Goethe instead of offering biographical or exegetic fragments; he keeps in the background and does not look on the subject as on an episode in his own development; and he introduces a new viewpoint into Goethe research by examining the poet's relevance for his own generation. In view of the critical spirit of his time, it was perhaps inevitable that Rosenkranz should have written a defence of Goethe as much as an introduction to him. Now and then this polemic tendency overshadows all else, as in the preface where the author gets so carried away by the problem of Prussia's relationship to the rest of Germany that he forcibly has to bring himself back to the subject at hand: 'But I shall make myself stop at this point, and [close with a quotation from Goethe].' In Rosenkranz's references to contemporary criticism, Gervinus is damned with faint praise, and Goethe's own attitude to political literature discussed at far greater length than the topic would warrant for us.

These minor defects are hardly surprising in a book written just before 1848. More serious are the limitations which spring from the author's Hegelian background, such as his insistence on philosophy as the proper organ for the interpretation of poetry, and his compulsion to force his material into categories. Thus Goethe's life is corseted into stages of Spontaneous Naturalism, Classical Idealism, and Eclectic Universalism, ominous-sounding concepts which are, in turn, neatly subdivided into secondary classifications. Rosenkranz's mania for symmetry is so strong that he refuses to accord any preponderant space to *Faust*, simply because 'it must not assume, in our account, an importance disproportionate to the care with which we have examined the other works',[1] even though the drama is elsewhere in the book acknowledged as Goethe's masterpiece. Another weakness, remedied in the later editions, had to do with the book's genesis. It grew out of lectures held at the University of Königsberg, as can clearly be seen from the abrupt transitions from topic to topic, and from a number of interjections like 'And now, gentlemen . . .', which in one intriguing instance was followed by 'since there are no ladies present . . .'(during the discussion of *Römische Elegien*).

Despite its excessively dialectic design, Rosenkranz's work offers a good deal more than does H. Viehoff's *Goethes Leben* (1847–8), which is no more than a detailed enumeration of the facts and dates of the poet's life. It was Viehoff's fate not to write, but merely to announce the great biography of the mid-nineteenth century. In the foreword to volume ii he expresses his dismay that the coming centennial of Goethe's birth— 'which, we hope, will be celebrated as a national event'—would not be greeted by a Goethe biography from the pen of any leading German author. It was to fill this vacuum that Viehoff, who either did not know of Rosenkranz, or perhaps did not consider him sufficiently eminent, decided to launch his own book at this juncture: because 'reports have been coming from across the Channel that an Englishman is getting ready to take from us the glory of a first biography'. Alas, Viehoff was wrong in assuming that the centennial of 1849 would be the signal for a nation-wide celebration. But he did correctly foretell that the first full-scale Goethe biography would be written by an Englishman.

Generations of German as well as English and American readers have owed their first acquaintance with the poet to

---

[1] *Göthe und seine Werke* (Königsberg, 1847), p. 387.

George Henry Lewes's *The Life and Works of Goethe*. Even today there exists, in the opinion of some, no better introduction to Goethe than this biography, originally published in 1855. The first great American biography, George H. Calvert's *The Life and Works of Goethe* (1875), was based on Lewes's book; so were the early French biographies by A. Hédouin and A. Mézières. Apart from its French version, Lewes's work, of which no less than 18 English editions had been published by 1900, was translated into Italian and Polish, and thrice into German (by Freese, Lippert, and Sydow). For a period of several decades, it was Lewes rather than any German writer who introduced Goethe to the world at large: a fact which no doubt prompted many Germans as well to take a closer look at this poet who was beginning to be so highly regarded abroad. Even in this century a scholar like Josef Hofmiller and a poet of the calibre of Rainer Maria Rilke owed their conversion to Goethe partly to this book.

Lewes's biography could hardly have failed to make a strong impression on the contemporary public. It was written by an author well known in his own right, who was a celebrity besides as the common-law husband of the novelist George Eliot; it was dedicated to the greatest of Goethe's English admirers, Thomas Carlyle, and published at a time when work on Goethe had almost reached a dead end in Germany itself. It is a scholarly biography, but never pedantic; it is elegantly if somewhat flamboyantly written, but does not sacrifice accuracy to mere chasing after literary effect. Lewes had an uncommon gift for the trenchant phrase, and where that gift is coupled with psychological and aesthetic insight, the result can be strikingly aphoristic: 'Experience is the most effective taskmaster, although, as Jean Paul says, "the schoolfees are somewhat heavy". Goethe was always willing to pay the fees, if he could but get the instruction'; 'Most poets describe objects by metaphors or comparisons; Goethe seldom tells you what an object is *like*, he tells you what it *is*. Shakespeare is very unlike Goethe in this respect'; 'All his poems grow out of occasions: they are the flowers of which circumstance is the earth.'[1]

While acknowledging Goethe's uniqueness throughout, Lewes none the less manages to bring his hero closer to the reader by

[1] *The Life and Works of Goethe* (3rd ed., Leipzig, 1882, 2 vols.), ii. 157; i. 66 and 95, respectively.

describing several of the great man's small foibles. He is one of
the few biographers to mention, with mild, urbane disapproval,
a weakness which the poet shared with many lesser mortals:
a great reluctance to return to their owners certain borrowed
objects to which he had taken a liking. (Knebel's engravings by
Dürer, Professor Büttner's optical instruments, and a bar of
platinum which the Czar had sent to the chemist Doebereiner
all ended up, by way of loan, in Goethe's house, from which
their owners later had great difficulty in retrieving them.) In
like manner, Lewes does not gloss over the fact that Goethe
was, at best, an average painter, and a shallow linguist. In a
characteristic aphorism he observes that 'there are men who learn
many languages, and never thoroughly master the grammar of
one. One of these was Goethe.'

Lewes does not hesitate to explain certain events in Goethe's
life by comparing them with analogous experiences of his own.
To the reader whose ear is attuned to the idolatrous lucubrations
of Goethe worship as practised in late nineteenth-century Germany, these references have a mutinous ring because they infer
that Goethe may have had more in common with the great
throng than is generally admitted. Doubting, for example, that
Goethe understood much of the French plays performed in
Frankfurt during the Seven Years War, Lewes describes an
occasion when he, too, as a child enjoyed the performance of a
French play, without understanding much of what was said.
The comment, properly tucked away in a footnote where it
belongs, is surely appropriate: Goethe was nine years old when
the French occupied his native city. In other observations of this
nature Lewes builds, whenever practicable, similar bridges of
understanding and sympathy between the subject and the
reader. Much of this is, of course, a question of taste and fashion.
It cannot be denied that Lewes was very much a rational Victor-
ian, and that the depths of Goethe's personality can never be
plumbed solely by means of such analogies. None the less,
Lewes's achievement is a real one: he manages to present his
subject without descending to the 'Dear Reader' type of
coyness, or, on the other hand, subscribing to the notion that the
secret of scholarly writing lies in enumerating, robot-fashion, a
series of facts.

To Lewes, a man like Menzel is 'radically incompetent to

appreciate a poet. I should as soon think of asking the first stalwart Kentish farmer for his opinion of the Parthenon.'[1] He is as wary of blind criticism as he is of blind adulation. Yet in trying to render a balanced account of Goethe, he often leans over too far in the direction opposite to the one followed in his day. Goethe's relationship with Christiane, for example, was more than the *mésalliance* it has often been called; but surely Lewes errs in endowing it with all the characteristics of a deep spiritual kinship. Likewise, whatever intricate motives have been imputed to Goethe to explain his sudden departure for Italy in 1786, they assuredly amounted to more than 'the gadfly of genius'.

More far-reaching than these distortions, and the author's refusal to credit Marianne von Willemer with any part of *Der westöstliche Divan*, has been Lewes's attempt to redress the balance between the Young Goethe and the Old. He is primarily interested in the former: 'It is Goethe's misfortune with posterity that he is mostly present to our minds as the calm old man, seldom as the glorious youth.'[2] However, in foreshortening the book towards the end so that the late years and works are given short shrift, Lewes has ignored the fact that the stress on the old poet was entirely natural at the time and could not be changed by arbitrarily telescoping the late works into a few pages of shallow analysis. Old men who have long been in the public eye necessarily acquire a protean reputation. Men of their own age fondly remember them as youngsters; they become older in the eyes of each successive generation, and the final verdict of history is not passed upon them until long after their death. Winston Churchill is such a man in our time. His public life has spanned three generations. He was a dashing young correspondent to the men who fought in the Spanish-American War, First Lord of the Admiralty to their sons, and to their grandsons who fought in the Second World War, an avuncular Grand Old Man. By the same token, Goethe was bound to be an old man in the eyes of Lewes's generation. Eckermann and Falk and Bettina and Riemer, as well as Lewes's friends and compatriots Carlyle and Thackeray, and all the others who after 1832 wrote down what they remembered about Goethe, necessarily described the venerable privy councillor who had still been alive in their youth. They could add but little to the image of their

[1] *The Life and Works of Goethe*, i. 327.   [2] Ibid. ii. 80.

fathers' contemporary who had talked with Napoleon, or their grandfathers' who had seen Marie Antoinette pass through Strassburg on her way to marry the Dauphin of France.

This young Goethe had by 1855 so far receded into the past that he had to be expressly rediscovered. Lewes could rediscover him for his own generation because some eighty years had elapsed in which works like *Götz* and *Werther* could be reassessed in their meaning for a changed world. It turned out that these and many other works of the young poet 'wore well', that they had stood the test of time and could now be assigned their niche in world literature. But the production of Goethe's old age, aside from being intrinsically harder to fathom, was still too recent for a definitive evaluation. Several decades still had to pass before works like *Faust* and *Wilhelm Meister* were beginning to be understood, and the picture of the calm old poet replaced by that of a man desperately struggling for equilibrium even at eighty. This weakness in an otherwise inspired biography clearly shows in the chapter on *Faust*. Unsure as to what to do with this late work, Lewes departs from his usual procedure of looking at Goethe as a sovereign entity; trying to find his way in the dark by reference to familiar constellations, he begins by comparing the work to *Hamlet* and ends by comparing it to Calderón's *El mágico prodigioso*.

Little biographical work of note was done on Goethe in the twenty years following the publication of Lewes's work. The men who wrote on recent German literature in the 1850's and 1860's—G. G. Gervinus, F. T. Vischer, August Koberstein, Otto Ludwig, Karl Goedeke, Hermann Hettner, Julian Schmidt—on the whole did so with a strong bias in favour of a nationally oriented and realistically conceived drama. In both these aspects Shakespeare and Schiller were clearly preferable to Goethe. The Schiller of these men, to be sure, was not the real Schiller but the idealized image of a philosopher-poet leading his people into the light. But if he was no better understood, he was at any rate better loved than Goethe, to whom Goedeke devoted a lacklustre biography and whose *Faust* even Vischer, for all his forceful lecturing and writing on the subject, sharply divided into a masterful first and an insultingly obscure second part, fit material for a parody.

These tendencies found concrete expression in the great Schiller celebrations of 1859 and the foundation of the German Shakespeare Society in 1864 after several attempts to establish a Goethe Society, although backed by men like Varnhagen von Ense, Franz Liszt, and Richard Wagner, had failed for lack of interest. It looked in those days as if Goethe were doomed to remain for ever the favourite author of an *élite* of discriminating readers; for the German people at large, he would live on as a formidable but lifeless item in the histories of literature. To designate the minority which even then looked up to Goethe both as a poet and as a guide through life, the discriminatory term 'Goethe congregation'—Goethegemeinde—came to be used more and more. Thus Hermann Marggraff in 1856 spoke of the courage required in openly acknowledging one's membership in that informal body, and as dedicated a devotee of the poet's as Gustav von Loeper expected no good to come from the establishment of a Goethe Society, because 'the Goethegemeinde, like the communion of the Christian Church, consists of the community of the believers, wherever these may happen to be'.[1]

However, the dawn of a new era of Goethe appreciation was just about to break even as these pessimistic ideas were being voiced. Among the factors which helped to usher in Goethe's rediscovery as one of the great authors of world literature was a biography which has not ceased to perplex the scholar and fascinate the reader since its first publication in 1876: Herman Grimm's *Goethe*.

Herman Grimm brought unique qualifications to the task of Goethe biography. The son of Wilhelm and nephew of Jacob, he had grown up in a household devoted to the study of German language and literature. His wife Gisela was Bettina von Arnim's youngest daughter. In her family as in his own, Goethe was read and discussed not only as a writer but as the intimate friend of the older generation. A number of talented men and women who had known Goethe personally became Grimm's friends in later life, and no doubt helped to strengthen the ties which bound him to the world of Weimar: Goethe's grandsons Walther and Wolfgang; Marianne von Willemer, who confided to Grimm the secret of her co-authorship of a part of *Der*

[1] Letter to W. von Biedermann, 19 Nov. 1869.

westöstliche Divan; Robert Schumann's widow Clara, who had played for Goethe in 1831; Alexander von Humboldt; the Empress Augusta, born and raised in Weimar; the painter Peter Cornelius, who had been one of the first to illustrate *Faust*. Steeped in the spirit of classical Weimar, Grimm none the less stood with both feet in the present: in the latter half of the nineteenth century, which to him was both a continuation of the Age of Classicism and a break with it—a continuation because Goethe shares with Dante and Shakespeare an immortality which among other things forces each successive generation to read his works and come to terms with them; a break because the German *Reich* of 1871, industrialized, increasingly urban, dedicated to technological progress, and a powerful political entity, necessarily lived by lights other than those which had illuminated Goethe's path. Grimm saw his century as divided into an Era of Goethe and an Era of Bismarck. It is a measure of the synthesis he achieved between the two that he edited a part of Bismarck's correspondence, amply and brilliantly wrote on Goethe, and in a lengthy novel (*Unüberwindliche Mächte*, 1867) frankly faced, and resolved in an affirmative sense, the question of Goethe's relevance to the modern world. At the same time Grimm's competence extended beyond an intimate knowledge of Goethe and an awareness of the changes which had taken place since 1832. He was a master of German prose; despite some mannerisms and a certain flavouring of Berlin dialect, his *Goethe* is stylistically one of the best biographies. The breadth of his interests in other fields is indicated by the fact that he was at home in half a dozen languages and civilizations, admired and translated Emerson, from a feeling of kinship with the American especially in regard to Goethe, and wrote a number of other biographical works which belong to the permanent achievements of German scholarship.

It is not surprising that a writer of such background and gifts should have left the imprint of his own personality even on his biography of another and greater man. To Grimm, Goethe was one of the high points in the development of mankind. His book is accordingly full, perhaps too full, of sweeping panoramas of entire periods of world history. With its widely ranging historical and philosophical reflections, it occasionally reminds one of the poet's own *Dichtung und Wahrheit*. Frankfurt, and the Free

Cities in general, are described in broad, yet detailed pictures; on the occasion of Goethe's Italian journey, we are treated to a synopsis of Roman history down the ages. Although Grimm tends to roam freely whenever he fills in the background of Goethe's life, he is none the less rigorous in restricting his delineation of the poet himself to only those factors which have directly affected the latter's development. Hence there is little mention of certain minor works (not a word on *Pandora* or the *Unterhaltungen deutscher Ausgewanderten*) or of such among Goethe's friends as Grimm thought unimportant. The Stolberg brothers, for example, are unceremoniously dropped when the author is through with them: 'We herewith leave the two counts to their own fate, since they are of no further importance for the consideration of Goethe's life.'[1] This is an arbitrary procedure, to be sure. But it was a necessary one in the days when the comma-counters reigned supreme in literary scholarship, when Heinrich Düntzer found it necessary to devote a footnote to the fact that the father of young Isenburg von Bury (an unimportant playmate of Goethe's when they were in their teens) was 'Friedrich Karl Buri, ennobled in 1753, first Directorial Councilor, then Privy Councilor of Isenburg-Birstein and Governmental Director'.[2]

Grimm's attitude toward the professional German scholars was one of thinly veiled contempt. He did not even deign to satirize the scholarly developments of his time: he ignored them. Perhaps the most important single discovery in the history of Goethe philology, that of one of the earliest versions of *Faust* (the so-called 'Urfaust', by Erich Schmidt in 1887), was never made as far as Grimm was concerned. Although this document has profoundly and permanently affected our understanding of the tragedy, Grimm never referred to it in the later editions of his book.[3] Typical of his disdain of the merely meticulous, library-bound researcher is also the challenge implicit in the title of the essay he wrote on the occasion of the 150th anniversary of the poet's birth in 1899: *Goethe unter freiem Himmel.* As a gentleman

---

[1] *Goethe. Vorlesungen gehalten an der Kgl. Universität zu Berlin* (8th ed., Berlin and Stuttgart, 1903, 2 vols.), i. 258.

[2] Cited from the English version, H. Düntzer, *The Life of Goethe* (New York, 1884), p. 46.

[3] When references to later developments seemed unavoidable, Grimm added nonchalant comments such as 'Thus in 1874. Today this would, of course, have to be amended' (Grimm, op. cit. ii. 256).

of the old school, independent in mind, manner, and means, Grimm had a cavalier familiarity with every station of the *grand tour* of the works and localities in which Western civilization had reached its fullest flowering. 'Who among us', he asks when comparing the reading of Homer with a walk on flowering meadows, 'has not plucked the anemones which in springtime grow in such profusion in the gardens of Roman villas?' Even in those halcyon days of cultural travel, such grandseigneurial offhandedness must have provoked a smile in some readers, and discomfort in others who had never walked in these enchanted gardens—or taken tea with the Empress Augusta, or talked with half a dozen friends of Goethe's.

The reader is entitled to expect much of so exclusive and discriminating an author. He is given much: a clearly focused, forcefully drawn portrait of Goethe, incorrect in some details but essentially as truthful as it could be made at the time, with many fine, original observations. For example, Grimm lays bare in masterly fashion the various springs which fed Goethe's language; the well-known debt to the Bible is clearly traced, as is the less-known influence which Lavater exerted in this respect. Wilhelm von Humboldt, usually relegated to a peripheral position in Goethe biographies, is here considered as Schiller's successor in the poet's esteem and affection. The Italian journey is seen not only as an escape from Weimar, but as Goethe's first real contact with the world at large. In this connexion Grimm at least touches on one of the great mysteries of Goethe's life: his astounding lack of interest in the great cultural centres of his time (aside from Rome, Goethe knew only one other metropolis, Berlin). Is it not odd, we may well ask, that this man of means and leisure who was obsessed with the urge to examine all sorts of phenomena, this poet with the universal mind who rarely looked at a cloud or a rock or a bone without reference to meteorology, mineralogy, or anatomy, this student of human nature who was intrigued by so many Frenchmen, Englishmen, and other foreigners of his acquaintance, should never have troubled to visit Paris, London, or even Vienna? Had his contemporaries Voltaire and Byron not ranged far over Europe, A. von Humboldt and Chamisso far over the globe? It is a question which Goethe's biographers have never answered.

Grimm changed the Goethe image of his generation in two important aspects. He secured for Frau von Stein an important and honourable place by Goethe's side, and relegated Schiller to a subordinate position as a poet and as a man. In the context of the biographer's own time, both adjustments were highly desirable. Goethe's correspondence with Charlotte von Stein had no sooner been published (1848–51) than people began to concern themselves with the question as to whether or not their relationship had been adulterous (Frau von Stein having, of course, been married at the time). For a public largely hostile to Goethe, such evidence of adultery as might have been found would have been telling proof of the immorality so often imputed to the poet. In postulating a Platonic relationship, and altogether in consigning the problem to the sphere of privacy where it belongs, Grimm succeeded in at least half-closing the door to a type of investigation as revolting as it was irrelevant. He did so on the basis not of prudery but of common-sense, and his argument was the more effective for its admixture of earthy humour. Explaining the poet's coolness toward Frau von Stein after his return from Italy, Grimm simply states that 'Charlotte von Stein . . . was, perhaps, the main reason why Goethe, surfeited with delicate sauces which left him un-nourished, now clasped under his arm a solid loaf of black bread [Christiane] into which he could sink his teeth as he wanted. . . .'[1]

Grimm's demotion of Schiller, which was to some extent rectified in the later editions of his work, also represents a reaction to a contemporary tendency: to the excessive Schiller-worship of the mid-nineteenth century. In asserting that Schiller's youth, unlike Goethe's, was in no sense 'a prologue to his later development', or that Schiller was throughout obsessed by the feeling that 'he could offer nothing . . . to Goethe', Grimm perhaps went farther than he had intended; at any rate, his disparagement of Schiller in the first version is one of the book's few weaknesses. Taken as such, this attitude of Grimm's is evidence of the fact that Goethe and Schiller used to play a mutually exclusive role in the German people's esteem. The

---

[1] Grimm, op. cit. ii. 94. Describing this juncture in Goethe's life, E. G. Kolben-heyer wrote in his *Karlsbader Novelle*: 'Die Zeit ist über den Minnedienst hinaus, Liebe will sie.'

public on the whole looked up to Schiller in times of stress and
national danger, as it did during the Napoleonic Wars and
again in the period 1848–71, and turned to Goethe in calmer
periods of history. For decades Schiller had been venerated as
the prophet of Germany's independence and greatness. Grimm's
book, published five years after the proclamation of the
Reich, marks the pendulum's swing in the opposite direction:
now that the nation's independence and greatness seemed assured for all time, Schiller's exhortations fell on the deaf ears of
a satiated audience. In the field of biographical writing Grimm
merely reflects a reversal of the two poets' roles which found
many other expressions as well: in the sudden phenomenal
demand for Goethe's works, of which no fewer than twenty-
seven different editions were published between 1868 and 1874
(as against a still respectable seventeen editions of Schiller); in
the shift, in German school texts, from Schiller to Goethe and to
modern authors; even in such details as the title of a course
offered at Heidelberg University, which in 1868–9 was announced as 'The Drama of Schiller and Goethe', and in 1869–
70 as 'The Drama of Goethe and Schiller'.[1] It was only in the
twentieth century that this see-saw ended in the minds of a great
part of the German public.

Grimm's book was published during the *Gründerjahre*, that
period of unparalleled prosperity and expansive optimism
which followed the Franco-Prussian War, when Germany
assumed world leadership in so many phases of industrial, military, technological, and academic activity. This biography is,
naturally enough, in part the literary refraction of an age when
few Germans had any reason to doubt the essential desirability
of the human condition, when progress (through science, education, social legislation, colonial expansion, or whatever) seemed
inevitable, when hardly anyone listened to Marx or Nietzsche,
when Freud and Einstein had not yet spoken. God was in His
Heaven, Bismarck in his *Reichstag*, Goethe on his Parnassus, and
all was well—in comparison, at least, to what had been (let
alone to what was to come). Small wonder, then, that Grimm's
Goethe is an optimist and primarily a young poet: Grimm, like

---

[1] It was at this time that Nietzsche's deep suspicion of Schiller made him ask:
'the Germans say Goethe *and* Schiller ... don't they *know* this Schiller yet?' (*Streif-
züge eines Unzeitgemässen*).

Lewes, dismisses the last twenty years in a few pages. This Goethe has a demonic side to him but is not really a problematical sort of person; for example, he is ever victorious against the onslaughts of the senses. (Ulrike von Levetzow, who as a young girl inspired in the seventy-four-year-old poet a last great love, a desperate and tragic emotional upheaval, is not mentioned in this biography.) In short, Goethe is a man who would do quite well if he were alive in Grimm's own time—not to mention Faust and Mephisto, capital fellows, who if they were to appear before the *Reichstag*, 'would immediately size up the situation, choose the right moment, and with a few penetrating ideas create for themselves an attentive audience!'[1] War and revolution, like poverty and disease, are not even clouds on the horizon. As for the Kant–Laplace Theory, according to which the world will in due course end when the burnt-out planet on which we live falls back into the sun, is its fatalism not more revolting, Grimm asks, than 'the bone of a carcass which not even a dog will touch'? It is not difficult to see how in the hands of biographers of less integrity and taste, this image of Goethe could eventually turn into the bland and preternaturally harmonious idol as which the poet was occasionally represented toward the end of the Wilhelmian Era.

No account of the Goethe renascence would be complete if it did not also record the shrilly dissenting voice of Father Alexander Baumgartner, S.J. His *Göthe. Sein Leben und seine Werke* (1885–6) was written with the express aim of stripping the poet of the quasi-divine attributes so lately bestowed upon him. Baumgartner felt that some biographers were establishing a sort of 'official' view of the poet (as reported above, Grimm had indeed suggested that Goethe would have felt at home in the new *Reich*), and that certain pernicious modern ideas such as Darwinism, Spinozism, and Naturalism were being smuggled into the German home and school under the guise of literature. Much of the violence of his protest no doubt sprang from his own exposed position: that of an embattled Jesuit tilting, at the height of the *Kulturkampf*, at the giants Goethe and Bismarck and demolishing the windmills Düntzer and Geiger. Yet his own methods were far from straightforward.

[1] Grimm, op. cit. ii. 220.

I am not at all the simpleton [he writes with artful *naïveté*] who in pharisaic self-righteousness looks down on the mad escapades of a great man, and solemnly exclaims 'I thank thee, O Lord, that I am not like this Göthe!' Nor am I like the frivolous Heine who deeply bowed before the Olympian, only to mock him the more shamelessly before all France. Still less do I agree with the turncoat Wolfgang Menzel, who, in order to rescue 'his' Christ [i.e. that of a militantly Protestant *Burschenschafter*], thought he had to deny Göthe his striking poetic gift and his other splendid talents.[1]

Having thus donned sheep's clothing by proclaiming himself a biographer *sine ira et studio*, the wolf set about attacking Goethe as 'a dilettante whose life has no task, who tries to keep himself amused with painting and poetry, reading, flirting, and gambling'; as a poet whose production was inspired by mere eroticism and as a man for whom life was only the raw material for his stories and plays, even if this meant ruining many women because he was 'far too clever and calculating a person to love honestly, or to make sacrifices for his love'. Furthermore, Goethe was an active Mason, which in this biographer's view was tantamount to being viciously anti-Catholic.

What made Baumgartner a formidable adversary of Goethe's apologists was his weapon. It was not the club once wielded by Menzel and Gervinus, but a rapier deadlier even than Heine's. Witness the way, for example, in which he disposes of an argument advanced by the hapless Düntzer: not by descending to the level of that scholar's pedantry, but by simply repeating Gretchen's cry 'Heinrich, you fill me with horror!' (Düntzer's, like Faust's, first name was Heinrich). Despite his fundamental bias, Baumgartner himself was a fine scholar of the school established by Scherer. His biography is as well documented as any of those which can claim literary status, and certain passages, such as the description of the social and human *milieu* which Goethe found on coming to Weimar, are little short of brilliant. The book also contains some valuable new material, such as an elaboration of the role played in Goethe's life by K. T. von Dalberg. Whether or not this information is provided intentionally (Dalberg was, after all, a major Catholic dignitary), it is only proper that it should have been given.

No one would dispute Baumgartner's right to examine

---

[1] *Göthe. Sein Leben und seine Werke* (2nd ed., Freiburg, 1885–6, 2 vols.), i. viii.

Goethe from an orthodox and even a doctrinaire viewpoint, or blame him for pointing out some aspects of the poet which may well give pause to deeply religious readers of whatever faith. He was neither the first nor the last Catholic writer to do so, and it was only a few decades ago that F. Muckermann and others accomplished a positive evaluation of Goethe from that quarter. The kind of partisanship practised by Baumgartner, however, becomes embarrassing when it swings from the field of ethics to that of literary aesthetics, as in the claim that F. Stolberg's account of his travels is superior to Goethe's *Die italienische Reise*, or in the praise bestowed on Görres as the peer of Dante and Goethe.

Not even Baumgartner, however, could appreciably stem the tide of Goethe enthusiasm which swept Germany toward the end of the nineteenth and the opening of the twentieth century. No less than eight major biographies were published in the years 1895–1909: those by Meyer, Heinemann, Wolff, Haarhaus, Witkowski, Geiger, Bielschowsky, and Engel. Despite their differences in style and outlook—Meyer's is the best written, Heinemann's somewhat school-teacherish, and Engel's annoyingly self-righteous—these works have a number of common denominators which may conveniently be traced by a short analysis of the one which best seems to have stood the test of time, Albert Bielschowsky's *Goethe. Sein Leben und seine Werke*.[1] The bulk of these two medium-sized volumes is made up of the plots and stories of Goethe's major works, as retold by the author. The latter furnishes this information not out of pedantry but because he feels constrained, with his too literal concept of Goethe the 'confessional' poet, to establish wherever possible a close identification between Goethe, or various persons close to him, and the heroes and heroines of the works. To Bielschowsky as to the great majority of his generation, Carlos *is* Merck; Iphigenie, Frau von Stein; and Leonore Sanvitale, the Duchess Anna Amalia ('. . . the same age, the same tastes [Ariosto-Wieland], the same enjoyment of life and happiness at being a patroness of the Muses; clever, refined, a little self-centred, yet

---

[1] The author died before he could finish the second volume, which was completed by other hands. By 1928, when a revised edition was published by W. Linden, 150,000 copies had been sold.

honest and kind').[1] Hand in hand with the over-emphasis of such parallels goes an occasional lack of emotional depth, a certain stuffiness, as evidenced by the author's incredulous head-shaking when he finds, in *Die Wahlverwandtschaften*, that Ottilie seems unaware of the many weaknesses in Eduard's character. Ottilie is a very young girl, in love for the first time, with a much older and worldlier man. To the post-Freudian reader their relationship does not seem so perplexing that 'we do not understand it'.

Bielschowsky is not altogether blind to Goethe's shortcomings. He castigates him for his neglect of his mother during the Weimar years, blames him for his obtuseness towards the French Revolution, and describes the liaison with, and marriage to, Christiane in what one suspects are its true colours, as a chafing yoke bravely borne. Yet many passages are suffused with an aura of adolescent hero worship. On the first seven pages alone Goethe appears as the 'master', the 'giant', and 'the most magnificent bearer of light'; later we come to 'tiny rascal', 'little fellow', and similar excrescences of misplaced coyness. This posture of idolatry leads Bielschowsky into some actual perversions of fact, such as imputing to Goethe the invention of a sort of Latin without Tears (he must surely have been the only man ever to 'master Latin with great ease without actually having grasped its grammar'), or suggesting that the poet acquired his profound familiarity with the main European cultures through his travels. No one will fail to credit him with that familiarity, or to see in the use to which he put it one of his finest achievements. But he gained this knowledge through his reading, his correspondence, and his many personal contacts with visitors to Weimar, all of which sparked his uncanny, intuitive perception of the *Gestalt* of other civilizations. He did not acquire it through his travels, which, with the sole exception of Italy, were restricted to the periphery of these spheres of cultural influence. It is not 'unfortunate' that he never published an account of what he observed on the day or two he spent in Cracow, in September 1790. On the contrary, it is reassuring to know that Goethe was too great a man to pronounce sentence on the Slavs (and this is clearly what Bielschowsky expected him to do) on that kind, and amount, of evidence.

[1] *Goethe. Sein Leben and seine Werke* (3rd ed., München, 1902–4, 2 vols.), i. 521.

These reservations should not blind us to the great merits of this biographer and of the others mentioned above. In retrospect, the image which these men drew of Goethe appears idealized and somewhat out of focus: not wrong, but incomplete. They loved the young, respected the classical, and did their best to understand the old poet. They tended to overlook the thinker, to dismiss the scientist as an amateur, and to censure the statesman as reactionary. They were inclined to turn the dynamic man who never ceased to work for the perfection of his own personality into the passive recipient of providential gifts. However, they drew their image of Goethe with loving attention to detail, with more than a little vision of the uniqueness of the man and poet, and with a truly encyclopedic knowledge. (In the footnotes to his work Bielschowsky made a considered attempt to keep the reader abreast of contemporary scholarly developments, a procedure which differs favourably not only from Herman Grimm's lordly indolence but from the self-intoxication of many more recent biographers.) That Bielschowsky, in particular, wrote *con brio e con amore* as well is shown by the following remarks, which could form a preface to any and all Goethe biographies:

Goethe was the most human of all men, because he had been endowed with a portion of everything human. His figure was typical in its mould, the very ideal of perfect man. Hence it was that all who came in touch with him had the feeling that they had never before seen such a complete man. There may have been others of clearer understanding, of greater energy, of deeper feelings, or of more vivid imagination, but it is quite certain that there never was an individual in whom all these faculties were united in such striking proportions. And, moreover, there has rarely been an individual of such highly developed powers of soul, whose physical life has so fully retained its independence and has so thoroughly permeated the spiritual. This wonderfully perfect amalgamation of Goethe's nature elevates it to the rank of the extraordinary, and, at the same time, accounts for its seemingly contradictory manifestations. But it is this seeming contradictoriness that has made it so difficult for most people to obtain a correct and adequate idea of him.

He observes color refractions like a physicist, examines bones and ligaments like an anatomist, and comments on bankrupt law like a jurist. Gifted with unusual clearness in the comprehension and analysis of men and things, his early appearance on the stage of action is marked by the wisdom and experience of a man of the world and a diplomat. And yet this same man writes poetry overflowing with imagination, goes about in the real world absorbed in dreams, sees many things and many people, not as they are, but in the light of his own fancy, is frequently incapable of making out a clear understanding of objects and their mutual relations, and stands in the midst of human activities a naïve and often helpless child. This man at one time grasps the world in the warm embrace of a Faust and again he spurns it with the annihilating contempt of a Mephistopheles.[1]

In these biographies the main results of contemporary Goethe research were made available to a reading public which, due to the general rise in Germany's population, the spreading of public instruction, and the establishment of German literature as an academic discipline, had greatly increased since 1871. It was for this audience that the most successful of Goethe's popularizers, Wilhelm Bode, wrote a number of monographs which were not strictly biographical but could be read as companion volumes to the works of Bielschowsky and his colleagues. Instead of delving into Goethe's life in the manner of an historian, Bode projected Goethe into his own time, into the first few years of the new century, by asking how the poet would have dealt with certain human situations typical of modern life. These questions he answered in books like *Goethes Lebenskunst* (1900) and *Goethes Gedanken* (1907), in which the poet appears not so much as a creative artist than as a man whose responses to various challenges of life are of universal interest and wide applicability. In thus addressing himself to the middle reaches of the public, Bode started a trend which has more recently been followed by a number of other men who have managed to combine sound erudition with a stylistic light touch and much human warmth.[2] The publishing industry helped in this by putting out several inexpensive editions of his works and of other classics. Reclam's Universal-Bibliothek began to come out in 1867, and was followed by the Sammlung Göschen in 1889. When Anton Kippenberg assumed control of the Inselverlag in 1905, he turned it into a publishing outlet not only of some distinguished contemporary writing, but of the fabulous 'Volksgoethe' and

[1] (Eng. tr. by W. A. Cooper, New York and London, 1905, 3 vols.), i. 1–2.
[2] J. Bab's *Goethes Leben in seinen Briefen*, E. Redslob's *Goethes Leben*, J. Hofmiller's *Wege zu Goethe*.

of Max Morris's revision of Hirzel's *Der junge Goethe*. Eugen
Diederichs, the brothers Karl and Wilhelm Langewiesche, and
Friedrich Lienhard were other publisher-writers who turned
their energies to the task of popularizing Goethe's work intelli-
gently and in good taste.

By 1900 the tide had turned completely. The century which
in its beginnings had seen such hostility to Goethe ended in an
almost universal acclaim of the great 'Olympian'. Before considering the forces which were to replace this concept with one
more meaningful for our own age, we must trace certain other
influences—some open, others almost subterranean—which
affected the Goethe revival.

IV

MUSIC, SCIENCE, AND *KULTURKRITIK*

Music must be played and heard, not written about. It is more profitable to trace Goethe's influence on the chief German composers of the nineteenth century (and the way in which their works have, in turn, reflected back on the German view of Goethe) than to enumerate, catalogue-fashion with more or less appropriately chosen adjectives for each item, all the important musical compositions which have been inspired by his works.[1] This is, perhaps, best done by disregarding completeness for its own sake and by concentrating on the works which have survived.

Goethe's own attitude to music is one of many aspects of his personality which have been subjected to the most contradictory interpretations. He has said so much about so many things that, given patience and a well-indexed edition of the works, conversations, and correspondence, one is truly free to draw the most diverse conclusions. There are those who insist that Goethe did not care for music at all. They buttress their argument with quotations like the following: 'You will find no word about music here, because that did not figure among my interests.'[2] Others, again, are fond of quoting the professional musician Zelter, who had called Goethe 'the only person whose judgment in musical matters I respect'; they deduce from this that the poet had a profound knowledge and appreciation of music. In view of these contradictions, a few dispassionate words may be in order about Goethe's contacts with music and musicians, the more so as his perplexing attitude to the composers of his own time is best understood in the light of his musical background and preferences.

Goethe's musical skills, tastes, and experiences were at least up to the average standards of the upper *bourgeoisie* of his time. He

---

[1] Perhaps the most recent list of compositions influenced by Goethe is that compiled by W. Schuh, at the end of vol. ii of the Artemis edition (Zürich, 1953).

[2] Eckermann, 3 Nov. 1823 (during a discussion of the notes Goethe had made on his Swiss journey of 1797).

had grown up in a family, and later himself presided over a household, where music was regularly performed. He played the piano, if only 'after a fashion'; he was able to read a score with some fluency, and had a fairly extensive, if sketchy, acquaintance with the operatic and symphonic repertory of his time. He was sufficiently interested to plan a Theory of Acoustics, which would perhaps have formed a pendant to the *Farbenlehre*; he counted many musicians among his friends, and in the course of his long life heard many of the foremost performers play: Mozart, Beethoven, Hummel, Maria Szymanowska, Paganini, Mendelssohn, Clara Wieck-Schumann. Certain limitations in his musical culture only appear to be such. Far from being an idiosyncracy of his, Goethe's preference for vocal as against instrumental music reflects a current of musical taste which was very strong in the pre-Beethoven era. Also common to Goethe's generation was an interest in musical expression, and the groping toward a definition of the essence of music, rather than a deep concern with questions of technique. Similarly his belated and rather weak interest in Johann Sebastian Bach was due not to obtuseness but to the popular preference then shown for other members of the Bach family, notably Philipp Emanuel. At the same time, it is reasonable to say that Goethe was not a profoundly musical person; music did not engage his loving attention as long or as intensely as did, for example, certain aspects of natural science. In various periods of his life, his interest in music was stimulated by experts who supplied him with technical information and with news of the main events in contemporary musical life: P. C. Kayser, whom the poet had in mind when he wrote *Jery und Bätely* and *Scherz, List und Rache*, and even as a composer of *Egmont*; J. F. Reichardt, who so strongly felt the adaptability of Goethe's poems to music that he seriously planned an all-inclusive, six-volume *Musik zu Goethes Werken*; and K. F. Zelter, less gifted perhaps than the others, but infinitely closer to Goethe as a friend. Between them, these men were the first to set to music a great many works of Goethe's although they were able to do justice only to some of the shorter poems. Nowadays their settings are largely forgotten, displaced in popular and professional esteem by the work of much greater composers.

Sometimes on his own, occasionally guided and advised by

these friends, Goethe not only followed attentively the musical advances of his time but took direct part in many of them. He encouraged composers by word and deed, through his operatic works which in varying degrees demand musical accompaniment. *Erwin und Elmire, Claudine von Villa Bella, Lila, Jery und Bätely,* and *Die Fischerin* all contain dialogue interrupted by songs, duets, arias; the Italianate *Scherz, List und Rache,* and the second versions of *Erwin* and *Claudine* with their recitative prose, were even more closely modelled on the operetta. With the exception of Hofmannsthal, Goethe was the only great German poet who set the full power of his genius to the writing of libretti: a literary sub-form whose low average quality represents the weak spot of many a great opera. He did so, moreover, with much consideration for the demands of his composers; he rarely overstrained the capabilities of the musicians, as he overstrained those of the actors of his time. Distinct from these direct contributions to the operetta was Goethe's activity as theatre director, in the course of which he also showed much comprehension of operatic music. If the importance of this work can be gauged from mere numbers, it might be pointed out that during his tenure (1791–1817), Mozart's operas alone were performed 280 times on the stages under Goethe's jurisdiction. He intended to write a sequel to *Die Zauberflöte,* and successfully adapted to the stage *Don Giovanni* and Gluck's *Iphigénie en Tauride.*

Not only the operettas but many of Goethe's other works contain entire passages for which he specified musical accompaniment: Klärchen's songs and the final apotheosis in *Egmont,* parts of Act II of *Das Erwachen des Epimenides,* entire scenes from both parts of *Faust,* and others. Most of these passages are, of course, lyrical in mood and form. It is to this lyric poetry that Goethe owes a distinction which is almost certainly his: that of having inspired more, and greater, composers than any other author in world literature. His short poems, whether interspersed in prose works like *Wilhelm Meister,* set in cycles like those of *Der westöstliche Divan,* or simply conceived and written as autonomous lyrical utterances, have fascinated musicians for almost two centuries. Some have been set to music over a hundred times. This is not because their author was famous (although this assured their availability in print, and perhaps influenced some non-German composers) but for very specific literary qualities which make them eminently suitable for composition. They are simple in form and diction and often have a compelling rhythm of their own; their emotional content is genuine and immediately 'transferable'; most importantly, their stanzas tend to be extraordinarily evenly balanced. Close to the end of his life, Brahms could only think of one instance where a poem of Goethe's had been truly improved, or 'raised', as he put it, by the music to which it was set; otherwise, he thought, Goethe's lyrics are 'so "finished" that music can add nothing to them'.[1] The earliest compositions in part or altogether based on Goethe date from the beginning of his literary career. The end of Goethe's influence on music is not yet in sight, although its high point has undoubtedly passed with the nineteenth century.

In view of this it is, perhaps, surprising that Goethe did not, like Wagner, create an altogether new type of musico-literary art work. It is not enough to say that he was no composer. Even as pure poet he might have found a musical *alter ego*, as Maeterlinck did in Debussy and Hofmannsthal in Richard Strauss. Goethe, unfortunately, never came close to the great composers who were active during his life span. Gluck was so old at the time that his veneration for Goethe could bear no fruit (unless it be Goethe's own monodrama *Proserpina*, written, at Gluck's request, as a memorial for the composer's niece Marianne). Except for some incidental music to *Götz von Berlichingen*, which is not definitely ascribed to him, there is not much evidence that Haydn, who lived until 1809 and thus was a contemporary for many years, was interested in Goethe. The same may be said of Weber, despite his frequent visits to Weimar and his plan of a *Faust* opera. Mozart died too soon to contribute more than the magnificent, if somewhat dramatized, setting of *Das Veilchen*. Beethoven did not come to Goethe's attention until late in the latter's life; by then, personality differences forestalled a collaboration which would have been unique in history. When Schubert was born, Goethe was approaching his fiftieth year. As it happened, the musicians with whom Goethe surrounded himself at various times—Kayser, the conductor Eberwein, Zelter, even the gifted and prolific Reichardt—were second-

---

[1] The exception was the last stanza of Schubert's setting of 'Was bedeutet die Bewegung' (M. Kalbeck, *Johannes Brahms* [3rd ed., Berlin, 1912, 3 vols.]), iii. 87.

rate. Thus *Faust* had to wait for Schumann (1844–53) to be worthily set to music; *Die [erste] Walpurgisnacht*, for Mendelssohn (1832 and 1843); *Harzreise im Winter*, for Brahms (1869); some of the *Lieder*, for Wolf (1889).

Among the great composers of the time, Mozart undoubtedly stood highest in Goethe's esteem. The poet had heard him play, in Frankfurt, as a child progidy of seven. The impression must have been strong because after more than sixty years he still remembered quite distinctly 'the little man with his wig and sword'. Goethe paid homage to Mozart in *Hermann und Dorothea*, had his operas performed on the stages of Weimar and Lauchstädt, and repeatedly expressed his belief that the creator of *Don Giovanni* would also have been the ideal composer for *Faust*, with which the opera has so much in common.

Beethoven admired Goethe from afar for years. He was confirmed in this by Bettina von Arnim, who sang Goethe's praises to Beethoven, Beethoven's to Goethe, and attempted to bring the two together. They finally made each other's acquaintance in July 1812, at the fashionable Bohemian spa of Teplitz, but did not advance beyond a pleasant exchange of formalities. It is said that on one occasion Goethe and Beethoven met, coming towards them on a narrow garden path, the Empress of Austria and her retinue. Goethe had no sooner recognized her than he respectfully stood aside, doffed his hat, and bowed. Beethoven, on the other hand, took no notice at all: head held high, he walked right through the group of courtiers . . . and afterwards berated Goethe for what he considered his servile behaviour. This well-known little anecdote epitomizes the difference between the two men, who after parting proceeded to express their opinion of one another to third parties.[1] Goethe thought that the composer may well have been right in thinking that the world was wretchedly unjust, but that he was only making things difficult for himself and for others by refusing to take life as it is. Beethoven, on his part, suspected that Goethe was fonder of keeping company with people of rank and position than befitted a poet

[1] One of the first to recognize the symptomatic character of this meeting was Nietzsche, who suggested that in order to understand the powerful but inarticulate nature of German music, one should 'imagine Beethoven next to Goethe, for example, at their meeting in Teplitz: semi-barbarism next to civilization, the people next to an aristocrat' (*Die fröhliche Wissenschaft*).

aware of his dignity. Despite these reservations, they continued to regard each other highly. Without at all grasping the revolutionary nature of Beethoven's compositions, Goethe at least respected him as an exceptionally dedicated artist and a skilled pianist. Beethoven also continued to admire Goethe, especially as a lyrical poet; his attitude as a professional musician, however, seems to have been shot through with the same sense of failure and frustration which is apparent in his personal relationship with the poet. His main Goethe setting is the incidental music to *Egmont* (op. 84), which contains not only the well-known overture but two *Lieder* of Klärchen, *entr'actes* and other short pieces, and the final Symphony of Victory. As composer of Goethe *Lieder*, however, Beethoven was far less successful, both in relation to his grandiose achievement in other fields and in comparison with the *Lied* production of later, and lesser, composers. The *Mailied* and a couple of others are fine settings, but the rest suffer from what undoubtedly was a lack of sympathy with and understanding of what Goethe had meant when he wrote, for example, 'Nur wer die Sehnsucht kennt'—which Beethoven set four different times without much success. The *Bundeslied* ('In allen guten Stunden') is equally unsatisfactory; the poem is, to be sure, no great jewel, but Reichardt composed it very creditably none the less. *Rastlose Liebe* was never finished; a *Faust* symphony never advanced beyond a few sketches; neither did *Der Erlkönig*. There is an element of the haphazard in these settings. The poems, one suspects, might as well have been written by someone else for all that Beethoven cared. (His music for the *Mailied* was, in fact, originally composed for an aria in Umlauf's *Die schöne Schusterin*. In much the same way, Mozart had come to set *Das Veilchen*: not because it was by Goethe, but because he happened to come across it in a collection of contemporary poems.)

Among Goethe's musical interpreters, Schubert was by far the most prolific. His eighty compositions outnumber even the production of Carl Loewe, who is chiefly remembered nowadays for his compositions from Goethe. Some of Schubert's settings are known the world over: *Das Heidenröslein, Gretchen am Spinnrad, Der König in Thule, Wanderers Nachtlied,* and of course his very first work, *Der Erlkönig*—whose locale is for some reason transferred to Italy, from alder trees to pines. Unlike many of his colleagues, Schubert went to great lengths to preserve the text and to avoid adapting the verse forcibly to the music, although this sometimes turned out to be to the detriment of the latter.[1] He was unique for his time also in his willingness to set to music not only the short lyrics which have always attracted composers, but even some of the longer, somewhat metaphysical works like *Prometheus*, *Grenzen der Menschheit*, or *Ganymed*. It would be difficult to imagine better settings of *Der Erlkönig* or *Gretchen am Spinnrad* than those we have by Schubert. Yet occasionally his very virtues become excesses: his tremendous melodic facility sometimes runs away with the topic at hand; individual words are misaccentuated, and false divisions made between stanzas which belong together by meaning; his faithfulness is often to the letter of the text rather than to the spirit. Some of Schubert's longer settings which require greater depth of understanding, and of general culture, are weak. If this composer had really grasped the psychological situation of the Harpist in *Wilhelm Meister*, his rendition of 'Wer nie sein Brot mit Tränen ass' (written at the optimistic age of nineteen) would not have ended on a note of almost serene complacency, but, like the poem, on one of bitterness and despair.

Schubert never received a reply to a very humble letter he sent Goethe in June 1825, together with his setting of three poems (now op. 19). Neither did J. von Spaun elicit any reaction when he had recommended the composer to Goethe a few years earlier. This silence is often explained by reference to the fact that the poet was overwhelmed with similar offerings by unknown young composers, and that his musical oracles in that period, Zelter and Eberwein, from all that is known of them presumably looked with disfavour on Schubert's unorthodox rendition of these poems (*An Mignon*, *An Schwager Kronos*, *Ganymed*). Perhaps it was mere coincidence that Beethoven had also remained without acknowledgement when he wrote, in 1823, to enlist Goethe's aid in interesting the court of Weimar in buying the *Missa Solemnis*, and that Berlioz, when he sent his *Huit Scènes de Faust*, also came up against a wall of silence. Perhaps these omissions indicate that Goethe was indifferent to the men and works concerned. He had, of course, no way of

---

[1] An interesting example of this, in regard to *Nähe des Geliebten*, is examined by W. Vetter in *Der Klassiker Schubert* (Leipzig, 1953, 2 vols.), i. 378–81.

knowing that Schubert's *Lieder* would soon sweep the country, and in this form popularize many of his own poems.

The only major contemporary composer with whom Goethe was on close terms personally was Mendelssohn, whose best-remembered Goethe work is the cantata op. 60, incidental music to *Die [erste] Walpurgisnacht*. Zelter had already introduced Felix Mendelssohn's father, Abraham, to Goethe in 1803; the boy's winning personality and pianistic skill won the poet over when he met him in 1821. It was after their last meeting, in 1830, that Goethe wrote the lines which indicate as clearly as anything else that his attitude to music was fundamentally an intellectual one:

'I was particularly happy to have him [Mendelssohn] here, because it made me realize that my outlook on music is unchanged. I listen to it with pleasure, interest, and reflection. I like the historical connotations it evokes: for how would it be possible to understand any phenomenon unless one entered into it through a consideration of its development?'

Goethe ended by saying that Mendelssohn (who had evidently played selections from various composers, arranged by period) 'starting with the Era of Bach, brought back to my mind . . . Haydn, Mozart, and Gluck, and gave me some idea of the great modern composers [significantly called *Techniker*]. . .'.[1]

With its great variety of mood and metre and its general appeal to the Romantic mind, Goethe's *Faust* became one of the nineteenth century's favourite musical subjects. Among the many settings of individual passages, Schumann's *Szenen aus Goethes 'Faust'* ranks high not only as a fine musical achievement but as a pioneering deed in regard to *Faust II*, which at the time (the overture, written last, was completed in 1853) was appreciated by only a few readers, let alone composers. The epilogue with its 'chorus mysticus' represents perhaps the most powerful rendition of any section of the Second Part. The cycle *Lieder und Gesänge aus 'Wilhelm Meister'* (op. 98a, 98b, *Requiem für Mignon*) has also long been part and parcel of the standard Goethe repertory. Schumann's opera, on the other hand, *Hermann und Dorothea*, never advanced beyond an indifferent overture which is so dominated by the *Marseillaise* theme that one wonders just what the connexion can have been between the composition and the epic on which it was supposedly based.

[1] Letter to Zelter, 3 June 1830.

Unlike Schubert (Goethe), Schumann (Heine), or Wolf (Mörike), Brahms does not seem to have had a favourite poet—unless it again was Goethe, who inspired him to two famous choral works, the [*Alto*]*Rhapsodie* after *Harzreise im Winter* and the *Gesang der Parzen* from *Iphigenie*, a worthy pendant to the rendition of Hölderlin's *Schicksalslied*. We also have a number of Goethe *Lieder* by Brahms, and the cantata op. 50, the only setting of *Rinaldo*. The story of Rinaldo and Armida had been the subject of several operas (Lully, Händel, Gluck, Haydn) when Goethe took it up, and in retelling it, subtly changed the emphasis from outward event to psychological inquiry by concentrating on the hero's torments in trying to free himself from the bonds of an unworthy love.

Aside from the competent Robert Franz, the composer most influenced by Goethe in the latter half of the century was Hugo Wolf. His *Lieder* from Goethe are somewhat more intellectual than were those of his predecessors, or his own cycles from Eichendorff and Mörike. Yet any comparison between the ten songs from *Wilhelm Meister* with which the cycle opens, and the parallel settings by Schubert and Schumann, shows that poetry is here neither the handmaiden of music, nor music inhibited by having to comply with the requirements of verse and metre. Both are truly wedded, not only in the songs themselves but with the story of Mignon and the Harpist as it unfolds in the novel. Wolf depicts both characters as Goethe had conceived them: the girl forlorn and pathetic, the old man sombre, mysterious, hovering on the verge of insanity. (Wolf's Harpist is perhaps the first 'neurotic' in modern music.) 'Kennst du das Land', 'Wer nie sein Brot', and the other songs are the creations of a musician himself sombre, neurotic, and quite literally hovering on the verge of insanity; of a man who had not 'happened upon' these poems, but who felt a deep affinity for the fate of their protagonists; of a man, also, who had absorbed the entire novel instead of restricting his attention to the lyrics only. His high general level of culture, the musical advances made since Romanticism and especially since Wagner, and the intoxicated concentration with which Wolf worked all contributed to the uniqueness of these creations. Wolf's success is the more remarkable because he realized that his version of these oft-composed *Lieder* would instantly be judged in relation to those of his well-known predecessors. He was frank in facing this prospect, and in the case of Schubert divided the latter's Goethe production into a group which he felt were perfect and should be left alone (e.g. *An Schwager Kronos, Geheimes*), and a number of others in which Schubert seemed to have misunderstood Goethe (e.g. *Prometheus, Grenzen der Menschheit*). These faithful, intelligent, musically superb renditions helped to keep Goethe's poems before the public. Wolf's special merit lies in his rediscovery of a hitherto neglected work, *Der westöstliche Divan*, which he made so come alive that the Vienna Goethe Club wrote him a note of thanks for having performed six of these songs in such a fashion as to have made the poems clearer through his music.

Apart from a few clear-cut acknowledgements of this nature, it is not easy to assess the precise effect which the work of these and other composers has had on the German image of Goethe. An audience bewitched by Schubert's *Erlkönig* is not *ipso facto* an audience of Goethe readers. Even the most attentive listener to Schubert's or Wolf's *Lieder* would at best become familiar with only a small portion of Goethe's work: with the lyric poems. There is nothing to show that a work like *Die Wahlverwandtschaften* has been, or can be, better understood and enjoyed with the aid of a musical rendition, not to mention the scientific, autobiographical, or yet other aspects of Goethe's production. Much depends, of course, on the extent to which a composition reflects a true image of the work on which it is ostensibly based. Certain musical works, like Schubert's and Wolf's *Lieder*, and even some instrumental pieces such as Liszt's *Faust* symphony, undoubtedly do communicate to us something of the essence of Goethe; others, like Berlioz's *La Damnation de Faust* or Boito's *Mefistofele*, are somewhat self-willed but still lineal descendants of Goethe's work; others again are like second cousins twice removed, and share with their august ancestor little more than a name: Liszt's symphonic poem *Tasso*, and a number of entirely non-German operas like Gounod's *Faust*, Thomas's *Mignon*, Massenet's *Werther*.

Despite these limitations, there is no doubt that musicians from the days of Mozart to Mahler, Pfitzner, and Richard Strauss in our own time have contributed to Goethe's fame, in

the sense of spreading it far and wide among a public which only
partially overlaps that which the poet could claim on the
strength of the written word alone. This especially applies to
the non-German public which has only limited access to his
works. The Schubertomania which swept France in the 1830's
helped also to introduce Goethe to that country; in many
contemporary Anglo-Saxon circles strong in stereophonic equip-
ment and weak in books, Goethe has at least joined Lorenzo da
Ponte and Hugo von Hofmannsthal in the limbo of vaguely-
heard-of authors who have 'somehow' inspired the great composers. It little matters that the real situation was quite the
opposite: that it was Goethe's poetry, and his great reputation, which helped many an able musician to become famous.
In Germany the composers helped to keep Goethe before the
public just when this was most needed, around the middle of
the nineteenth century. In view of this great accomplishment,
the objection is quite irrelevant that the composite 'musical
Goethe' bears many distinctly Romantic traits. Under the
circumstances, he could hardly fail to do so.

There is, however, a second and far more direct way in which
two major German composers affected their contemporaries'
view of Goethe. Liszt and Wagner stand apart from their
fellow musicians because their interest in the poet far transcended professional bounds. Liszt, by then the foremost musical
celebrity of his time, had settled in Weimar in 1848. Near by, his
friend Karoline von Sayn-Wittgenstein was assembling at the
Altenburg a brilliant group of men, much as Goethe himself had
done at Weimar, or Mme de Staël at Coppet. Berlioz, Brahms,
and Schumann were her guests at one time or another, as were
the painters Schwindt, Richter, and Menzel, the writers Hebbel,
Heyse, and Freytag, and the sculptor Ernst Rietschel who later
created the Weimar Goethe–Schiller monument. In the 1850's
the sleepy little town on the Ilm once more rose to be a centre of
European culture. It was no coincidence either in place or date
that Liszt, in his capacity as opera director, performed the
world première of Wagner's *Lohengrin* in Weimar, in honour of
the 101st return of Goethe's birth, on 28 August 1850. On the
same occasion of Goethe's anniversary, a number of prominent
German men of letters, among them A. von Humboldt and
Varnhagen von Ense, had published in various newspapers an

appeal for funds for the establishment of a foundation designed, in Goethe's name, 'to further and enliven artistic creation in Germany, and to strengthen its formative influence on the nation's moral development'. Liszt found this proposal too hazy, and in a pamphlet developed his own project of a Goethe Foundation which was to hold yearly competitions in music, painting, plastic arts, and poetry, in rotation so that each art form would have its turn every four years. The foundation, Liszt thought, should acquire the best works in painting and sculpture for exhibition in a special museum, and produce the prize-winning entries in music and literature in the form of a festival.

This ambitious plan to make Weimar the site of a sort of artistic Olympiad elicited very little response. As has been pointed out, the broad public at the time took little interest in anything connected with the name of Goethe. The Grand Duke Carl Alexander, without whose active support nothing could be done, was lukewarm, for fiscal and other reasons. Even Liszt's friend Wagner thought that a new competition for artists would only duplicate other such projects which were already in operation. He wanted to see the plan focused instead on the establishment of a German National Theatre, a first-rate stage able to perform, regardless of financial consideration, idealistic and experimental plays.

In later years Liszt himself described his design as a utopia: 'At a certain time. . . I had visions of a new art period for Weimar, not unlike that of Karl August, in which Wagner and I would have been the leaders, as Goethe and Schiller were before; but unfavourable circumstances have prevented the realization of this dream.'[1] Wagner evidently had harboured similar thoughts when he wrote Liszt, a few years earlier, that 'the correspondence between Goethe and Schiller . . . pleased me very much; it reminded me of our relationship, and showed me the precious fruits which, in favourable circumstances, might spring from our working together'.[2] The point is well taken, for there was much in Liszt's calm guidance of the proud and impetuous Wagner, and in his selfless efforts by way of helping the younger man find a stage and a public for his theatrical creations, which reminds one of the helping hand which Goethe had

---

[1] Letter to the Princess Wittgenstein, 14 Sept. 1860.
[2] Letter of 16 Dec. 1856 (tr. F. Hueffer).

extended to Schiller some sixty years before. Making allowance
for different personalities and changed conditions, there is some
similarity even between Karl August's relationship to Goethe
and Carl Alexander's to Liszt. These similarities did not escape
the contemporary public: when Fanny Lewald, a popular
authoress of the time, wanted to console Liszt for the lack of
public response to his project, she quite naturally did so by
saying that the people of Weimar had made life difficult for
Goethe also.

It is indicative of the profound interest which Liszt and
Wagner took in Goethe that it extended to their private lives as
well. Their championship of the poet even affected their
relationship to the women they loved at the time. Karoline von
Sayn-Wittgenstein for some reason detested Goethe so much
that the very name could not safely be mentioned in her presence;
her total lack of interest in the Goethe Foundation probably contributed to its early demise. In Wagner's case, *Faust* played,
with less fatal but equally dramatic results, the role of Galeotto
in Dante's episode of Paolo and Francesca. When the Wagners
lived in Zürich as guests of the Wesendoncks (1857–8) and the
composer worked on *Tristan und Isolde*, his friendship with
Mathilde Wesendonck quickly ripened into love.[1] On the
morning of 7 April 1858 Wagner sent her the first draft of the
prelude to the opera, together with a letter which was intercep-
ted, and retained, by his jealous wife Minna—who, in turn, was
ungallant enough to show it to Mathilde's husband. After some
unpleasant scenes the two families became estranged, and
Wagner shortly afterwards divorced Minna. The body of this
letter, entitled 'Morning Confession', deals with Goethe's *Faust*,
which the two near-lovers had discussed the previous evening.
Wagner's arguments are too involved, and too much tied up
with Mathilde and himself, to be conveniently reproduced here.
One may conclude from them that he had studied the work very
carefully and admired it greatly, but was baffled by Gretchen's
intercession at the end. He was perturbed, furthermore, by what

[1] In *Tristan und Isolde* a direct Goethean influence can perhaps be found in the
very short lyrics which condense a mood in a very few words, e.g. 'Bist du mein?/Darf
ich dich fassen?/Hab' ich dich wieder?/Kann ich mir trauen?' (II. ii). At any rate,
it is certain that the composer knew Goethe's poetry extremely well, and that such
lyrics did not exist in German literature prior to Goethe's Storm and Stress period,
or in the German opera before Wagner.

the scholars and critics were doing to the poet, and greatly over-estimated the danger of having the entire image of Goethe perverted by the Philistines of his time. (Wagner, it will be remembered, seldom passed up a chance to *épater le bourgeois*.)

This was by no means the only instance where Goethe figured prominently in the composer's life and thought. He had done so at the beginning of Wagner's artistic career when the schoolboy wrote a tragedy (now lost), *Leubald und Adelaide*, which according to his autobiography was deeply indebted to Shakespeare and *Götz von Berlichingen*. The name Adelaide was, of course, borrowed from the third guiding star in Wagner's firmament, along with Goethe and Schiller: Beethoven. The combination of Goethe and Beethoven accompanied and symbolized the composer's growth like a true *Leitmotiv*. The boy had been so overwhelmed by the *Egmont* score that he 'would not dream of launching [his] just-completed tragedy unless it would be equipped with similar music'.[1] The young man's greatest musical experience was the performance of the Ninth Symphony at Dresden, on Palm Sunday 1849, which so moved him that he wrote a commentary to it in which he characterized each movement by prefacing it, by way of motto, with quotations from *Faust*. The mature artist's greatest essay, *Beethoven*, contains many fine observations on Goethe as well.

Wagner's interest in Goethe was fed by two springs: early familiarity with the poet's work, and a strong identification with him especially in matters theatrical. Unlike the great majority of musicians, he had had a thorough literary training both at home and in school. He cannot possibly have remembered his father, who died a few months after Richard's birth; but the father had been sufficiently interested in the theatre to travel to Lauch-städt for the première of Schiller's *Die Braut von Messina* (with the composer's mother, whom he upbraided for not knowing who Goethe and Schiller were). Wagner's stepfather Ludwig Geyer was a professional actor, and from all accounts a good one. His uncle Adolf Wagner had been a writer of some minor note who had once received a silver cup from Goethe, as acknowledgement for a poem he had dedicated to him. These influences were strengthened in school. Wagner did not seriously become interested in music until he was eighteen; being thus

[1] R. Wagner, *Gesammelte Schriften und Dichtungen* (Leipzig, 1871–83, 10 vols.), i. 9.

spared the tremendous outlay in time, effort, and nervous energy
which is attendant on the early mastering of a musical instru-
ment, he was able to concentrate on his literary studies. Since
his youthful inclinations were towards poetic, and especially
dramatic, rather than musical expression, he was naturally
guided to Goethe and Schiller. Given his thorough knowledge of
both authors, he was able to elucidate their similarities and dis-
similarities in a number of apt comments, particularly in letters
and in the essays *Beethoven* and *Über Schauspieler und Sänger*.
Turning, for example, against the habit which historians of
literature had, and still have, of designating Goethe as 'realist'
and Schiller as 'idealist', Wagner pointed out that the opposite
would be more appropriate: in regard to the theatre, at any
rate, Goethe was the more idealistic in that he refused to adapt
his own production to the low standard of the German stage of
his time. In the field of music, on the other hand, Schiller is
credited with deeper feeling and greater comprehension while
Goethe is taken to task for the frivolity of his operettas: 'Goethe
thought he had to lower his productive standards when he wrote
operatic texts.'

Wagner's self-identification with Goethe stems from the similarity in their fate as dramatic poets: both wrote plays which
were vastly superior to the customary fare of the period; both
struggled for years trying to train their performers in presenting
these plays adequately; both spent much of their energy, Sisy-
phus-like in Goethe's case and with not much more success in the
pre-Bayreuth Wagner, in endeavouring to elevate their public
to a state of intelligent receptivity. Such points of contact could
not fail to impress Wagner; he, too, just like the Goethe of the
classicist period, wrote not only for his self-release but *sub specie
aeternitatis*: ever aware, with the reflective part of his being, of
the total cultural picture of Germany.

Above all it was *Faust* which fascinated Wagner time and
again. He attempted to cope with it musically in op. 5 (five
Lieder and two non-vocal settings of different scenes) and in
Eine Faust-Ouvertüre, which gives a general impression of Goethe's
Faust in his solitude, without reference to Gretchen. What
particularly infuriated Wagner was the popular belief that
Geothe was an incompetent theatre poet because the Second
Part transcends the abilities of almost any actor. He felt so

strongly about this point that it provoked him into making one of the most categorical statements ever made on the tragedy: 'In Goethe's *Faust*, I can show our German actors a play of the highest conceivable literary value, in which they should none-theless be able, by sheer natural endowment, to play every role and to speak every part—provided they have any gift for the theatre at all.'[1] To judge the importance of this assertion we must remember that Wagner had himself achieved the near-impossible in creating, and successfully performing on the stage, a new type of drama; that he was, to millions of his compatriots, a demigod, second only to Bismarck among the great men of the age; and that these words were written when the second part of *Faust*, far from being held up as the touchstone of an actor's accomplishment, was more often than not indulgently dismissed as the product of an old man's ravings. Only a little more than two decades before, Hebbel had closed his review of a perform-ance in Vienna with the words: 'I do not want to criticize the acting as such, since *Faust* is hardly a test for the mimic artist; in part it acts itself, in part it cannot be acted at all.'[2] There is little doubt that Hebbel was wrong in this, and Wagner right. Great as the latter's demands are, they should not be incapable of fulfilment because the tragedy does, in fact, range over the entire spectrum of human emotion.

In the eyes of a superficial and statistically minded observer, Goethe's position in German life must have looked impressive indeed at the end of the nineteenth century. The works were being bought as quickly as the presses could turn them out in a variety of editions, from the paper-bound, pocket-size Reclam copy of almost every individual play to the several monumental Collected Works. If some of the latter seemed destined not so much to be read as to slumber, as status symbols, in glass-fronted parlour bookcases, that surely could have been dismissed as a concession to a public taste which ran to the monumental and pretentious in all its expressions. Wide currency was being given to the somewhat bland, but lovingly drawn, Goethe image of the great positivistic biographers. Goethe had become firmly established in the school, the university, the concert hall, and on

---

[1] R. Wagner, op. cit. ix. 221.
[2] F. Hebbel, *Sämtliche Werke* (Berlin, 1904–7, 24 vols.), xi. 338.

the stage. Popular essayists as well as serious scholars were ex-
pending oceans of ink on his behalf. To be sure, a few small
voices cried out even then against the idol of the 'prince of poets'
who from somewhere (embarrassingly enough, he had neglected
to make sure of his place in either the Protestant or the Catholic
paradise, but wasn't German Classicism almost a religion in
itself, and Goethe its high priest?) benignly smiled down at his
people who had meanwhile reached such heights of wealth and
power. Baumgartner's hostile biography was followed by two
small brochures, published in 1892 and 1899 respectively, which
attacked the prevailing view of Goethe as a mockery of both
poet and public: F. Braitmaier's *Goethekult und Goethephilologie*,
and R. Huch's *Mehr Goethe*. But despite their provocative titles,
these exceptions only seemed to confirm the rule: Goethe, like
almost everyone else in the new *Reich*, had 'arrived'. His popularity as a dramatist had not been impaired by the end of the
court and municipal theatres' monopoly in 1871, and the subsequent multiplication of the country's stages under a manage-
ment of business men. Everybody who was anybody among the
new *élite* either belonged to the Goethe Society, or otherwise
made his bow toward Weimar. Even the Iron Chancellor had
done so when he said that he did not like *Die Wahlverwandtschaften* because Eduard was so spineless, but that otherwise,
'Goethe is altogether to my taste'.[1] In 1889 the young Emperor
had been graciously pleased to visit the Weimar Goethehaus in
person. Ten years later innumerable festive addresses were
given on the occasion of the 150th anniversary of the poet's
birth, and earlier omissions made good through the unveiling of
no less than three major Goethe monuments, in Leipzig, Strassburg, and Wetzlar. If all these statues showed the poet as a
young man, that, too, was as it should be: he had just weathered
the most recent attack made against traditional literature, that
of the Naturalists and early Expressionists, who had no liking at
all for the classical Goethe but found that the young poet had in
part anticipated their own programme, with its socialist tendencies (or at least its marked sympathy with the downtrodden),
its forceful and original language, and its impatience to throw
off the fetters of a decadent civilization in order to return to
Nature. No matter to what kind of writing our observer might

[1] O. von Bismarck, *Tischgespräche* (ed. H. von Poschinger), Jan. 1891.

have turned, he was bound to come up against a ready-made image of Goethe: that drawn by the Naturalists, who thought that Weimar and Italy had corrupted a youthful titan; that of the traditionalist craftsmen like Paul Heyse, whose intellectual and aesthetic habitat was a watered-down Classicism, elegant in diction, elegiac in mood, smoothed in contour; that of Impressionists like Dehmel and Liliencron, who saw in Goethe an ally in their fight against the Philistines; or even that of the truly great writers of the nineteenth century, of Grillparzer, Stifter, Hebbel, Keller, and Raabe, who were only now beginning to come into their own and who appeared differently but no less deeply indebted to Goethe.

Yet these appearances were misleading. The forces which were to shatter the German view of life of the late nineteenth century, and with it the prevailing image of Goethe, were already at work. It was in the victorious scientific camp itself that serious doubts were beginning to be expressed not only about Goethe's role in German science, but altogether about the adequacy of that mechanistic thought system which had achieved such triumphs. The advances recently made in medicine, the growing acceptance of the theory of evolution and its gradual extension to disciplines other than biology, the discovery of X-rays and of the radioactive elements, the improvements made in means of communication, the steadily growing utilization of electricity, and other developments of the kind had all seemed to portend that the day was not far distant when the very processes of Life would be explained, and perhaps controlled and artificially reproduced, to the satisfaction of all. The humanities, on the other hand, had long been on the defensive in the university curriculum and in terms of public support and interest. Their advocates and practitioners had themselves fallen under the spell of scientific methodology and terminology, until they began to consider history as a social 'science', wrote Zola-esque novels of 'scientific' Naturalism, and engaged in 'Literatur-wissenschaft'. Yet the more perceptive and imaginative scientists had meanwhile begun to ask themselves whether their experimental procedures really came much closer to solving the basic problems of Nature and of human existence than the speculative methods of idealistic philosophy had done half a century before.

In retrospect, it seems clear that Planck's and Einstein's theories about the nature and behaviour of the physical universe, as well as Freud's views on the nature and behaviour of Man, merely dealt the death blow to a structure which had long been under stress. They did so, of course, by showing that the ideology of scientific materialism had been built on faulty premises, and that neither the physical world nor the moral and behavioural fundament of man were so constructed that their workings could be explained solely in terms of an unbroken chain of causative connexions. As a result of this development, those among the German scientists who gave free rein to their speculative tendencies soon split into various factions. Some continued to cling to the belief that despite the limits set to our perception of the world around us, the factors which directly affect human existence could still eventually be reduced to a body of formulated laws. Many among these men, especially the followers of Ernst Haeckel, the 'German Darwin', banded together in the *Monistenbund*. They rejected all divine revelation, cultivated a type of pantheism in which God and Nature were truly one, and, of course, believed in the Darwinian development theory. Against them was arrayed the *Keplerbund*, founded in 1907 by scientists committed to finding a synthesis between modern technological civilization on one hand, and the precepts of the Christian faith on the other. Others, again, were proselytizing on behalf of their own individual philosophies. Wilhelm Ostwald, for example, the chemist who won a Nobel Prize in 1909, preached 'Energetics', according to which not only the physical universe but even our cultural and artistic values are, at bottom, emanations of energy: 'What is, is energy.' In similar fashion Max Wundt examined the effect of thought processes on the nervous system, and came to claim for experimental psychology the status of a panacea. Among the social scientists, finally, the Protestant theologian Friedrich Naumann advocated the equalization of social burdens as the first task of the age.

The figure of Goethe, both as poet and scientist, loomed large in all these developments. In *Die Welträtsel* (1899) Haeckel claimed the poet for the cause of Darwinism; with little justification, since the developmental aspects of Nature had interested Goethe far less than the aesthetic and morphological ones. At the same time, Naumann saw in him a forerunner of Christian socialism, and Rudolf Steiner, a proto-anthroposophist (see below). It was, however, a physiologist who most directly took issue with Goethe's scientific work: Emil Dubois-Reymond. In a paper read to a medical convention in 1872, he had compared the modern scientist with a great general like Alexander or Caesar, who on a day of rest surveys his territories to see what could still be conquered and what would forever remain outside of his domain. He had come to the conclusion that no matter what advances might still be made, two questions would always be beyond the domain of scientific cognition: a philosophical definition of matter (as opposed to a merely physical one, by which, for example, a constant amount of matter may be considered as bearer of a constant amount of potential and kinetic energy), and a definition of the nature of consciousness (by which he meant any mental process). The origin of organic life, Dubois-Reymond thought, could perhaps in time be explained; it may turn out to be no more than 'an exceedingly difficult mechanical problem'.[1] But the real nature of matter and of consciousness would never be determined. Dubois-Reymond enjoined his audience to face these facts, and to admit, in a famous formulation which quickly became a slogan, that 'Ignorabimus'—we shall never know.

Dubois-Reymond was one of the great specialists of his time, J. von Müller's successor as professor of physiology at Berlin University, author of a standard work on animal electricity, and a spokesman for German science at international meetings in Paris and London. The shock which his revelations had caused had barely subsided when he delivered another sensational lecture, *Goethe und kein Ende* (1882), in which he criticized the poet for having led German scientists astray by his example of a graphic rather than mechanical description of natural phenomena. Goethe's scientific work, in particular his *Farbenlehre*, was no more than 'the stillborn pastime of a self-taught dilettante',[2] because he had pursued his investigations without reference to the law of causality. By restricting himself to the field of descriptive morphology, Goethe had disregarded the far more fruitful inquiry into growth, locomotion, and other distinguishing features of organic life from which natural laws

[1] *Über die Grenzen des Naturerkennens* (Leipzig, 1872), p. 15.
[2] *Goethe und kein Ende* (Leipzig, 1883), p. 29.

might be formulated. These statements, made on the solemn
occasion of Dubois-Reymond's installation as *Rektor* of Berlin
University, called forth a flood of rectifications on the part of
other scientists, who insisted that Goethe's investigations were no
less valid than those of researchers of a more experimental bent.[1]
The most forceful defence of Goethe was that offered by Rudolf
Steiner, then engaged in editing the poet's scientific works for
the *Weimarausgabe*. In later years Steiner was to develop, in
his celebrated anthroposophy, an entire philosophical system
founded on the antithesis impressed on him when he was working on Goethe: that between the mechanical element in Nature
which can be reduced to laws, and the organic, for the cognition of which we can only operate by means of ideas. His later
mysticism, however, and his manner of imputing to Goethe's
scientific views a supernatural power, do not lessen the value
of his earlier accomplishments. He was one of the first to define
Goethe's characteristic method of *schauen*, i.e. his intuitive and
inductive viewing of natural phenomena with the aim of arriving at widely applicable symbols and ideas, which in turn must
stand up under precise investigation. Steiner also stressed most
forcibly that this process of *schauen* sprang from a concept of
Nature as something not mechanistic, but divine or at least
spiritual in origin, and that a knowledge of the manner in which
his natural studies affected Goethe was not merely desirable, but
indispensable for the full understanding of his poetic works.

While these problems were agitating the scientific community,
a number of creative spirits were subjecting the entire relationship of 'Natur- und Geisteswissenschaften' (corresponding,
roughly, to natural sciences as against the humanities) to a
searching analysis. It is significant that the men who clarified
the basic differences between these fields in aim and method,
again frequently did so by reference to Goethe. This was the case
with the philosopher Wilhelm Windelband, who defined the
sciences as 'nomotheistic' or law-giving, and the humanities as

---

[1] For example, H. Helmholtz's address on *Goethes Vorahnungen kommender natur-
wissenschaftlicher Ideen* (1892) and J. Langbehn's *Rembrandt als Erzieher* (1890), where
Dubois-Reymond's 'microscopic' view of Nature is contrasted with the 'macro-
scopic' one held by Goethe, and a synthesis advocated between the poet's subjective
procedures and the experimental techniques of a Newton or Helmholtz (chapter
'Deutsche Wissenschaft').

'idiographic' or descriptive and individualizing; with the *Faust*-interpreter Heinrich Rickert; and above all with Wilhelm Dilthey, one of the pioneers of the concept of the History of Ideas, and the man who at the time did more than anyone else to give back to the historians of German literature a sense of pride and confidence in their craft. In the epoch-making essay on *Goethe und die dichterische Phantasie*, originally published in 1877 and reissued in 1905 as the pivotal part of *Das Erlebnis und die Dichtung*, Dilthey applied to Goethe the descriptive psychology with which he hoped to delve deeply into the secret of artistic creation. The great achievement of what he called the German Movement, which began with Lessing and the Storm and Stress and ended with Hegel and the Romanticists, lay in the unfettering of the creative imagination from abstract rationalism and from the dictates of mere good taste. Goethe represents the high point of this intellectual movement—the most significant yet to have taken place on German soil—because with him creative imagination formed the very mainspring of art. Even more than other poets, he must be judged not in terms of the average human being, but in terms of the psychological organization particular to the creative artist: he did not have more of what all men have in varying degrees, but gifts of a different nature. If it is the task of great literature to describe not reality but the writer's experience and concept of life, then Goethe was fortunate in being able to experience the world with particular intensity. His way of experiencing the world was, in fact, symptomatic for the process as such, which 'must be intensely felt; it must not merely be received passively but rather transformed actively; it must engage or involve the whole man, the basic unity of what Dilthey calls life'.[1] However, the metamorphosis by which he turned his life-experience into works of art went far beyond the mnemonic re-creation of which all human beings are capable to some extent, because it included a stage of thinking in images, until it became a force spontaneously active by itself in dreams as well as conscious states. This explains Goethe's inability to 'command the Muse' like Schiller, or, conversely, to turn off the stream of poetic imagination. Hence the creation of *Werther* within a few weeks, without notes or preliminary drafts,

[1] R. Wellek, 'Wilhelm Dilthey's Poetics and Literary Theory' (in *Festschrift für Hermann J. Weigand* [New Haven, 1957]), p. 122.

and the similar genesis of *Hermann und Dorothea*. Hence also the poet's involvement in his own creations, epitomized in the incident when he read aloud from the last-named work and broke out in tears.

With these and many other observations of similar nature, Dilthey proclaimed anew the autonomy of the creative writer and his independence of any and all scientific procedures. He went further and designed a whole typology of the artistic mind, according to which Goethe was not only the standard-bearer of the German Movement but the prototype of what he called the 'Goethean' form of Man. In the essay under discussion Dilthey set off this type on the one hand from the Shakespearian, on the other from the Rousseauan type. Shakespeare was fascinated by life, seemingly unconcerned with mastering it, and uncritical of the injustices and of the *homo homini lupus* which characterized the world around him. He was interested only in understanding and describing that world; active, inclined to do the wrong thing rather than nothing, devoid of introspective or reformist tendencies. At the opposite pole stands Rousseau, the first European writer who, especially in *La Nouvelle Héloïse*, formed characters entirely out of his own imagination. Between them stands Goethe, absorbed by what goes on inside him, yet intent also on mastering his own life and shaping his own personality in a world about whose imperfections he harboured no illusion.

Dilthey's yeoman service on behalf of a better understanding of Goethe, and of all literature, is best judged by keeping in mind that it was performed at a time when the writer was rarely credited with being a law unto himself, and when his work, instead of being taken as achievement *sui generis*, was 'measured' by means of various scientific valuations and procedures: as result of his environment, as effect to the cause of a particular event in the poet's life, and by similar tokens. It is only natural that Dilthey's insistence on the 'otherness' of the man of letters (which brought about, among other things, a vindication of Goethe's great contemporary Hölderlin, who had been all but forgotten because he would not fit into any traditionally accepted system of literary criticism) was slow in taking effect. Perhaps the first great scholarly work directly influenced by it was Georg Simmel's *Goethe* (1913), an inspired attempt to achieve a philosophical definition of the poet's intellectual type, of the 'idea' Goethe (contrasted, in Simmel's dialectic fashion, with that of Kant). Simmel stressed the complete harmoniousness in Goethe between the objective reality of the world and the system of subjective valuations, moral, aesthetic, and other, by which men live. In expressing his own individuality during different stages of his life, Goethe never ran counter to the structure of the external world, in the manner of Kleist or Hölderlin. On the contrary, Goethe's whole development represents a continuously heightened synthesis between mind and matter. This synthesis was achieved by a normal and typical human being who fulfilled all the potential functions given to Man. Simmel, however, was merely a forerunner of modern psychology and sociology; it was only after the First War that the History of Ideas, and with it literary typology and morphology, really became familiar tools in Goethe scholarship, in the works of such men as H. A. Korff and R. Unger.

By friend and foe alike, Goethe was thus assigned a central position in the intellectual movements which stirred Germany around the turn of the century. Before discussing the great biographies of Chamberlain and Gundolf, in which the recent discoveries about the nature of the creative process were applied to Goethe and bore magnificent fruit, it is essential to determine the role which Goethe played in the thought of Friedrich Nietzsche. In his own time this philosopher was not as well known as some other contemporary social critics like Paul de Lagarde, or Julius Langbehn, the 'Rembrandt-German'. In retrospect, however, he appears far greater than they, as a thinker and writer, and particularly in regard to his effect on posterity. Nor did his views on Goethe very materially differ from those of Lagarde and Langbehn; their impression of the poet, like Nietzsche's own, was conditioned by the dislike, fear, and despair which their own times inspired in them.

As a poet Nietzsche never ceased to admire Goethe, to whose example his free verse and prose owe a great deal. As an historian he knew himself to be one with Goethe in rejecting the claims which its contemporary practitioners were advancing on behalf of 'scientific' historiology. As a classical philologist he detected certain limitations in Goethe's understanding of the Greeks and of their tragic art. As a social critic, finally, Nietzsche

claimed to be a descendant of Goethe's, especially in his attitude
to the German people and to the Christian religions. The
frequent and detailed references to Goethe throughout his
writings are evidence of Nietzsche's preoccupation with this
poet, the only great figure of the past whom he regarded all his
life as an embodiment of European culture at its best, whom he
never pushed off his pedestal or 'revaluated'. Because of Nietzsche's role as mentor of a large section of the intellectual *élite* of
twentieth-century Germany, his views have had a permanent
effect on the German image of Goethe. In Thomas Mann,
Nietzsche was to live on as the prophetic warner against all that
had become problematic in German life; in Stefan George, as a
proclaimer of the pre-eminence of the form-conscious artist;
in Oswald Spengler, as the herald of a dynamic concept of
history. With these men and many other modern writers and
thinkers, Nietzsche's vision of Goethe loomed behind the
philosopher's own ambiguous figure, and in the end perhaps
overshadowed it altogether.

It is one of the main theses of *Vom Nutzen und Nachteil der
Historie für das Leben* that the acquisition of historical knowledge
as such is a useless if not altogether harmful pursuit, and that the
study of Man's past is profitable only where it can be made to
enhance the reader's own powers. As a rule this can only happen
with men who are strong enough to maintain their own individualities against the onrush of historical ideas and ideologies: men
who neither glorify the past at the expense of the present, as the
Romanticists had done, nor project their hopes, as many of
Nietzsche's contemporaries were wont to do, into a paradisaical
future of Christian, socialist, technological, or otherwise idealized aspect. Goethe was such a man. He disliked the pragmatic
and didactic historiography of his time, and took little interest
in historical, or any other, knowledge unless he could turn it into
a productive force in his own existence. This, Nietzsche found,
was the case especially with the poet's knowledge of classical
antiquity, which was less thorough than that of a philologist, but
'sufficient to let him wrestle with it profitably'.[1] Historical
truth, then, is fundamentally that part of the past which lives
on, as the Greeks lived on in Goethe. It is irrelevant in this connexion that Nietzsche, like Goethe before him and such histor-

---

[1] F. Nietzsche, *Werke* (Leipzig and Stuttgart, 1901–22, 20 vols.), x. 410.

ians as Carlyle and Churchill afterwards, was attacked for this stress on the inspirational power of historiography.

Although he claimed Goethe as an ally in his fight against positivistic historians, and specifically quoted him in the preface to *Vom Nutzen und Nachteil der Historie*, Nietzsche upbraided the poet for exercising the selectivity which he had himself advocated. Goethe's idea of the Greek world was a one-sided one which ignored the emotional, almost neurotic basis of that people's philosophy and art, particularly that 'delight in tragedy' which Nietzsche regarded as the most characteristic feature not only of pre-Socratic Greece, but altogether of creative historical periods. Being 'Apollinian', Goethe concentrated his affection on the harmony of Greek plastic art. He rejected, as alien to his nature, that 'Dionysian' element whose definition was one of Nietzsche's great accomplishments: the orgiastic component, derived not from harmony but from an experience of suffering and existential anxiety, which was the source of the Greek ideal of beauty. The reason for this lay, of course, in Goethe's conciliatory concept of the tragic, which he regarded not as a means of raising Man to a higher sensitivity and perception, but as an undesirable, and often avoidable, imperilment of his inner balance. This difference of opinion gave rise to Nietzsche's criticism of *Faust*:

A little seamstress is seduced and made unhappy; the culprit is a great scholar and graduate of all four faculties. Surely there must be something uncanny about that? Indeed there is! The great scholar could not have managed all this without the help of the devil himself. Should this really be Germany's greatest 'tragic idea'. . .? But for Goethe, even this idea was still too frightful [so that he ended by reuniting the lovers in Heaven].[1]

Denying as he did the possibility or even desirability of a metaphysical existence, Nietzsche was bound to consider Faust's salvation as altogether inadmissible. More than that: the whole antinomy between instinct and reason on which Goethe had based his drama was repulsive to Nietzsche, who liked his tragedy 'straight' and preferred Byron's *Manfred* for that reason, just as he thought highly of Kleist's *Penthesilea*, and would surely have approved of Mann's *Doktor Faustus*. In fact, as Bergen-

[1] Ibid. iii. 264. See also the parody 'An Goethe' in *Lieder des Prinzen Vogelfrei*.

gruen has pointed out, there is a striking similarity between the late nineteenth century's image of the Olympian Goethe and the poet's own concept of a preternaturally harmonious Greek civilization.[1]

These disagreements did not affect Nietzsche's great veneration for Goethe, whom he regarded not only as a good man and one gifted with 'a universal understanding and approval [of life], a readiness to let things come close to him, a daring realism coupled with reverence for all that exists',[2] but as an entire civilization in himself. Nevertheless, Goethe only represented in German history an 'event without consequences', so that his works are not really living literature like those of Schiller, or even Lessing. It was Kotzebue, Nietzsche thought, who had expressed the true aspirations of the Germans of the classical period, and, next to him, Schiller who had attracted the adolescents by making himself the mouthpiece of their moral indignation. Goethe, on the other hand, had 'stood above the Germans in every respect, and still does so today: he will never be one of them. . . Just as Beethoven wrote his music and Schopenhauer formulated his philosophy above their heads, so did Goethe write his *Tasso* and *Iphigenie* above their heads'.[3] The real Goethe, Nietzsche felt, would only be understood much later. In the meantime he symbolized the very opposite of all that the Germans of Bismarck's *Reich* prided themselves on: the very antithesis of their philistine 'culture-business', their pragmatic scientism, their patriotic self-satisfaction and religious hypocrisy. It need hardly be pointed out that this estimate of Goethe was a highly subjective one. Every quotation with which Nietzsche supported his criticism of the Germany of his time could easily be cancelled out by a different selection. This is even more the case with his remarks on Christianity, about which Goethe had far more complex and ambivalent ideas than those imputed to him by Nietzsche, who must have known that he had no right to claim that 'Goethe and I are of one opinion in regard to the crucifix'. Nietzsche's subjectivity is noticeable also in his blindness toward the pre-classical poet, whom he

[1] W. Bergengruen, *Rede über Goethe* (Marburg/Lahn, 1949), p. 8.
[2] *Werke*, viii. 164. This characterization of Goethe's outlook on life is strikingly similar to that which Keller gave in *Der grüne Heinrich*. (See p. 143.)
[3] *Werke*, iii. 89.

practically ignores in favour of the author of *Tasso*, *Iphigenie*, and
his particular favourite, the *Novelle*. Nietzsche's acute feeling for
literary form, coupled with his belief in the necessity of dramatic
and epic discipline and his cult of the strong and self-sufficient
personality, seems to have predisposed him, even in his youth,
to an exclusive admiration for the Goethe who comes to life for
us in Eckermann's *Gespräche*, 'the best book ever written in
German'.[1] This was the Goethe whom Nietzsche treasured
more deeply than Schopenhauer and longer than Wagner: the
mature poet whose art he defined as describing

not individuals, but more or less ideally designed masks; not realism,
but an allegorical generality; topical characters and local colours
softened to near-invisibility, and rendered mythical; the sensibilities
of the time and problems of contemporary society restricted to their
fundamentals, and divested of all that is merely titillating, thrilling,
or pathological ... no new subjects or characters, but the traditional
ones in continuous reanimation and transformation: that is art as
Goethe later conceived it, as the Greeks and even the French practised it.[2]

If Nietzsche had contributed no more to the German image of
Goethe than this classic definition of the classicist poet, he
would still be assured of a place in the annals of German
literature.

[1] Ibid. 257.   [2] Ibid. ii. 205-6.

V

THE GOETHE SOCIETY

IN considering the last phase of our subject, from the Goethe renascence to the present, we must depart from the chronological sequence of narration and, at the risk of occasionally getting ahead of our story, turn to various factors which have simultaneously acted upon the German view of Goethe. Foremost among these stands an organization which dates from the 1880's and is unique in the history of literature: the Goethe Society. Most of the modern German work done on Goethe has been undertaken by men connected with this body, which in turn has been the channel through which their opinions have reached an audience of special interest to us: Goethe's modern and contemporary public.

The public is important because literature, seen as organic process, 'occurs' whenever a writer communicates his thoughts and impressions to his readers. Like most of their brethren in literary criticism, the Goethe scholars have primarily busied themselves with the originator of the communication and with its content and form: with the poet and his works. In tending to take the public for granted, they have forgotten Whitman's observation that 'to have great poets, there must be great audiences, too'. Yet the days are long past, in Germany as elsewhere, when the interest or even the existence of 'great audiences' for classical literature could be taken for granted. It is time, then, that we paid some attention also to the recipient of the literary communication, to the reader, without whose reaction even the greatest book is but a number of bound sheets covered with printer's symbols. So much has been written about Goethe himself that his public has been largely ignored—as if the fact that Goethe is still read were not partly due to the efforts of previous generations in publishing, explaining, and recommending his works, and handing them down to us intact and accessible. Until the Gallup Poll in the fullness of time takes an interest in German literature, any answer to the question 'Who reads

Goethe?' must remain incomplete. This does not mean that we should refrain from giving a partial answer, any more than the anthropologist should eschew speculation about the Neanderthal man merely because no complete specimen has ever been found. Our prototype, the composite German Goethe reader of the past seventy years, can be partially reconstructed by an examination of the Goethe Society and its members, an examination which provides an outline both of the modern Goethe image itself and of the public for which it was drawn.

Walther Wolfgang von Goethe, the poet's last surviving descendant, died on 15 April 1885. In accordance with his last will and testament, the Goethehaus with its collections thereupon passed into the possession of the Grand Duchy of Sachsen-Weimar. Grand Duchess Sophie personally was named trustee of the Goethe family archives, i.e. of all manuscripts and other papers (literary, scientific, and personal) left by the poet and his family. She accepted this legacy with the understanding that the archives were to be made available to the scholars of the day, for classification, research, and publication. This in turn led to the organization, by a group of Goethe experts and interested laymen, of the 'Goethe-Gesellschaft in Weimar', which constituted itself as such at a meeting held in Weimar on 21 June 1885. It was destined to become Germany's largest, and quite possibly most influential, learned society.

A rudimentary programme for the Society was outlined in a public appeal for membership, *To All Admirers of Goethe*, issued in July 1885 and carried by most German newspapers. Priority was given to the sifting and examination of the unpublished papers and to the preparation of a new, complete edition of the works. The Weimar Goethehaus was to be transformed into a permanent museum, which would thus become a centre for Goethe studies the world over.[1] Payment of the yearly dues of

[1] Another such centre is the Frankfurt Goethemuseum, seat of the Freies Deutsches Hochstift founded by Otto Volger in 1859, as a 'democratic' academy distinct from the dynastically endowed ones in such court cities as Berlin, Dresden, and München. In 1863 Volger bought the house where Goethe was born and raised. Since the purchase of this building (now the Goethemuseum, destroyed in World War II and rebuilt soon afterwards), the Hochstift has become an organization primarily devoted to Goethe studies. After some early friction, its relations with the Goethe Society have been most cordial. A third important repository of Goethe documents is the Vienna Goethemuseum, opened in 1907.

ten marks entitled a member to a vote in the general meeting
held in Weimar every year, to free use of the library, and to a
free copy of the *Goethe-Jahrbuch*.[1] Members were also accorded a
reduction in the price of the Society's other publications, such
as the forthcoming edition of the works or the *Schriften der Goethe-
Gesellschaft*, i.e. the projected annual issue of a book, brochure,
or reprint dealing with Goethe. Largely as the result of this
appeal, 1,359 men and women had joined the Goethe Society
by the end of 1885; by 1 March 1886 the total for Germany had
risen to 1,660.

The quality of the Society's early backers was no less impressive than their quantity. Leading Goethe scholars of the time,
men like Fischer, Scherer, and von Loeper, willingly served on
the executive committee; the most promising of all, Erich
Schmidt, left the University of Vienna to become director of the
archives and editor-in-chief of the Society's publications. E. von
Simson, a national figure since his presidency of the Frankfurt
Parliament in late 1848, and later Chief Justice of Germany, was
made the Society's president; Grand Duke Carl Alexander of
Sachsen-Weimar-Eisenach consented to be its patron-in-chief.
An even brighter augury for the future was an application for
membership received from Augusta, Empress of Germany, who
had been reared in Weimar and whose grandson, Wilhelm II,
was soon to begin his reign as Germany's last emperor. But this
distinguished patronage was not the only social conquest made
by the Goethe Society, a list of whose members from the ruling
houses of Europe read like a page from the *Almanach de Gotha*:

'His Imperial and Royal Majesty Wilhelm II, Emperor of
Germany and King of Prussia;

Her Imperial and Royal Majesty Augusta Victoria, Empress
of Germany and Queen of Prussia;

Her Imperial and Royal Majesty Victoria, Empress and
Queen Friedrich;[2]

[1] This journal, a compendium of essays, papers, and news items about Goethe
scholarship, had been founded in 1880. Five years later the Goethe Society adopted
it as its official organ. It appeared annually until 1914, when the Society launched
its own *Jahrbuch der Goethe-Gesellschaft*. This, in turn, was discontinued in 1935 to
make way for the quarterly *Goethe*, which in 1938 was changed into a publication
issued three times a year. Since the war it has for all practical purposes reverted
to the form of a yearbook.

[2] Queen Victoria's eldest daughter, Wilhelm II's mother, who after her con-
sort's death took the title 'Königin Friedrich'.

His Imperial and Royal Apostolic Majesty, the Emperor of
Austria, King of Hungary;
His Majesty the King of Sweden;
His Majesty the King of Württemberg;
Her Majesty the Queen of Italy;
Her Majesty the Queen of Rumania;
Her Imperial Highness the Grand Duchess Elisabeth Mauri-
kiewna of Russia. . .'

There followed, in order of precedence, the names and titles
of thirty-two lesser princes and princesses.[1]

The Society was thus assured from its beginnings of the co-
operation of Germany's most prominent literary scholars and of
the interest of her social *élite*. It was no less fortunate in enlisting
the support of leaders in other walks of life. P. Heyse was among
the founding members; T. Storm, F. Spielhagen, L. Fulda, and
a host of lesser writers followed suit. The membership of 1885
furthermore included the historian Theodor Mommsen and
his son-in-law, the classical philologist U. von Wilamowitz-
Moellendorff, the archaeologist A. Furtwängler (the conductor's
father) and the zoologist E. Haeckel, the philosopher R. Eucken
and the violinist J. Joachim, the actor J. Kainz and the indus-
trialist L. Merck (whose brother Georg established the American
branch of the pharmaceutical concern of Merck & Co.), the
physiologist H. von Helmholtz and the egyptologist G. Ebers. It
is an indication of the eminence of these sponsors that although
the Nobel Prize was not instituted until 1901, when some of
these men were no longer living, three of them—Mommsen,
Eucken, and Heyse—were among the early recipients of that
prize.

It is clear that the founding of the Goethe Society met a need
long felt by the educated classes of Germany, and indeed by those
of other countries, where 270 members were enrolled during the
first year.[2] It is no coincidence that this need should have been
so acutely felt in 1885. In philosophy and history, in the natural
sciences, and in what had just established itself as 'Literaturwissenschaft', precise investigation had replaced speculation.

[1] 'Jahresbericht der Goethe-Gesellschaft' (*Goethe-Jahrbuch*, ix, 1890), pp. 18–19.
[2] As if to stress the universality of Goethe's appeal in those days, the English
Goethe Society, independent of the German parent organization but affiliated with
it, was founded one year later. The Vienna Goethe Club had been established as
early as 1878.

Philologists and historians of literature took over where the philosophers, most recently the Hegelians, had left off. By the time the Goethe Society was established, much of the philological spade work had been done on the material then available. Some of it, like Scherer's work, was good and has stood the test of time; much of it, like Düntzer's commentaries, was merely conscientious. Common to all Goethe scholars of the time, however, was the realization that the material they worked on must needs remain fragmentary until, presumably with the extinction of the poet's family, the archives would somehow become available to the public. This, as we have seen, had come about in 1885. Impetus was also given to the Goethe renascence by the group of brilliant amateur and professional scholars who now devoted their labour to the work of reviving interest in the poet: Grimm, Hehn, Bernays, and their colleagues who by background, training, and, as it were, academic bedside manner were admirably suited to the demands of intellectual leadership. Yet even the efforts of these men would have been in vain if the period of their greatest activity, and the founding of the Society on whose behalf they laboured, had not coincided with the creation and early growth of the German Empire. Following upon the victorious wars of 1864, 1866, 1870–1, the three last decades of the nineteenth century were, for Germany, a period of national muscle-flexing, of which the very founding of the Goethe Society was a minor but not insignificant expression. Indeed, a strong current of nationalism was evident in the Society's early history. The *mésalliance* between scholarship and chauvinism is found as early as 1885, in the appeal *To All Admirers of Goethe*, where the timeliness of the venture is stressed not in terms of intellectual significance or artistic appeal, but as a demand of *Realpolitik*. The appeal reads, in part:

With the new German *Reich* the time has arrived for a ... national and political way of thinking, in which those limitations have ceased to exist which in past decades have kept many from duly knowing and appreciating Goethe. A great national state knows how to esteem in his whole worth the greatest of its poets. The establishment and preservation of our people's political greatness goes hand in hand with the cultivation and strengthening of our spiritual values.

Only one member of the committee by whose vote the appeal was given to the Press objected to the inclusion of these sentiments. The literary scholar and lifelong Liberal G. von Rümelin remarked that a knowledge and appreciation of Goethe had nothing whatever to do with the new German Empire—which, he added, was in any case already fifteen years old—and that others whose native tongue was German, in Switzerland and Austria, had quite as much right to claim Goethe as their poet as did the *Reichsdeutschen*. He did not bother to point out that Goethe himself had not been at all worried about the lack, in his own time, of a 'great national state' in Germany.

The Goethe Society thus owed its establishment in 1885 to a coincidence of propitious factors: the death of the last Goethe and his bequest of the archives to a German princess of rare intelligence and initiative; the flowering of a group of singularly gifted and articulate Goethe scholars; and the foundation of Bismarck's Empire, which created not only a heightened awareness of Germany's cultural traditions, but a widely distributed material wealth by means of which many families were enabled to support literary and scholarly activities for the first time.

Launched under these auspicious circumstances, the Society has followed three distinct but related lines of action to implement its programme. First of all, it published works by Goethe and works about Goethe. Secondly, it acquired and cared for physical as well as intellectual monuments of Weimar's classical period: houses, statues, collections, memorial tablets, &c. Finally, through the sheer impact of its activities on the placid world of scholars and readers, the Goethe Society has come to be the world's foremost promoter—the word is used advisedly— of German literature in general. Its officials have dined in the Waldorf-Astoria (as guests of the American Goethe Society) and spoken over the Japanese radio (by courtesy of Kyoto University and Nihon Goethe Kyotai, the Japanese Goethe Society); they have encouraged German studies in Addis Ababa and organized a Goethe Memorial Exhibition in Buenos Aires; they have introduced Arab princes, Soviet generals, and British business-men not only to Goethe, but to Germany.

Before it could even think of engaging in these far-flung enterprises, the Society had to establish itself firmly in the world of German scholarship. Its most urgent task was that of preparing a complete and dependable edition of Goethe's works, including those which had been found in the archives. This was accomplished in the *Sophienausgabe*, so called in honour of the Grand Duchess to whom the archives had been bequeathed and by whose order the work was begun. In one of the great publishing ventures of history, a committee of the Society's scholars supervised the annual issue of four to six volumes, until in 1919, thirty-three years after its inception, the edition was thought to have been completed with the publication of the 133rd volume. Thus Goethe's total literary output, divided into four sections (Literary Works, Writings on Natural Science, Diaries, Letters), was laid before the public in a definitive edition. The Russian occupation of 1945 and the subsequent opening of the Thuringian State Archives have made available to scholars many documents written by Goethe in his capacity as government official; these papers are to be added to the edition as a fifth section, Official Writings, of which the first volume appeared in 1951. Counting from 1886, three-quarters of a century may well have gone by before the *Sophienausgabe* will finally be completed. Although already in some ways obsolete, notably in the orthography, which the editors stubbornly refused to modernize, it is to this day the basic edition of Goethe's works.

When the publication of this series was well under way, suggestions began to be made at the Society's annual meetings for bringing out an inexpensive edition of the main works. After consultation with the Inselverlag, a special committee decided that six cardboard-bound volumes would best satisfy the need for a really popular or 'Volksgoethe'. At its meeting in 1908, the Society voted a special grant of 20,000 marks to help the publishers bridge the gap between production costs and sales price. *Goethes Werke* ('im Auftrage der Goethe-Gesellschaft ausgewählt und herausgegeben von Erich Schmidt') accordingly appeared in 1909. Unlike the scholarly *Sophienausgabe*, which is bare of all exegesis, the new edition was destined for the intelligent layman. The first volume contained a biographical sketch of Goethe, written in a way that takes for granted very little previous knowledge on the reader's part. At the price of six marks for the six-volume set, the 'Volksgoethe' was a true best seller. Aside from the copies distributed free to members of the Society, in lieu of the twenty-fourth annual issue of *Schriften der Goethe-Gesellschaft*, the first printing of 20,000 sold out within a few months. A second printing of 30,000 in 1910, and a third of 20,000 four years later, were exhausted almost as quickly. The popularity of this edition has survived into our days: a revised and enlarged issue, again in six volumes, was brought out in 1949–50. Since World War I the Society has occasionally donated sets of this edition to selected German schools for distribution, as graduation prizes, to promising students. The 'Volksgoethe' thus offers a striking example of the Society's success in broadening Goethe's public. Unimpeachable scholarship (the edition has stood the test of forty years of Goethe research), great financial daring (the subsidy to the Inselverlag amounted to almost a fourth of the Society's total assests at the time), and imaginative promotion (among teenagers whose literary preferences were still unsettled) were here combined on behalf of a 'classical' author. The result must have been gratifying to every member of the Society: the total number of sets sold by 1951 exceeded 100,000 in five printings.

With the Society's example before them, several German publishing houses launched Goethe editions of their own in the years before 1914. The Bibliographic Institute in Leipzig (30 volumes), J. G. Cotta & Successors in Stuttgart (the *Jubiläums-ausgabe* of 41 volumes), and G. Müller & Co. in Munich (the chronological *Propyläenausgabe* in 45 volumes) all attempted to strike a mean, in thoroughness and appearance, between the ponderous *Sophienausgabe* and the streamlined 'Volksgoethe'. That they succeeded in doing so without sacrificing sound editorial and printing workmanship, and thereby raised ever higher the standards and reputation of the German publishing industry of those years, is again to some extent due to the Goethe Society. Almost all editors and publishers of Goethe's works in the past sixty years belonged to it and benefited from its facilities and from the encouragement of their fellow members. Thanks in part to its connexion with the Society, the generation of 1895–1930 has produced not only more first-rate biographies but more good editions of Goethe than any other before or since.

Apart from the works and the *Goethe-Jahrbuch*, the Society has so far issued more than fifty of its *Schriften*. This is a series of books, albums, reprints, and brochures dealing with a variety of topics more or less closely related to Goethe. Distributed free to members and nowhere to be had for sale, these 'bonuses' were originally scheduled to appear at the rate of one a year; however, the two wars and the attendant breakdown of the German economy have caused the cancellation or postponement of several projected issues. With their purposely restricted public and the magnificent make-up of many of the early volumes, the *Schriften der Goethe-Gesellschaft* represent the trend toward 'carriage trade appeal' which was so marked in German publishing before 1914.

The maintenance of buildings and collections ranked second only to publishing among the Society's activities. This was, perhaps, a natural result of the last Goethe's bequest of his grandfather's house to the Grand Duchy, and of the family archives—a collection—to the Grand Duchess. Since the administration of bequests and estates is not a primary function either of states or their rulers, the Society stepped into the breach and became *de facto* trustee of house and archives. After being thoroughly renovated and converted into a national shrine, the house came to be called 'Goethe-Nationalmuseum' and as such was permanently opened to the public on 3 July 1886. Within five years of its inauguration, the museum had been visited by over thirty thousand people. In 1914 and 1935 two annexes were built to house Goethe's collections (except the family archives), which was fortunate because the main building was partially destroyed in an air raid on 9 February 1945. With the permission of the Russian authorities, a rebuilt Goethe-Nationalmuseum, still administered by the Society, was opened to the public on the 196th anniversary of Goethe's birth, on 28 August 1945. A result of the abdication of the Grand Ducal House in 1918 was the last reigning duke's bequest of the so-called Dornburg châteaux to the Society. Situated high above the river Saale not far from Jena, these three buildings, two small castles and a country house, had been a favourite retreat for Karl August and Goethe, who wrote a good many poems there as well as working on the first version of *Iphigenie* and revising part of *Wilhelm Meister*. Under the supervision of a board of trustees which for a time included Stefan Zweig and Gustav Stresemann, buildings and grounds were carefully restored to their condition in Goethe's time.

Similar work had in the meantime been undertaken in Austria.

There, the Vienna Goethe Club—Wiener Goethe-Verein—
had originally been founded with a view to organizing support
for the erection of a Goethe monument. This aim was achieved
with the unveiling, on 15 December 1900, of Hellmer's statue,
which shows Goethe seated in an armchair and pensively gazing
straight ahead: a most appropriate posture for the reflective
poet, here shown in the fullness of his years. The Club also
devoted its energies to the establishment of its own Goethemuseum, opened in 1907, and to the *Chronik des Wiener Goethe-
Vereins*. Unlike the *Goethe-Jahrbuch*, the *Chronik* (founded in 1886)
had no large body of posthumous or otherwise unpublished
documents to draw on; in its pages, scholarly contributions have
therefore predominated from the very beginning over the publication of hitherto unknown material. However, the editors
have made a virtue out of necessity by devoting many of their
offerings to a specific topic: Goethe's relationship with Austria.
Indeed, it is only when examining the *Chronik* that one fully
realizes the great importance of that country and its people in
Goethe's life and in the propagation of his posthumous fame.
It is true that his involvement with Austria took place at a later
stage in his life, and perhaps for that reason was less dramatic,
than his discovery of France and of Italy. Yet the human element in his relationship with Austria and Austrians was far
greater than in the case of the Latin nations. Neither the French
nor the Italians (nor yet the English) played a role in Goethe's
life comparable to that played by Ulrike von Levetzow and
Marianne von Willemer, Grillparzer and Beethoven, Metternich and the Empress Maria Ludovica. The relationship of
these and other Austrians to Goethe has been described in the
Chronik in loving detail, as have his visits to Karlsbad and Teplitz, his journeys to Galicia and the Tirol, and Ottilie von
Goethe's long residence in Vienna, where her daughter Alma,
the poet's granddaughter, had died in 1844.

Beginning with the Goethe family archives, the German
Goethe Society has been throughout its existence the recipient
and trustee, if not always the owner, of Goetheana of every
description. Manuscripts, coins, letters, statues, and paintings
were given to or acquired by it for safekeeping and often for
exhibition. From 1885, when a first grant was made to the

Library Committee for book purchases, the Society has been a powerful magnet which has slowly but inexorably attracted to itself, at auctions, by way of bequest, on loan or by purchase, most of the artistic and literary monuments of the Goethe period which had hitherto been in private hands. The Society bought its first Goethe portrait, Kolbe's painting of 1822, as early as 1886. Nine years later 15,000 marks were set aside toward the acquisition of Goethe's letters to Frau von Stein, for which the latter's hardheaded heirs had asked 70,000. The balance was raised by a group of subscribers whose composition shows how strongly the Society's work was backed by prominent Germans in various walks of life. Among the contributors to this fund, the German dynasties were represented by Wilhelm II and the Grand Duke of Baden; big business by Friedrich Krupp; publishing by E. Paetel; the diplomatic corps by the honorary consuls-general of Sweden-Norway and of Belgium; the *haut monde* by a Dumba in Vienna and a Mendelssohn-Bartholdy in Berlin. In their name and in that of the other donors, the seven volumes of correspondence, the most famous love letters in German literature, were presented to the Grand Duchess in 1896 for inclusion in the archives.

Even more valuable than these and similar acquisitions, and more continuous because they were not limited in scope by the Society's financial position at a given time, were the bequests and other gifts received from friends and members. By far the most important of these donations was that of Schiller's library and papers, made in 1889 by his great-grandson, K. A. von Gleichen-Russwurm. The archives and their accretions were now enlarged to form a body of documents called 'Goethe and Schiller Archives', a name which soon came to be applied as well to the magnificent building erected by the Grand Duchess in 1893–6, to which these treasures were transferred from the Weimar castle for permanent safekeeping. The Society's library was also placed in this building, which contains ample facilities for scholarly and administrative work.

Thus enlarged, the Archives were intended to serve as a repository not only for Goethe's and Schiller's manuscripts, but for those of Weimar's classical period as a whole. Thanks to the generosity of their respective descendants, Herder's correspondence with Caroline Flachsland, Wieland's translation of

Cicero's letters, and many other such items soon joined Goethe's and Schiller's papers in the Archives. In the course of time these were further enlarged to include documents relating to later German literature; by the end of the century, manuscripts and papers by Keller, Auerbach, Hebbel, Geibel, Heyse, Mörike, Immermann, Ludwig, and others had been donated to the Archives, and in a few cases purchased for them by the owner (the Grand Duchess) or the administrator (the Goethe Society). After Sophie's death in 1897, the Archives, as perpetual family entail of the Grand Ducal House, were nominally taken over by her grandson, Duke Wilhelm Ernst. The latter agreed after his abdication in 1918 to share both ownership and maintenance costs with the Goethe Society and the *Land* of Thuringia, in an arrangement designed to forestall the dissolution of the Archives and their possible removal (except, of course, for the building) from Weimar. Like the Nationalmuseum and the Society's library, the Archives continue to receive donations from various sources. As late as 1937, no less than three established authors, Agnes Miegel, Börries von Münchhausen, and Johannes Schlaf, contributed manuscripts of their own works to this ever-growing collection.

The Society's work of publication and preservation, which also included the upkeep of monuments and graves of persons close to Goethe, was largely done by 1914. It was in the nature of this work that it should have been limited in time and space, that it should in the main have been confined to Weimar and its surroundings and to the publishing centres of central Germany: Leipzig, Berlin, Stuttgart, and Frankfurt. The Society's widespread activities by way of promotion, on the other hand, correspond to a later stage in its history and in the history of the German image of Goethe. Since the end of World War I, the Goethe Society has increasingly tended to consolidate its scholarly and other achievements and to make the results of its labours known to the general public. In 1917 a first local group of Goethe enthusiasts was started in Munich; Berlin followed in 1919, Essen and Hamburg in 1920.[1] These local branches, officially devoted, as is the national body, to the propagation of interest in Goethe, were in some cases very active. They organized,

---

[1] In 1938 the appellation 'Ortsgruppe' had to be changed to 'Ortsvereinigung' because the former term had been pre-empted by the Nazi Party for its local units.

generally during the winter months, a number of lectures, concerts, and theatre performances of which the Society itself might well have been proud. The local branch in Mülheim/ Ruhr, for example, presented in 1921 three recitation evenings, six guest lectures, and several concerts. In view of the fact that this branch alone counted 850 members and had as vice-president one of Germany's wealthiest women, Mrs. Hugo Stinnes, it is not surprising that friction should have developed between the regional and the national organization: the parent, in the small and far from prosperous town of Weimar, was in danger of being devoured by its offspring. There was also the distinct possibility that the encouragement of Goethe studies would be forgotten altogether, and that fashionable *soirées* and other social events would replace the more academic work. A compromise was finally worked out by means of which the largest local branch represented all regional organizations through its president. The latter was an *ex officio* member of the national executive, which thus retained some measure of over-all control. Since 1918 the Society has also strengthened wherever possible its connexion with other organizations of similar nature. As early as 1898 it had joined the Deutsche Shakespeare-Gesellschaft, founded at Weimar in 1864, in a successful appeal to the Grand Duchy's Diet for a complete tax exemption for both learned bodies. Over the years the Goethe Society has also contributed considerable sums to the Schiller-Stiftung, which provides financial support for needy writers, and to the Deutsche Dichter Gedächtnis-Stiftung, established in 1901 for the dissemination of good literature. An exchange of publications has long been under way between the Goethe Society and such organizations as the Kleist-Gesellschaft, the Herder-Stiftung, and the Wiener Goethe-Verein. The last-named organization, in fact, to some extent surpassed the Goethe Society in the scope of its 'promotional' activities: being located in Vienna, it was able to engage, for lectures and readings, the services of many members of the Burgtheater, at the time the finest ensemble of German-speaking actors anywhere.

In the course of time the Goethe Society has come to be regarded as a last court of appeal in many questions relating to Goethe scholarship. This was, perhaps, a natural consequence of its eminence in that field. Whatever the reason, it was at any rate highly desirable that a universally recognized authority of this kind should exist, especially during the Nazi period when the image of Goethe which had been painstakingly elaborated by generations of capable and self-effacing scholars was subjected to many partisan distortions. For example, when the Nazi drive against free-masonry got under way, a rumour was spread that Goethe, in his capacity as freemason, had caused or at least welcomed Schiller's death. The Society was forced to go to the trouble of publicly refuting this charge, along with others, advanced by the widow of the redoubtable General Ludendorff, that Goethe had been a willing tool in a number of vaguely sinister Masonic intrigues. Soon afterwards, several German newspapers were castigated for printing a flood of cheaply sentimental stories set in an utterly disfigured, saccharine version of classical Weimar.

The old work of research and publication went on and goes on still. A *Welt-Goethe-Ausgabe*, jointly sponsored by the Society and the City of Mainz (in honour of its most famous son, Johann Gutenberg), had barely begun to appear when the outbreak of war in 1939 caused it to be suspended. A similar fate overtook the *Nationalausgabe der Werke Friedrich Schillers*, which was to do for Schiller what the *Sophienausgabe* had done for Goethe. By and large, however, the Society's more recent activity has been that of a 'defender of the faith' rather than one of creative scholarship.

It is clear that efforts of this nature originated with, and were executed by, a different segment of the Society's membership than that which had laid the scholarly foundation. Acting as a technical adviser to a producer about to make a *Faust* film,[1]

---

[1] One of the earliest of all motion pictures was L. Lumière's *Faust* (1896), which was soon followed by a number of other treatments of the same topic: G. Mélié's *Faust et Marguérite* (1897), *La Damnation de Faust* (1904), and *Faust* (1904). The first American picture of *Faust* was made in 1908, and the first German one two years later, with Henny Porten as Gretchen. In the most successful of all silent film versions of *Faust* (1925, directed by F. Murnau), Emil Jannings played Mephisto, Yvette Guilbert Marthe, and Gerhart Hauptmann furnished the subtitles. It was, perhaps, an inevitable consequence of the silent pictures with their piano accompaniment that the hero should have turned out, in all these films, to be the romanticized Faust of Thomas, Gounod, and Berlioz. Even after the introduction of sound, Goethe films continued to be heavily indebted to music: *Le Roi des Aulnes* (made in 1930 by Jean Renoir's wife Marie-Louise Iribe) and *Wer her* (1938) both drew heavily on compositions by Schubert, Mozart, and even Bach. Perhaps the best of the motion pictures made for the memorial years 1932 and 1949 was a faithful biographical 'documentary' on the poet himself, *Goethe lebt* (1932).

delivering a radio talk on the attractions of classical literature, taking part in a person-to-person membership drive (which the Society had carefully refrained from doing in the old days) is not the kind of work relished, or capably performed, by the traditional German scholar. These activities resulted, in large measure, from a change in the composition of the Society's membership and of Goethe's public in general. This change is clearly reflected in the tables on pp. 133 and 134, which represent a cross-section of the membership at twenty-year intervals from the first full year of the Society's existence to the last date for which a complete list exists. It must be pointed out that the information here given, while accurate for the Goethe Society, is of necessity no more than a rough yardstick with which to measure Goethe's public as a whole. The men and women whose professional data are analysed below were the leaders, not the rank and file, of the modern 'Goethegemeinde'. To be sure, much lip-service has been offered at Goethe's altar along with the incense, but the question remains: what manner of people found it necessary to pay even that tribute to Goethe? It must also be stressed, however, that membership in this organization was open to anyone on payment of ten marks, and thus transcended the boundaries which so closely limit the composition of other learned societies. In this respect the Goethe Society bears no resemblance to the Académie Française or the Royal Society, with their professionally, socially, and in the former case even morally circumscribed membership. An organization devoted to the propagation of classical literature which counts in its ranks a thousand business-men is, at any rate, not only a literary but also a sociological phenomenon of some importance.

The most startling change that has taken place in the over-all composition of the membership concerns the relative importance of the Business and Education groups. In 1886 over a third of all members listing their profession were engaged in academic work; by 1926 less than a fourth were so employed. The percentage of business men, on the other hand, increased from roughly a sixth to well over one-fourth. The proportion of medical men, and of libraries and clubs, went up by about a third. Lawyers have held their own, while government officials, clergymen, journalists, and artists were somewhat less prominent among the membership of 1926 than their predecessors had been forty years earlier. Court officials naturally ceased to be an active factor after 1918. The other professional group directly affected by the lost war, the military, shows a remarkable tenacity in holding on to their membership: their number in 1926 is smaller than in 1886, in relation to the total, but not by much—

TABLE A

	1886	1906	1926
Members in Germany	1,359	2,282	5,192
Members abroad	270	486	319
Total membership	1,629	2,768	5,511
German membership by profession, in percentages[1]			
No profession listed	32·2	33·2	32·5
Of the remainder:			
Business	17·2	19·5	28·4
Medicine	6·2	6·0	9·9
Law	13·2	12·7	13·2
Government	9·8	6·8	8·2
Court officials	2·2	1·3	0·2
Military	2·8	1·8	1·9
Education	34·0	28·3	22·9
Journalism	1·8	1·6	1·0
Clergy	1·8	1·5	1·5
The Arts	5·3	7·0	4·5
Libraries, Organizations, Clubs . . .	5·7	13·5	8·3
	100·0	100·0	100·0

perhaps not at all if one remembers the reduction of the German army to 100,000 which was stipulated at Versailles.

While in Table A 'Business' is used generically to distinguish its representatives from the professional men with a generally

---

[1] For the membership of 1886, see *Goethe-Jahrb.* vii, Appendix, pp. 18–51; for that of 1906, *Goethe-Jahrb.* xxvii, Appendix, pp. 18–68. The list for 1926 was printed separately as a supplement to vol. xii of *Jahrbuch der G.-G.* (Weimar, 1926).

Members are listed (*a*) according to location, and (*b*) within a given locality, alphabetically by name. The profession, where given, follows the name and initial(s). It is not always easy to determine, in the Wilhelmian period, whether a German title other than one of nobility has been conferred upon its holder on a basis of professional excellence or by way of social distinction. A *Hofrat* or *Geheimrat* may be a privy councillor in some branch of the government, or else a successful professional man with a purely honorary title. The same problem arises in the evaluation of titles like *Konsul* or *Kommerzienrat*. For the purposes of this study, some arbitrary adjustments had to be made on a basis of probability. Cases thus adjusted do not exceed 2 per cent. of the total.

more humanistic background, Table B brings out the difference between business proper—Industry and Commerce—and some allied occupations.

Here again, the relative position of the two largest groups has been reversed: Industry and Commerce has replaced Publishing as the largest section. The reason for the strong representation of publishers among the membership before 1914 is twofold. There existed among the ranks of German publishers a large group of highly cultured men to whom Goethe scholarship,

TABLE B

Breakdown of 'Business'

	1886	1906	1926
Banking and Finance	12·5	14·1	11·9
Publishing	41·5	26·5	16·9
Agriculture, Forestry, Mining	3·2	8·1	4·8
Architecture and Engineering	7·0	7·0	9·4
Chemistry, Applied Sciences	0·6	0·7	2·2
Industry and Commerce	35·2	43·6	54·8
	100·0	100·0	100·0

and by extension the Goethe Society, owes much: Salomon Hirzel, Eugen Diederichs, and above all Anton Kippenberg of the Inselverlag, friend and mentor to Rilke, Stefan Zweig, Hofmannsthal, and a host of other contemporaries, owner of the world's largest private Goethe collection, and president of the Goethe Society from 1938 to 1950. These men and others undoubtedly set an intellectual trend within the profession and encouraged their fellow publishers to read and study Goethe. The other reason for the great interest shown by the book world seems to have been a commercial one: rendering assistance to an organization whose avowed aim was the stimulation of interest in an author who, as the 'Volksgoethe' was to show, could be turned into a veritable gold mine. In enlightened self-interest, German publishers backed the Goethe Society much as the modern pharmaceutical industry is not indifferent to the welfare of learned societies in the biological field. As Germany became saturated with Goethe editions, interest on the publishers' part lessened appreciably. Geographically this interest was largely centred in Leipzig, long the country's book capital;

as late as 1926, 30 out of 246 members in that city were publishing houses, including not only those which brought out
editions of Goethe's works (Insel, Bibliographisches Institut),
but others whose world-wide reputation is built on an entirely
different basis (e.g. Brockhaus, Baedeker). The radical change
in the relative position of Publishing and Industry-and-Commerce contrasts with the passivity of the other groups in Table
B. Banking and Finance has held its own; Agriculture, Forestry
and Mining has made but little permanent gain; the slow increase in members engaged in architecture, engineering, and
other applied sciences reflects only very slightly the tremendous
increase since 1886 in the number of persons engaged in these
professions. In this respect the composition of the membership
mirrors social changes less than it does, for example, in regard
to the women of Germany. The working women of 1886, a bare
couple of dozen, were without exception artists, mainly actresses.
In 1926 several hundred listed professions other than the
arts.

The essentially middle-class composition of the membership is
borne out not only by the vertical grouping of professions in the
two tables, but even more by the 'horizontal' distribution, as it
were, of members within a given profession.[1] The continued
presence among the members of a substantial number of doctors,
lawyers, professors, and clergymen goes hand in hand with a high
average professional standing in the case of those members whose
work is not necessarily an index of their social position. Both the
chief editor and the youngest copyboy on a newspaper are engaged
in Journalism; the fact is that more than half of the membership
in that field consists of editorial writers and editors: a significant
fact, in the light of the Society's promotional work. The bank
president and the teller are both in Banking; here again, the
membership abounds in presidents and other executives, with
only a handful of men in subordinate positions. Among the

---

[1] Learned societies as such are not necessarily middle-class institutions; the
'Sprachgesellschaften' of the German Baroque had an entirely different composition, as has the present Academie Française. The remarkable feature of the Goethe
Society is not its middle-class foundation but its ubiquitousness within that class. It
would be hard to imagine any other organization uniting under its banner, as the
Goethe Society did in 1926, such disparate figures as G. Krupp von Bohlen-Halbach, Thomas Mann, Hugo Gropius, Admiral Scheer, Theodor Wolff, Gustav
Stresemann, and the Mayor of Hamburg.

military, not one non-commissioned member can be found in the
three years for which data have been collected. Their median
rank is the respectable one of Lieutenant-Colonel, and the best-
known representative is no less a man than Admiral Scheer,
who commanded the High Seas Fleet at the Battle of Jutland.
Similarly the great expansion of the Business group in Table A
is due to the interest taken in the Society not by the rank and
file, but by the leaders of the German business world. The vast
majority of members in the Industry and Commerce division of
Table B are men of executive rank: agency managers, vice-
presidents and treasurers of corporations, advertising men, &c.
At the top of the business pyramid one finds the great indus-
trialists whose names used to be household words in Europe:
Krupp, Stinnes, Borsig, Siemens.

There is practically no working-class interest in the Goethe
Society.[1] Among its 5,192 members in the Germany of 1926 we
find one plumber, one mechanic, one electrician, and two minor
union officials. Thus it is clear that the Society's periodic attempts at investing Goethe with working-class appeal have met
with little success. A hesitating first step in this direction had
been taken during the War of 1914–18, when the Society did its
level best to awaken an interest in German classicism among the
men in the trenches and factories. A more articulate endeavour
was the 'Goethe Festival in the Ruhr' (Bochum, 20–26 October
1928), in the course of which the guest of honour, Gerhart
Hauptmann, pointed out that Goethe's popularity among the
working classes left much to be desired, especially in comparison to Schiller's, and that 'Goethe the Worker' ought to be
an organic part of the German working man's emotional and
intellectual experience. A more recent experiment along the
same lines was undertaken in 1937, when the 'Reichsführer-
lager' of the Hitler Youth movement, convened in Weimar, went
through what can only be called a Goethe Indoctrination
Course. Time will show the degree of success of these endeavours
and of similar ones presently being undertaken in the German
Democratic Republic, to gain for Goethe a public composed of

---

[1] This does not mean that there is no interest, on the part of the working class,
in Goethe himself. There is some evidence that he is presently being read by men
and women who cannot remotely be called 'intellectual' or 'bourgeois' (e.g. the
twenty-five essays in *Goethe in unserm Leben* [Willsbach, 1947]).

younger and socially less privileged readers, a public more similar to that of Dante in Italy or Shakespeare in the Anglo-Saxon countries.

If we now define, with all due reservations, the composite modern Goethe reader whose existence was postulated in the beginning of this chapter, we find that while he was formerly most likely to be found in the ranks of the learned professions, our prototype is now, more often than not, a business-man. He tends to live in the large cities, especially in the industrial centres whose population contains a prosperous managerial stratum: in places like Chemnitz, Essen, Gelsenkirchen, Leipzig, Hamburg, Dessau, all of which in 1930 harboured local branches of the Goethe Society (the world-renowned intellectual centres of Heidelberg and Tübingen had none). Judging, again with due caution, from name, profession, and geographical location, one is tempted to say that the serious reader of Goethe is still probably Protestant, quite possibly Jewish (before 1933), rather unlikely to be Catholic. Unlike the (hypothetically 'typical') Rilke reader, the Goethe reader is far more likely to be a man than a woman—although the women did not leave their interest in Goethe behind when they left their sheltered homes and went to work in the years after 1918. Unlike the (hypothetically 'typical') Schiller reader, the Goethe reader is unlikely to be a student, and practically never a working man. More often than not he is a mature person carrying on his shoulders a good deal of civic and professional responsibility. He is essentially a leader: the nucleus of Goethe readers and enthusiasts, whether genuine or not, within any given profession comes close to being identical with the locally and nationally leading members of that profession. Many no doubt joined the Goethe Society because that was a fashionable thing to do in certain circles. Nevertheless the modern Goethe reader seems to be less motivated by academic, social, or nationalistic pressures than his father or grandfather had been. The redoubtable 'Herren Professoren' who questioned the wisdom of admitting the general public to the sacred precincts of Goethe scholarship (a point hotly debated in 1885), the *jeunesse dorée* of Potsdam whose knowledge of Goethe was highly precarious, the chauvinists to whom Goethe was primarily Germany's answer to Shakespeare—these and similar relics of former times have all but disappeared from the membership lists. In terms of Whitman's postulate of a great poet's great audience, it is clear that as the animosities of the nineteenth century have receded into the past, Goethe's particular audience has increased in stature as well as in size.

VI

THE LITERARY IMAGE

GOETHE's influence on the German writers who came after him has been as profound as it was elusive. Unlike their predecessors in the time of Romanticism and Young Germany, the authors of the later nineteenth century wrote relatively little that deals with Goethe directly. Some merely devoted an essay or two to him, as Fontane did on the occasion of the centennial of 1849. Others, like Raabe in *Abu Telfan* or Keller in *Der grüne Heinrich*, indirectly paid tribute to him through the characters which they created and endowed with speech. Others again, like Grillparzer in *Sappho* and Stifter in *Der Nachsommer*, wrote works which are by no means imitative, but carry an unmistakably Goethean flavour. Along with Storm, Spielhagen, Freytag, and so many others, these authors, no less than the great nineteenth-century composers, have at one time or the other in their lives 'discovered' Goethe. We can here follow this discovery in only a few striking instances, in order to underline the fact that even in the years of public hostility, Goethe occupied a central position in German letters. He did so not only as an author of academic interest but as a living force in the intellectual, human, and artistic growth of the *élite*. The depth of the poet's influence necessarily varied with the individual reader. Its scope extended from the sublime to the ridiculous, from considering Goethe as interpreter of Life itself to calling on him for strength when faced with the tragicomic problem of How to Stop Smoking.[1]

Franz Grillparzer's conversion to Goethe was sudden, violent, and definitive. By the time he was nineteen, he had written *Blanka von Kastilien* and was well on the way to becoming an historical dramatist in Schiller's manner. However, in early

---

[1] In his diary Hebbel mentions a civil servant by the name of Marschall, who was so awed by Goethe's condemnation of tobacco (*Venezianische Epigramme*, No. 66) that he decided forthwith to give up smoking. When Hebbel made the entry, the gallant man had six weeks to his credit (*Tagebuch*, 3 May 1861).

1810 he suddenly found unbearable Schiller's 'claim' to be reckoned among the leaders of his nation, his 'ridiculous and pretentious yearning to play the philosopher', and the 'bombastic verbosity' of a play like *Die Braut von Messina*. What had happened? Grillparzer had discovered his very own image in Faust, 'the daring, fascinating man in whom I had so often found myself', and in Tasso, where he thought it was himself who spoke, acted, and loved, so that Goethe had only 'lent words to my feelings'.[1] He reacted to the dramas much as the sentimental readers of 1774 had reacted to *Werther*: not so much aesthetically impressed as touched to the quick emotionally. His self-identification with Tasso and Faust aggravated his morbid tendencies, not surprisingly, since at the end of the drama Tasso remains suspended in an agony of indecision, while Faust was not incontrovertibly saved until the publication of Part II. These works *are* depressing if one fails to realize, as Grillparzer did at first, that Goethe had also shown, in Antonio and Mephisto, an opposite view of life which was no less valid for being commonsensical and realistic. There is something curiously feminine about the violence of Grillparzer's scorn for Schiller, the man he had adored but yesterday, and his discovery—'on the rebound', as it were—of Goethe. Like most experiences in his life, it left him with a strong feeling of inadequacy. He knew that he could write in Schiller's manner, and possibly even in the fashion of *Götz von Berlichingen*; yet the rhetorical *Blanka von Kastilien* now seemed to him crude and obvious. He was an ambitious author in his youth, and fully conscious of his extraordinary gifts. At the same time, he was too clear-eyed a critic not to realize that the transparent perfection of an *Iphigenie* or a *Tasso* represented an unattainable peak in dramatic creation. He could not then have known that his own achievements, in the building up of psychological suspense, the delineation of women in love, and the mastering of stage craft, were quite great enough to secure him a position next only to Goethe and Schiller themselves in the annals of the German theatre. He was, furthermore, unduly influenced by friends, the two closest of whom unhappily pulled in different directions. G. Altmütter was a Schiller enthusiast, who con-

---

[1] *Sämtliche Werke* (Stuttgart, no date [Cotta'sche Bibliothek der Weltliteratur], 20 vols.), Ergänzungsband ii. 28–29.

firmed Grillparzer in his belief that the prolonged study of
Goethe would end by undermining his precarious self-con-
fidence as an author. J. Schreyvogel, on the other hand, had
just been instrumental in introducing Goethe to Vienna, in the
pages of the *Sonntagsblatt* (1807–9). There he prepared the
ground for the Viennese Goethe cult of the early nineteenth
century, which was to unite such disparate figures as Beethoven,
Gentz, Stifter, Schubert, Metternich, and Grillparzer himself.

The high point in the poet's relationship with Goethe was his
visit to Weimar in 1826. He has left a description of it in his
posthumous autobiography, one of the few such works which
do not aim, no matter how subtly, at safeguarding their author's
reputation with posterity. Grillparzer wrote it only for his own
eyes, and it is therefore doubly interesting to see that Goethe at
first made as formidable an impression on the self-effacing
Austrian as he had made on the insolent Heine (who had told
him that he, too, was busy working on a *Faust*). Grillparzer, by
then well known as the author of *Die Ahnfrau*, *Sappho*, *Das Goldene
Vliess*, and *König Ottokars Glück und Ende*, and a poet who had
long found his own 'tone', was one of a good many guests
assembled at a reception when Goethe appeared, 'dressed in
black, on his chest the star of an order, holding himself straight
and a little stiffly... like a monarch granting an audience'.
Inevitably, disenchantment was the result of this meeting, as
it had been in the case of Heine and so many others who came
away overwhelmed by the ceremonious exterior: 'I admit that I
returned to my hotel with a highly unpleasant impression. Not
that my vanity was offended; on the contrary, Goethe had
treated me with more kindness and consideration than I had
expected. But to see the ideal of my youth, the author of *Faust*,
Clavigo, and *Egmont*, as a stiff minister... was a rude awakening.'[1]
Yet at lunch the next day Goethe led his visitor, so much his
junior in age, rank, and worldly fame, to the table in person—
a sign of solicitude which brought tears to Grillparzer's eyes.
This revised impression of a man who on closer acquaintance
proved to be as thoughtful as he was great, was strengthened by
Goethe's praise of *Sappho*, his interest in Austrian letters, and his
veiled invitation to Grillparzer to remain in Weimar. In one of
his periodic attacks of self-deprecation, the young dramatist

[1] Ibid. xix. 134.

later turned down a suggestion that he visit Goethe again the following evening, when he would find him alone.

Grillparzer has contributed much to the comparative evaluation of Goethe and Schiller. It has long become commonplace to say that Schiller appeals to the young and Goethe to the mature, that the former was a very great dramatist and the latter a supreme poet in many genres, or that Schiller tends to be 'idealistic' and Goethe 'realistic'. It was Grillparzer who first formulated these and similar points of contact and contrast. A substantial portion of his informal *Studien* is devoted to an analysis of these two authors, who seem to have been bracketed together in his mind from the days of his youth, when he rashly hailed Adolf Müllner as Germany's leading dramatist 'now that Schiller is physically, and Goethe creatively dead', to his old age when he proclaimed Goethe as the greater poet, but Schiller as 'belonging more to the nation'. Grillparzer became an embittered man early in life, and his observations occasionally suffer from being caustic and overstated; it may be witty, but it is also unfair to say that Goethe should have remained a poet at thirty and become a minister at sixty, instead of the other way round. Despite this sometimes jaundiced view and his lack of interest in the very late works, Grillparzer openly acknowledged Goethe as his mentor, and defended him against those who belaboured him for his alleged lack of patriotism. Although he had suffered much under Metternich's censorship, Grillparzer was perhaps the only leading European author who not only took no part whatever in the revolution of 1848 but publicly supported the established order. Aside from aesthetic views and practices which lie outside the scope of this study, it was here, in the belief in peaceful adjustment and the horror of radicals of any sort, that the patriotic Austrian monarchist came closest to the German cosmopolite. Some of his political poems of the 1840's and 1850's—e.g. *Deutsche Bewegung*, or *Der liberale Journalist*—resemble Goethe's *Venezianische Epigramme* so strongly in form and tone that it would be hard to tell them apart in an anthology.

If politics thus formed a bond of sympathy between the conservatives Grillparzer and Goethe, they represented a formidable wall between Goethe and the liberal Gottfried Keller. In *Der grüne Heinrich* Keller's hero Heinrich Lee, on returning from a visit to the country, finds in his room a parcel delivered in his absence: a complete set of Goethe's Works. Heinrich spends the next forty days reading, and emerges from his solitude with a new conception of how the writer and painter should look at the world: with a 'selfless love for all that has become and is, a love which honours the right and the significance of every individual object, and acknowledges the interdependence of things and the depths of the universe'.[1] He then asks himself to what extent the artist should let himself become involved in the events of his time, and arrives at an answer totally at variance with what Goethe thought. Heinrich finds that while the creative person is by nature passive and receptive—'the man who marches along in a festive procession cannot describe it as well as he who looks on from the sidelines'—he will nonetheless in time be forced to join in, precisely because he has the gift of close observation and knows when the moment for action has come.

Keller shared with Goethe a certain coyness in now conceding, at other times denying the autobiographical dimension of certain of his works. Whatever the degree to which Heinrich Lee may be equated with Gottfried Keller, there is no doubt that the author here expressed his own convictions. The passage was not only left intact when he rewrote the novel for its second, and definitive, edition; it is also in tune with his often reiterated belief that no man has the right to abdicate his civic responsibilities. It closely corresponds, furthermore, to an entry which Keller made in his diary when, at the height of his liberal involvement, he came up against the Goethe problem of his whole generation: how to combine the literary man's admiration for Goethe with the need for political action felt by so many of the best minds of the time.

Börne is a regular Goethophobe [he wrote on 15 August 1843] . . . one can't help but agree with much that he says. . . . I don't know just what it is that bothers me about [Goethe]. Is it the fact that the author of *Faust, Tasso, Iphigenie*, etc. was such a self-centred fuss-budget, or is it that such a hoarder—Hamster—should have been the author of *Faust, Tasso*, etc.? I don't know which pains me more: that Goethe was such a great genius, or that the great genius had, as private person, such a character, or rather, non-character.

[1] *Sämtliche Werke* (Bern and Leipzig, 1926–49, 22 vols.), v. 5.

It was not until he lived in Berlin, in the early 1850's, that Keller arrived at a more harmonious view of Goethe. In that period he developed the thesis that the beliefs and literary practices of German Classicism had lost much of their validity, and that the modern author, instead of trying to emulate Lessing, Goethe, Schiller, and Tieck, must strive to express his own ideals and those of times yet to come. Having thus rationalized away, as it were, his reservations, Keller was free to appreciate the many personal and artistic traits which he shared with Goethe, from a pantheistic outlook on life and an ability to find solace in nature to a predilection for painting: a discipline in which he did not credit Goethe with much competence.[1] If there is no evidence that any work of Goethe's ever swept him off his feet as *Wilhelm Tell* had Heinrich Lee, there is none, either, that he persevered in his former hostility. On the contrary; in *Der Apotheker von Chamounix* both Goethe and Schiller are shown in a pose which, except for the parodistic circumstances (Heinrich Heine dreams of ascending to Heaven), was nothing if not impressive: as Olympian gods of incomparable wisdom and dignity.

Friedrich Hebbel, the son of a poor bricklayer in a small town in Schleswig-Holstein, had little access to books during his formative years. When he did manage to procure a copy of *Faust*, he was able to keep it for only a few hours: a friend, who had himself 'borrowed' the volume from the library of a greatly feared local clergyman, lent it to Hebbel on condition that the latter accompany him to the house of a young lady whom he was too bashful to visit alone. Hebbel accordingly played the chaperone for three hours and afterwards collected his reward in the form of *Faust*, which he quickly read through before the clergyman would return and notice that the copy was missing. There is nothing to show that this hurried first exposure to Goethe weaned the young student away from his predilection for Schiller, Uhland, and Jean Paul Richter. He had not yet read the second part of *Faust* when he reviewed, in Hamburg

---

[1] In an interesting aside on the psychology of the artist, E. Ermatinger observes that Keller, who modestly discouraged all *literary* comparisons between himself and Goethe, nonetheless felt superior to him as a *painter* ('Gottfried Keller und Goethe', *Publications of the Modern Language Association of America*, lxiv, 1949, p. 85).

some years later, a friend's essay on a recently published *Faust* commentary. Characteristically, it was Hebbel himself who pointed out that his remarks were inconclusive because he had not read the entire work. His real acquaintance with Goethe began when he studied at the universities of Heidelberg and Munich. Although desperately poor, he repeatedly spent what little money he had on the purchase of books by Goethe. As he gradually gained an understanding of these works—through reading, by reviewing books dealing with them, later in attempting to clarify, in letters, diaries, and theoretical treatises, his own ideas about literature—Hebbel developed a profound respect for Goethe. In 1849, when he was himself an author of considerable fame, he helped organize the celebration of Goethe's 100th birthday in Vienna's Theater am Kärtnertor, and publicly documented his admiration for the poet in a prologue written for the occasion.

What particularly attracted him to Goethe was the latter's striving for harmoniousness and universality. These aspects could not fail to impress Hebbel: not only was harmony to him 'a state difficult of attainment, and indeed rarely attained',[1] but his own culture was so autodidactic and incomplete that he felt occasional twinges of envy in regard to Goethe, on whom 'all the flowers have been scattered which life has to bestow . . . while another man, with a soul equally full of seed, might have to drag his existence along behind him. . .'. When he decided to give up the study of law and to devote himself entirely to writing, Hebbel took pains to point out that he was renouncing only jurisprudence, not the pursuit of knowledge as such. At this critical juncture in his life, a friend tried to cheer him up by saying that book learning had never yet augmented a man's inborn poetic gift. The budding author agreed, but insisted that the literary man's knowledge must nonetheless be as extensive as it is possible for him to make it, for 'Goethe was an encyclopedia, and Shakespeare is a fountainhead of English history'. Similar reflections on the manysidedness of Goethe's interests and accomplishments led him to defend the poet against the reproach that his preoccupation with nature, and his reliance on what he could perceive with his senses, had made him disregard

---

[1] E. Purdie, 'Hebbel's Portrait of Goethe' (in *The Era of Goethe*, Oxford, 1959), p. 137.

philosophy and other abstract achievements of the human mind. In Hebbel's phrase, Goethe knew full well that 'one has to water the roots of the tree if one wants to see the branches grow'.[1]

But it was not only when he decided to become an author that Hebbel remembered Goethe. He drew strength from him at other times as well. He was, perhaps, the first major German writer who saw in Goethe not only a standard in questions of aesthetics and literature but a beacon by which to chart his own course in life. It was under the influence of *Dichtung und Wahrheit* that he began in 1842, and again in 1856, to compose his own fragmentary autobiography, which was likewise intended to be not a photographic rendition of episodes from his youth, still less an attempt at total recall, but an account of the significant experiences which had guided his development. In the same manner, he approvingly quoted Goethe's enumeration of various kinds of ingratitude, in *Dichtung und Wahrheit*, when he set down on paper the reasons which made him break with his long-time benefactress, Amalie Schoppe. Much as Goethe had done in regard to Herder, Hebbel, in looking back on his own past, came to feel that his youth had been made miserable by the demands of his benefactors as much as by outward want and necessity.

Hebbel was primarily a dramatist, and it was as such that he felt himself most directly to be a successor to Goethe. Not that his plays have much in common with the latter's; they resemble Schiller's much more in the philosophical grounding, and Kleist's in the dialectic rigidity, of their plots. But Hebbel did share with Grillparzer an occasionally nightmarish feeling that Goethe's life work was a tremendous burden which he would somehow have to roll off his chest if he ever were to breathe freely. Hebbel expressed this obsession in a variety of aphoristic remarks in his essays and diaries. It was, at bottom, the realization that his own works would inevitably be held up in comparison with those of his great predecessor, and that they might be crushed by the sheer weight of the older man's reputation. Goethe had, in a sense, anticipated this problem which has beset many of those who came after him, when he declared himself lucky not to have been born an Englishman, because the

[1] *Sämtliche Werke* (Berlin, 1904–7, 24 vols.), xi. 114.

very excellence of that nation's literature, from Shakespeare on down, would have inhibited his own development.[1] It is entirely understandable in view of this that Hebbel frequently and bitingly commented on the incense burned at Goethe's altar by the early idolators, and made fun of those who would shut off their critical faculties and prostrate themselves before the 'Dalai Lama'.

Two historical periods, Hebbel thought, have brought forth the highest form of dramatic literature: the age of classical Greece, at the moment when that people's naive view of life began to be corroded by reflection, and Elizabethan England. In *King Oedipus* the individual is represented as the plaything of fate; in *Hamlet* the individual is emancipated, and the tragic conflict is no longer between Man and Fate but within the hero himself. In *Faust* and in *Die Wahlverwandtschaften* ('which are rightly called dramatic') Goethe has made a further advance in making the idea of the drama itself the dialectic battlefield, although he did not do this as rigorously as Hebbel would have wished, or did in his own dramas. *Faust I* is, then, the high point of the German drama. Its spiritual ancestor is neither Marlowe's play nor Calderón's *El mágico prodigoso* but *Hamlet*; one of its greatest qualities lies in the mirroring of medieval life; it is, furthermore, a characteristically German work, so that the reader can tell himself that 'this is all part of your nation, and therefore a part of you too'. *Faust II*, on the other hand, is an abomination. It can at best evoke 'cold respect', for we do not go to the theatre, or even read at home, in order to be confronted with riddles; in the Second Part Goethe did no more than 'relieve himself spiritually. . . of a store of ideas and opinions on various subjects' which have no organic connexion with the work as a whole. It cannot even be said, as Varnhagen von Ense had done, that it has some positive value because much of it dates from Goethe's best period: works like *Der Bürgergeneral* and *Der Gross-Kophta* show that Goethe had some 'very bad hours' even at the height of his creative powers.

If these are some of the ways in which Hebbel has enriched and modified the Goethe image of his time, we may also ask, conversely, in what way Goethe has influenced Hebbel. The paradoxical answer 'everywhere and nowhere' would be only a

[1] Eckermann, 2 Jan. 1824.

slight exaggeration. No single dramatic creation of Hebbel's
was, as such, an offspring of Goethe's; but his entire production
was predicated on the need he felt of leading the drama out of
the untragic, and occasionally undramatic, dead end in which
Goethe had left it. The author tells us that Goethe was before
his mind's eye not only when he visited Weimar, but on the top
of the Strassburg cathedral and in the midst of the Roman
crowds. His entire life and literary creation took place in
Goethe's shadow: from the moment of near self-deletion when
he read some supposedly Goethean poems to Adam Oehlen-
schläger (and when the old man applauded, admitted that they
were his own) to the opposite pole—the realization, in Rome,
that he was cut of quite different cloth because the plastic arts
which had so absorbed Goethe interested him not at all.

Like all great writers, Grillparzer, Keller, and Hebbel in part
belonged to their age and in part stood above it. They shared
with their lesser contemporaries a number of attitudes characteristic of the mid-nineteenth-century German view of Goethe.
These may be defined as a coolness toward the post-Storm and
Stress poet, and a corresponding early enthusiasm for Schiller at
his most rhetorical; an indifference to certain vital aspects of
Goethe (religious and philosophical views, natural sciences, the
arts), and a burning interest in a minor detail of his life: his
political and social views. They also had in common with their
age a dislike of *Faust II*, and to a lesser extent of *Wilhelm Meister*
and of the entire late lyrical production, as well as a suspicion
that the old poet, who according to Hebbel 'should have been
hanged after *Die Wahlverwandtschaften*', had suffered from harden-
ing of the artistic arteries. They rose above the Menzels and
Gervinuses in their conviction (individually arrived at in un-
propitious times) that Goethe is one of the four or five great
literary figures who will live forever; that the entire period to
which he gave his name represented a standard of perfection
which, regardless of what it may or may not mean to a particular generation, is in itself absolute and indisputable; that
Goethe is an ethical phenomenon as well as a literary one; and
that these truths were in danger of being perverted by a section
of Goethe's contemporary public: by the Goethe Philistines and
Goethe Pedants of whom Keller made fun in two venomous
poems.

The German authors of the twentieth century, too, may be grouped according to their relative closeness to Goethe as well as by any other token. The result of such a grouping could be likened to a spectrum, at one end of which are found those who have given evidence—direct or indirect, in their works or through specific statements to this effect—of having been influenced by Goethe or of otherwise having taken up a definite position toward him. This group includes Naturalists like Hauptmann, Neoclassicists like Binding, Impressionists like Hofmannsthal, Symbolists like George, Expressionists like Benn, as well as representatives of less recognized trends. It includes novelists like Thomas Mann and Wassermann, dramatists like Hauptmann and Hofmannsthal, lyric poets like George and Dehmel. It includes members of the generation which made its debut in the last century (Hauptmann, Hofmannsthal), and others who did not begin to write until the present (Bergengruen, Carossa). It includes writers of wide fame, like the Nobel laureates Hauptmann, Mann, and Hesse, and some of more modest reputation, like Beer-Hofmann, Bahr, and Kolbenheyer. It includes some who have survived an individual experience of chaos, like Hofmannsthal, Rilke, or Mann, and others to whom fate or faith has granted a less precarious inner existence, as it did to Hauptmann and George. It even ignores the Great Divide of the years 1933–45: Thomas Mann, Arnold Zweig, and other enemies of the Nazi régime belong to it no less than do Hauptmann and Carossa. All these writers are rooted in the Western humanistic tradition and thus beholden, in greatly varying measure, to the aesthetic tenets which grew out of classical antiquity, to the ethical postulates of Christianity and idealistic philosophy, and to the social and intellectual programmes which reflect, from the Reformation to the French Revolution and beyond, the main stages in the rational emancipation of the individual. They all consider Goethe, with greatly varying emphasis, as the most recent and perhaps the last embodiment which this tradition has found in the realm of letters. Despite differences which in other respects would make them seem as disparate a group as any to be found in literary history, they have all undergone, at one time or another, the experience of coming face to face with Goethe—an experience which one of them has thus described at its most ecstatic: 'Trying to account for one's connexion with Goethe is like trying to define one's relationship to air and light, to the very elements in which we live. There exist forces and objects which are so all-pervasive that it is impossible to gauge just how intimately we are connected with and dependent on them.'[1]

In the centre of the spectrum is found a broad band of authors who have expressed few if any opinions on the poet, and whose work gives no evidence of an indisputably Goethean influence. Arthur Schnitzler belongs to this group, as does Ernst Wiechert and a large number of Expressionists. Although these men have for all practical purposes maintained silence on the subject of Goethe, the tenor and form of their work show them to be so indebted to the humanistic tradition that their silence should not be interpreted as hostility. It is, rather, at the other end of the spectrum that we find such hostility, or at least an imperviousness to Goethe, among a group of writers who for a variety of reasons have broken with this tradition. We can, indeed, expect little enlightenment about Goethe from such authors as Wedekind, Heym, Trakl, Kafka, Ernst Jünger, or Borchert. They are spiritual descendants not of Goethe but of Pascal, Kierkegaard, Strindberg, and others for whom man is essentially out of step with the world in which he finds himself.

At first sight Gerhart Hauptmann would appear to be the most representative protagonist of the first-named group. His acquaintance and partial identification with Goethe covered almost his entire life span, from the age of eight when he first saw part of *Faust* on the stage to that of eighty-two when he finished *Mignon*. It has found a reflection not only in his works, many of which are continuations or modifications of Goethean subjects—even where, as in the *Iphigenie* tetralogy, the relationship is one of motif rather than spirit—but in several direct acknowledgements on Hauptmann's part of what Goethe has meant to him. It extends even to such imponderables of existence as a similar background, a life of comparable circumstances and almost equal length, and a marked physical resemblance (which Hauptmann enhanced by occasionally affecting Goethean garb). Nonetheless, Hauptmann's kinship with Goethe was

---

[1] Ricarda Huch, 'Ansprache bei Verleihung des Goethepreises am 28. August 1931' (*Jahrbuch des Freien Deutschen Hochstifts*, 1931), p. 323.

extensive rather than intensive. For all his works which to some extent parallel those of Goethe (as *Florian Geyer* does *Götz*, or *Anna, Hermann und Dorothea*) or represent analogous stages in his development (*Griechischer Frühling* in many ways corresponds to *Die italienische Reise*, and *Das Abenteuer meiner Jugend* to *Dichtung und Wahrheit*), and despite the public addresses he gave on the poet, Hauptmann has made a less original contribution to the Goethe image than have less creative but mentally more agile writers.

One of the ablest of these was Hans Carossa, who in his address on *Wirkungen Goethes in der Gegenwart* (1938) sounded a most timely warning: namely that the young generation, then already enmeshed in totalitarian doctrines, must for its own sake not be allowed to lose sight of two Goethean traits—a distrust of what is obvious and merely well-said, and that feeling of awe before the mysteries of existence which made Faust say:

> Doch im Erstarren such' ich nicht mein Heil,
> Das Schaudern ist der Menschheit bestes Teil.

Equally thoughtful, and necessary because the Nazi Party so artfully flattered the conceits of youth, was Carossa's observation that the poet has given a new and positive meaning to old age, because 'since his time, we believe in the old man who . . . again and again overcomes [the infirmities and diminutions of old age]. . ., in the old clairvoyant who, unbroken and unbowed, still watches over us all while many a man born after him has already gone to sleep again'.[1] Among Carossa's contemporaries, the novelists Werner Bergengruen and Frank Thiess also have shown a deep and true understanding of Goethe. In modifying Carus's concept of the 'healthy' Goethe, Bergengruen felt that such favourite Goethean terms as 'clear, clean, neat, capable, fruitful, well-formed' are to some extent synonymous with health, and that this health of Goethe's, which is 'the realization of [one's] yearning for a balance of all functions, coupled with the power to recreate oneself and to maintain one's identity'[2]

---

[1] 'Wirkungen Goethes in der Gegenwart' (*Goethe* [Viermonatsschrift der Goethe-Gesellschaft], iii. 1938), p. 121.

[2] *Rede über Goethe* (Marburg, 1949), p. 9. One of the most original comments made on Goethe's health in this sense is the following by F. Servaes: 'The bright, satiated, joyous element in his works is undoubtedly in part due to the time of day in which they were composed. On the other hand, it is surely no coincidence that Ibsen is a nocturnal producer' (*Goethe am Ausgang des Jahrhunderts* [Berlin, 1897], p. 23).

is that aspect of his personality which is worthiest of imitation on the part of those who are at all receptive to Goethe. What we need are not new revelations about him from this source or that, or a return to conditions which favoured the training of numerous Goethe experts, but the strength to follow his example in the achievement and preservation of such health, and in the daily task of self-discipline and self-application to useful work. If Bergengruen thus considers Goethe's present-day significance from the individual's viewpoint, Frank Thiess interprets it from an ethnic one. It is not by coincidence, he explained in *Goethe als Symbol* (1947), that the Chinese venerated K'ung Fu-Tse as the epitome of their national virtues, or the Greeks Plato, and the Romans Caesar—although the Chinese and Greeks, too, had famous generals, and Romans great poets and thinkers. Goethe's symbolic meaning for his people was that he represented in his person the yearning for unity which characterized the nineteenth century in Germany. It does not matter that they understood him only imperfectly and did not share all his enthusiasms. What made him a national symbol, and does so even now, is that the German people saw in him 'themselves, their own higher self; they saw realized in him that which they could not realize themselves'.

One could easily lose one's way in endeavouring to report on the modifications of the Goethe image which have been suggested by these authors and by others of similar stature—for example, R. A. Schröder, R. Beer-Hofmann, G. Benn—who have written on Goethe briefly but wisely. The literary Goethe image of our time is so complex and many-faced a phenomenon that it is impossible to do it full justice. In territory which is largely uncharted, however, a sketch is better than no map at all. In our case, any such sketch must mark the precise position which those writers have taken up toward Goethe whose work is certain to survive into the future: not only Stefan George but Rainer Maria Rilke, Hugo von Hofmannsthal, Thomas Mann, and Hermann Hesse. It has already been pointed out that the spectrum of closeness to Goethe transcends the standard classifications of literary history and that a substantial number of major modern authors 'face away from' Goethe, not from hostility but out of indifference to the ideals for which he stands.

The depth no less than extent of his influence is indicated by the fact that the truly great writers of our time do not look at Goethe from the viewpoints which governed such relationships in the past. They are not primarily concerned with his religion, his patriotism, his attitude toward women, his position in intellectual history or even his aesthetic beliefs and practices. Instead they have looked for, and found in him, an answer to the most pressing problems of their individual existence.

Rilke was born in 1875, and the Goethe to whom he was introduced in his youth was 'the Olympian who moves in other regions'.[1] It is not likely that this formidable figure elicited any response beyond some routine acknowledgements, such as Rilke's plan to set down his impressions of *Wilhelm Meister*, or a reference to Goethe's description of Venice which the young traveller consulted prior to his own first visit there. The only early mention of Goethe which bears a more personal note concerns *Die Wahlverwandtschaften*, over which Rilke, then seventeen, cried a whole evening; however, the circumstances attendant on this scene lead one to suspect that the novel was the occasion but not the cause of his grief. Rilke's critical analysis of Goethe for all practical purposes began with the passage in *Die Aufzeichnungen des Malte Laurids Brigge* (1909) in which the (unnamed) 'greatest poet' is censured for having taken Bettina von Arnim's love too lightly:

Perhaps it will one day become clear that this was where his greatness fell short. This lover was imposed on him as a supreme test, and he was not equal to it. What does it help to say that he could not requite her love? Such love needs no requiting, it has the mating-cry and the response too within itself. But he ought to have humbled himself before it in all his glory, going down on his knees and writing with both hands what it dictated to him, like St. John on Patmos. It was not for him to pick and choose before this voice that 'performed the office of the angels', who had come to enshroud him and transport him to eternity. Here was the chariot for his fiery flight to Heaven. Here had the darkling myth been prepared for his death, and he left it empty.[2]

[1] Quoted, without source, by C. Sieber, 'Rilkes äusserer Weg zu Goethe' (*Dichtung und Volkstum*, xxxvii, 1936), p. 54.

[2] *Gesammelte Werke* (Leipzig, 1927, 6 vols.), v. 241. Translated by E. C. Mason, to whose article 'Rilke and Goethe' (*Publications of the English Goethe Society*, new series xvii, 1948) the present account is indebted in several points.

Instead of humbly accepting Bettina's love, Goethe had reacted
as privy councillor: by saying how much he enjoyed her letters,
and how they reminded him of his own youth.

The argument is a precarious one, even though Rilke reiterated it in a letter to his wife, and left it unchanged even after
he had come to see that the real Bettina was quite different
from the vision that had appeared to Malte. It is a valid viewpoint only in the context of Rilke's conviction that a woman's
love, especially a thwarted love which reaches a higher pitch
of intensity for being deprived of its natural fulfilment, is of
necessity deeper and more valuable than a man's. In the poet's
constellation of women whose love represents the quintessence of
their worth and fate, Bettina thus took her place at the side of
Marianna Alcoforado, Louize Labée, and Gaspara Stampa.

About a year after this passage-at-arms Rilke spent some time
in the home of his friend and publisher Anton Kippenberg,
director of the Inselverlag and Goethe collector extraordinary.
Kippenberg and his wife Katherina introduced him to some of
the early works of their favourite poet, so successfully that somewhat later, Rilke himself asked to be sent a copy of the 'Volksgoethe' because 'it is now time for me to read more of the Goethe
of those years, 1775–80'. The *Tagebücher* and *Tag- und Jahreshefte* moved him to confess that 'from *these* writings I can get
quite near to Goethe, and *then* he puts up with me, just as though
it were really meant to be so'[1]—an oddly and characteristically
Rilkean turn of phrase, which surely means that he had discovered the living Goethe behind the Olympian façade. Despite
some relapses into his earlier reserve, and the decidedly circumspect tone of his statements on this point, he developed in the
end a great respect for Goethe, mediated in part by Lewes's and
Gundolf's biographies.

What strikes one about this development is its eclectic nature.
Unlike Hofmannsthal and Mann, Rilke did not come by his
concept of Goethe in the normal course of events in that he
'inherited' him along with the other classics of German literature; or rather, the Goethe whom he did thus inherit remained
sterile, a schoolboy's required reading, and sank no roots in the
creative layers of his mind. When they took their own place in

---

[1] Letter to Kippenberg, 11 Feb. 1910. Translation, and italics, by Mason (op.
cit., p. 108).

the German literary tradition, Mann and Hofmannsthal (and George and so many others) imperceptibly, and at first perhaps unconsciously, began to question the image of Goethe which had been handed down to them, until they ended by modifying it according to their own lights. But Rilke remained outside of this communal *Goethe-Erlebnis*, as he remained outside of the main currents of the entire German tradition. He oriented himself by modern Scandinavian and Russian authors, by the Worpswede painters, by Rodin. The traditional turn-of-the-century Goethe image (the great humanist, the master of form, the advocate of self-limitation, the last universal genius) was bound to mean less to him than to most others. His case once more illustrates the truth of the observation that not only every generation but every individual takes from Goethe that which is germane to his own nature, and disregards the rest. On the face of it, no one has disregarded more than Rilke: all that which Bielschowsky's generation had found most impressive in Goethe. Rilke's comments on *Faust* and on the other great dramas are, accordingly, sparse and insignificant; it is very likely that a novel like Jens Peter Jacobsen's *Niels Lyhne* meant more to him than all of Goethe's prose; even most of the better-known poems failed to strike a responsive chord in him. Nor can there be any question of a Goethean 'influence' on Rilke, except, perhaps, in regard to some very specific words and images.

This is not to say that Rilke found nothing in Goethe that was germane to him. His utterly uncompromising drive beyond hitherto accepted limits, in thought, in form, in language itself, is in a way more Faust-like than Goethe's own stately advance toward resignation.[1] What Rilke lacked, however, and to an extent learned from Goethe, has little to do with Faustian striving. Although his comments on Goethe are scattered throughout his correspondence and prose, and characterized by a similar lack of intermediary stages between *Erlebnis* and *Dichtung* as that which makes his poetry capable of being interpreted on so many different levels, it is more than likely that such

[1] In *Goethe und die Demokratie*, Thomas Mann cites, with evident delight, Fairley's contention that Goethe 'did not foresee the coming, in the century after him, of a point of view that would have preferred to have him go to pieces at all costs like a good poet rather than make a success of things' (*A Study of Goethe*, Oxford, 1947, p. 271). Yet in his own way, and under much more difficult circumstances than those which had faced Goethe, Rilke, too, refused to 'go to pieces'.

documents as Goethe's letters to Auguste zu Stolberg, these buoyantly effusive 'radiations of youth',[1] taught Rilke that the pursuit of the highest art need not separate a man from life and atrophy his social function. Similarly Rilke's admiration for *Harzreise im Winter* and, conversely, his dislike of *Tasso*—a 'peevish, badtempered book' in whose hero he quite possibly recognized a potential image of himself—surely sprang from Goethe's warning that a retreat from the realities of the world is bound to lead to self-isolation and a scorn for mankind.

Hofmannsthal, who is said to have remarked of himself that he had never really felt any great joy or pain, also seems far removed, at first sight, from the author of *Werther*. Young Loris, with his precocious *déjà vu* and his mystical knowledge of things never yet experienced in the flesh, seems to stand at the opposite pole from Goethe, the 'confessional' poet. Even the similarities between *Der Tor und der Tod* and *Faust*, or *Die Frau ohne Schatten* and *Das Märchen*, are similarities of the letter rather than the spirit. The contrast is still sharper when we think of Hofmannsthal's adaptations from Sophocles and Euripides; his Greece, like Hauptmann's, is clearly that of Nietzsche and Bachofen. Nonetheless Hofmannsthal has held, ever since he grew beyond the aestheticism of his early twenties, a 'dialogue with Goethe', which can be so called even in regard to the antithetical form of the respective writings. It is not too much to say that he found himself in the course of that dialogue, which was made doubly fruitful by his awareness of the gulf which separated him and his world from the spirit of Weimar. This awareness has, among other things, enabled him to define the difficulties which confront the modern reader when he turns to Goethe, as well as the rewards which await those among us who are willing to make the transition from our sphere to his:

He ... who wants to reabsorb one of Goethe's works ... must approach the book with senses already purified. He must leave much of himself, of the atmosphere of his life behind. He must forget the big city. He must cut through ten thousand threads of the feeling, thinking, and wishing of the moment. ... Once he has achieved this, however, it is of little importance which of Goethe's works he opens. Everywhere he is enveloped by the same enhanced and transfigured

[1] Letter to Kippenberg, 28 Sept. 1911.

reality; he is truly surrounded by a world, a spirit in itself a world. . . .
The immense calm of an immense wealth descends almost oppres-
sively on his soul, in order to raise this soul again to a state of bliss.
But this arm which can raise to the stars does not embrace everyone.
The living Goethe, too, gave himself only to a few and to these not at
any hour. To him who reaches out for it with a nervous hand, a
creation such as *Die Wahlverwandtschaften* snaps shut like the shell of an
oyster. . . .[1]

The salient point in Hofmannsthal's dialogue with Goethe was
the realization of the 'otherness' of his own nature, which he
turned into a productive factor by learning from Goethe that
polarities need not lead to destruction. They had threatened to
do so in the time of the *Brief des Lord Chandos*, whose fictitious
writer was torn asunder by the sudden antinomy between his
own self and an outside world which could no longer be reached
through mere words. Yet Hofmannsthal overcame this paralysis
of his creative powers, and learned from Goethe the secret of
dissolving such a polarity by identifying his conjectural self with
the phenomenal world around him. He has, furthermore, described for us, in the magnificent imagery which was his,
that other side of Goethe whose mere existence had once been
prettified beyond recognition.

But you must also admit [he has Balzac say in the imaginary
dialogue *Über Charaktere im Roman und im Drama*] that your German
Apollo, your Olympian, that your wizard of Weimar was a demon,
and not one of the least awe-inspiring. I will not judge him by his
Werther: he has repudiated this fever of his youth. But the whole man,
the whole poet, the whole Being! I could imagine having known him:
his eye must have been more uncanny than that of Klingsor the
magician, than that of Merlin of whom they said it reached down,
like a bottomless pit, into the depths of hell; more uncanny than that
of Medusa. He could kill, this prodigious man, with one glance, ...
with one lift of his Olympian shoulders: he could turn a human heart
to stone; he could kill a soul and then turn his back on it as if nothing
had happened, and then walk off to his plants, to his stones, to his
colours. . . . There were times when men would have burned him,
and there were other times when he would have been worshipped.
He allowed his destiny, which was his nature, to bring to that

---

[1] H. von Hofmannsthal, *Gesammelte Werke in Einzelausgaben* (Frankfurt a. M.
1946–), Prosa ii. 381. Tr. by T. and S. Stern.

nature—that is, his destiny—all the sacrifices demons require. . . .
And this glittering enchanted castle which he fashioned out of
immortal substance—do you imagine it had no dungeons where
prisoners moaned their way toward a lingering death?. . . He is
bigger and more sinister than the Trojan Horse, but I will break down
the doorposts of my work and lead him in.[1]

The high points of Hofmannsthal's dialogue with the poet are
the introductory essay *Goethes 'Westöstlicher Divan'*, the fictitious
Unterhaltung über den 'Tasso' von Goethe, and the Goethe passages
in the posthumous *Das Buch der Freunde*. The introduction to the
Divan is another expression of that characteristic note in Hofmannsthal's attitude to Goethe which was already evident in the
above quotation from the essay *Balzac*: a preoccupation with
helping the modern reader break down the invisible walls
which stand between him and the poet's word.[2] From the exoti-
cism of the title to the fact that the whole *Divan* is so spiritual in
mood that it requires a reader who is himself in a state of exalta-
tion, Hofmannsthal discusses, and banishes, most of the reservations which a certain type of reader harbours in regard to the
work. The *Unterhaltung über den 'Tasso' von Goethe* (1906) centres
not on the dichotomy between Tasso and Antonio but on the
most passive character in the drama, on the figure of the Princess,
who is so transparently noble, resigned, and simple: 'We hear
so much talk about simplicity; all parents want to raise their
children to be simple—but how seldom do we acknowledge that
complete simplicity is an extreme and exposed condition! It is a
determined nobility of mind, a renunciation of all endeavour.
Anyone who undertakes or seeks something can easily appear
adventurous or snobbish by contrast. Such simplicity is a
triumph of one's whole being, a triumph of good breeding—but
a dangerous and quite possibly pitiable triumph.'[3] It is this
'extreme and exposed' simplicity of the Princess which makes
Tasso's embrace so grievous an offence: an affront to a person
whose only shield is a sort of aprioristically granted inviolability.
There is a perfect blending of minds and styles in this imaginary
conversation between two married couples, an enamel-like

---

[1] H. von Hofmannsthal, *Gesammelte Werke*, &c., Prosa ii. 53–55. Tr. by T. and
S. Stern.

[2] The problem of how best to approach Goethe is also touched upon in *Die Briefe
des jungen Goethe* and *'Wilhelm Meister' in der Urform*.

[3] *Gesammelte Werke*, &c., Prosa ii. 224.

smoothness and an evanescent, Old-Austrian gentility which softens but does not de-individualize four people who could have stepped out of *Die Wahlverwandtschaften* or the *Novelle*, even down to their anonymity as Poet, Baron, Baroness, and Hostess. In their conversation following a *Tasso* performance in which the great Kainz had played the title role, and in the letter which may or may not have been written by the Baroness, these four figures represent so many different ways of looking at Tasso's relationship with the Princess. Hofmannsthal came so close to Goethe here that he recreated even the most ineffable of the latter's achievements, that of endowing his characters with a marked personality of their own, and a no less distinct symbolic meaning.

Das Buch der Freunde, a collection of aphoristic diary jottings, contains Hofmannsthal's most private reflections on Goethe. These are as spontaneous as the essay on *Tasso* is polished, and it seems almost unbelievable that these flamboyant *aperçus* should have come from the hand which composed some of the most delicately chiselled prose in German. Yet one cannot mistake, underneath the pithy formulation, Hofmannsthal's own tone of love and nostalgia for Goethe in remarks like these: 'We have no modern literature. We have Goethe, and some beginnings', or 'Goethe is not the source of this or that in our modern litera-ture, but a huge mountain, and the fountainhead of all our modern writing'.

Thomas Mann, like Rilke, came to Goethe late in life. From the first short stories to *Betrachtungen eines Unpolitischen* (1918), his work offers no comments on Goethe comparable in depth and sympathy to those he made on Schopenhauer, Wagner, Nietzsche, or even Lessing, Kleist, and Eichendorff Whatever Goethean influences on style and subject matter may be traced in the early production, they are surely insignificant beside the obvious debt which the author owes to the great French and Russian novelists of the later nineteenth century. Even in the *Betrach-tungen*, Mann's painstaking and courageous analysis of the heri-tage of an embattled Germany, Goethe appears not as a poet but as supreme representative of those who believed in, and practised, that dissociation of 'Kultur' from the problems of daily political life which the book advocates. The author's preoccupation with Goethe began with the essay *Goethe und Tolstoi* (1922), culminated in the best work of fiction ever written on the poet, the novel *Lotte in Weimar* (1939), and continued unabated until Mann's death in 1955.

The dialectic nature of Mann's approach to Goethe is already evident in that first essay, which compares the 'European humanist and confirmed pagan' with the 'anarchic primeval Christian of the East'.[1] Mann illustrates the community of interests, viewpoints, and character traits in Goethe and Tolstoy by contrasting it with a similar community found in their antipodes Schiller and Dostoevsky. These latter are 'children of the mind', while Goethe and Tolstoy belong to the 'children of nature': a distinction which largely but not altogether overlaps that which Schiller himself had drawn between the Naive and the Sentimental Poet. The 'children of nature' are so designated by certain gifts and attitudes which were first defined in this essay, and reinterpreted many times in Mann's later contributions to literary criticism (for all their originality and elegance of diction, Mann's Goethe studies are also extraordinarily repetitive). The following anecdote, for example, epitomizes a number of Goethean attitudes which Mann not only admired but in large measure shared.

'Now Sömmering has died . . . just a paltry 75 years old. What rascals people are, that they do not have the courage to hold on longer than that! I must say I admire my friend [Jeremy] Bentham, that very radical old fool; he is getting along nicely, and he is even a few weeks older than I!' Eckermann, to whom these remarks were addressed, suggested that Goethe, too, might have been a radical if he had lived in England. 'What do you take me for?' replied Goethe, '. . . if I had been born in England I would have been a wealthy duke, or rather, a bishop with a yearly income of thirty thousand pounds.' Eckermann agreed that this was all very well, but what if Goethe had drawn a blank in life's lottery and remained poor? 'Not everybody, my good friend, is made to win first prize. Do you think I would have been fool enough to draw a blank?' (In Eckermann's account of 17 March 1830 the poet went on to express his confidence that

---

[1] 'Goethe und Tolstoi' (in *Adel des Geistes*), p. 161. All quotations are from the individually published volumes of the 'Stockholmer Gesamtausgabe der Werke von Thomas Mann'.

he would have got to the top in England also, and would have 'left nothing undone to maintain myself there'.)

Why did this story so impress Mann that he repeated it not only in this essay, but in *Goethe als Repräsentant des bürgerlichen Zeitalters, Lotte in Weimar, Phantasie über Goethe,* and *Goethe und die Demokratie?* To begin with, there is Goethe's boasting about his longevity, and the affected scorn for a youngster of seventy-five who had the effrontery to die; but these are merely examples of a frequent and rather engaging weakness of very old men. More specifically Goethean is the combination of seemingly incompatible attributes, as in 'radical old fool': whether or not radicalism is tantamount to foolishness is a matter of opinion, but it surely is a trait far more frequently attributed to youth than old age. The Goethe of the late Weimar years was a masterful coiner of such hybrid formulations, which reach from the bantering tone of this example right up to the incredible compounds of words, moods, and meanings in the third act of *Faust II.* Mann had a similar inventiveness and penchant for the paradoxical, which he put to good use in *Lotte in Weimar* and elsewhere. Furthermore the epithet 'radical old fool', goodnaturedly contemptuous, reflects in its application to a social reformer an attitude of tolerant conservatism in such matters which resembles Mann's own (even if in the latter's case both tolerance and conservatism were severely strained as the skies gradually darkened over his homeland). However, what most fascinated Mann was, no doubt, Goethe's bland assumption that life would not have given him short change no matter where and under what circumstances he had lived it. The poet has expressed this conviction in another paradoxical saying dear to Mann's heart: that there exist 'innate merits' which are the endowment of those who are destined to succeed. Outrageous and 'undemocratic' as it sounds to our age, the idea is a modification of the concept of 'well-born' which Carus had first applied to Goethe —a mythical but unmistakable peculiarity of those who have an aristocratic fate, a quality which has only the most tenuous of connexions with ordinary good fortune, or with such measurable aristocracies as those of birth, wealth, or even talents. Goethe, whose 'rejoicing in an aristocratic exceptionality [and] a distinguished injustice' Mann has celebrated elsewhere, and Tolstoy who was similarly endowed, are set apart from Schiller and Dostoevsky by this and many other traits: by their physical vitality, their Anteus-like reliance on the earth as source of creative strength, their cheerful and occasionally priapic hedonism, their curious mixture of friendliness and ice-cold reserve. If Mann thus makes use of Goethe's principle of polarity in characterizing the essence of a phenomenon (here, the writer as personality type) by bracketing it within the extremes to which it can extend, he likewise applies the complementary concept of intensification: both groups enhance their faculties by following the attraction exerted on them by their opposites. (These need not always be embodied in the same antipodes; in one of the parallels drawn in this essay, it is not Schiller and Dostoevsky, but Merck and Turgenev respectively who urge the minister Goethe and the judge Tolstoy to return to literary production.)

A different kind of antithesis governs the essays *Goethe als Repräsentant des bürgerlichen Zeitalters* and *Goethes Laufbahn als Schriftsteller* (both 1932). In the opening paragraphs of the first-named work Mann has set down, in a passage which forms a key to his entire *Goethe-Erlebnis*, the sensation of profound and immediate familiarity which overcame him on his first visit, years before, to the Goethemuseum in Frankfurt.

I cannot speak of Goethe [he concludes his memories of that occasion] except with love; that is, on the basis of an intimacy which is rendered less questionable by [my] very lively awareness of [his] incomparable stature. I modestly leave it to others, to commentators, historians of literature, and those who feel capable of intuitively doing justice to the highest, to make pronouncements about the peaks [of his achievement]. This is quite a different matter from sharing with him a part of his substance, and deriving from this fact only . . . a right and an opportunity to participate in the discussion about him.[1]

Having thus introduced himself as a lesser man than Goethe but as not unlike him in nature (and having elsewhere interpreted the 'bourgeois era' as the period of middle-class ascendancy which extended from the Renaissance through the French Revolution up to the beginning of the present century), the author proceeds to examine another complex of attitudes: those which have a bearing on Goethe's existence as a social being and as a professional writer. To no one's surprise, the

[1] pp. 90–91.

touches here pencilled into the Goethe image tend to underline such idiosyncrasies as have affected the manner in which the poet solved a problem which has long intrigued Mann himself: the seemingly irreconcilable conflict between the artist and the bourgeois. Here we encounter, on one level, a predilection for good food and sundry other creature comforts, a neatness bordering on the fastidious, an insistence on getting paid for work done as handsomely as the trade will allow, a drive to finish what has been started even at the risk of merely 'going through the motions', and other such traits which would have made men like Johann Buddenbrook, and perhaps even Gustav von Aschenbach and Hans Castorp, feel very much at home in Weimar. Yet for all the loving care which Mann expands on this account of Goethe *en bourgeois*, there shines through again and again an inkling of the other level of the poet's being, of his spirit of contradiction and negation, his at times frightening lack of enthusiam and human warmth, his 'Protean nature. . . which was ironical and bizarre rather than comfortable, more negative than positive, facetious rather than cheerful'.[1] With eyes sharpened by his own precarious defence against the nihilistic undercurrents of modern life, Mann perceives in Goethe a number of inclinations which, had they been allowed to go unchecked, would have turned the man who harboured them into a monstrous persiflage of a great creator: a demoniacal egocentricity, a corroding lack of faith in God, himself, and the world, and a ruthless rejection of those among the younger generation who tried to approach him on their own terms.

It is this image of Goethe struggling against self-obliteration which the author has enshrined in the novel *Lotte in Weimar*. In telling his very simple plot—Lotte Kestner, *née* Buff, visits Weimar in late 1816 and meets Goethe again after more than forty years—Mann has bent his formidable epic and analytical skill to the task of presenting a psychological X-ray picture taken from various perspectives. In the centre of the book stands the poet himself, who bares to us, in one of the few convincing stream-of-consciousness passages in the German language, the infinity of thoughts and sensations which flood his mind on some outwardly nondescript morning. Mann artfully leads us up to this pivotal seventh chapter by making us follow for a while along the path of several minor characters who orbit,

[1] *Goethe als Repräsentant, &c.*, p. 111.

as it were, around this sun whose emanations are so strong
that even those who live remote from it, like Lotte and her
daughter, or who possess, like the hotel factotum Mager, little
specific weight of their own, have taken on Goethe's mannerisms
of speech and demeanour. In this galaxy we meet the young
Scotswoman, Miss Cuzzle, who insists on drawing a portrait of
the worthy matron who once was 'Werther's Lotte'. Here, too,
we meet the ponderous Riemer, Goethe's 'purveyor of information'—Wissenslieferant—who is too ambitious to be able to
subordinate himself gracefully to his employer, yet too subaltern
a character to break out of the gravitational field which holds
him imprisoned in Weimar; and Johanna Schopenhauer, who
with the devastating insight of an intelligent but unattractive
young woman dissects the miseries of His Excellency's domestic
life, the double isolation resulting from the marriage to Christiane and the refusal to be drawn into the Wars of Liberation.
In giving vent to her forebodings about the impending marriage
of her confidante and friend Ottilie von Pogwisch, she sets the
stage for our acquaintance with the bridegroom, August von
Goethe, the not altogether unworthy but somehow pitifully
inadequate son of a very great father. But above all, it is through
the eyes of Lotte herself that we see both the young Goethe
about whom she reminisces in various conversations, and the old
poet whom she twice meets in person. In her unclouded vision
we behold a man of gigantic stature, grandiose even in his
pettiness, who is characterized in some particularly apt observations: as so nervous and 'charged' in temperament in his
younger years that one would expect to 'get a shock if one were
to touch him'; as a demigod who descends Zeus-like to the
mortal sphere of Lotte and Kestner and parasitically feeds his
emotions on their engagement, because he is really incapable of
giving himself completely; but also as a man who in a myriad
ways has to pay the full price of greatness.

Delightful as the novel is, one might almost wish that a lesser
author had written it. The very depth of Mann's familiarity
with Goethe's work and whole aura of life, as well as the perfect
fusing of his own style with that of the old Goethe, so obliterates
the line between author and subject that the ironical tone of the
book occasionally skirts the parodistic. The account of the poet's
morning ablutions, for example, with its reference to the physio-

logical and psychological effects of squeezing out a sponge over one's neck and letting the icy drops trickle down one's back, is more likely to evoke the shades of such determined masochists as Detlev Spinell and Gustav von Aschenbach than that of Goethe.

With the exception of this novel whose hero is, for sound epic reasons, almost hermetically sealed off from the world around him, Mann's works on Goethe present the poet as deeply affected by the intellectual currents of the past, and, in turn, influencing those of modern times. This happened not by chance but because it corresponds to two overriding characteristics of the novelist and essayist Thomas Mann: an extraordinary degree of artistic consciousness coupled with a correspondingly high skill in the evocation of experiences not of war, love, religion, or social conditions, but of intellectual vistas. The 'Bildungserlebnis'—one of his own in the numerous autobiographical fragments, or that of a Thomas Buddenbrook, Kröger, Castorp, or Leverkühn— is surely Mann's favourite topic. His Goethe experience was the opening up of precisely such an intellectual vista. It was, to use his own expression from *Der Tod in Venedig*, an 'adventure of the mind'. The cerebral density of his art enabled and perhaps caused him to describe in some detail not only the effect which the 'adventures' of Schopenhauer, Wagner, Nietzsche, and Goethe had on him, but also the circumstances under which he came up against these adventures. A classic example of this is the description, in *Betrachtungen eines Unpolitischen*, of his discovery or rediscovery of Wagner among the irreverent Roman crowds. Other such instances are the above passage from *Goethe als Repräsentant des bürgerlichen Zeitalters*, the inclusion of the poet among those who had been attracted to the story of the Biblical Joseph, the coy observation (made when he was already at work on his own novel) that 'a thought-provoking tale, in fact a novel' might be written about Lotte's visit to Weimar,[1] and last but not least, the well-considered audacity with which Mann returned to the Faust-theme and restored to it its traditional tragic connotation.

Mann, by all accounts the most articulate among the modern German authors who have written on Goethe, has never ceased to strive for a precise delineation of the poet's role in the unfolding of German culture. Whether he sees in Goethe's aloofness

[1] 'Goethes Werther' (in *Altes und Neues*), p. 214.

from the French Revolution a parallel to Erasmus's coolness toward the Reformation, or in Goethe's character a synthesis of the Nordic and the Mediterranean psyche and a combination of the demoniac and the urbane, or in his outlook on life a positive and democratic counterweight to the Romanticist, Wagnerian, and aristocratic death-wish which he considered a typically and fatally German trait, Mann has never tired of examining Goethe with the eyes of a psychologist and cultural historian. Despite the variety of such cultural perspectives (of which the above represent only a small selection), his view of Goethe is basically a very consistent one. Thomas Mann's Goethe is that of the late Weimar period; a 'good' German, but not a narrowly patriotic one; with the exception of *Faust*, a novelist rather than poet; a creative spirit for whom art was less a vehicle of self-expression than an aid in the shaping of his personality; a man who neither flinched in the face of nothingness nor sat back in the expectation that grace would seek him out from above; and a highly problematical person whose taming as well as intensifying of great natural endowments has set an example for posterity.

Hermann Hesse, Mann's friend and contemporary, has also documented his admiration for Goethe. Even more than in the case of Mann, many facets of Hesse's life and work are so reminiscent of Goethe's that certain similarities can and have been traced. One may compare his pietistic upbringing with Goethe's early exposure to that movement, find a similarity in the two men's somewhat circuitous route toward the literary life, or comment on Hesse's preoccupation with Indian and oriental philosophy and the corresponding stage in Goethe's life. It might even be argued that both Mann and Hesse share with Goethe some experiences which have been the common lot of many Germans —such as the early and lasting disillusionment with institutionalized education—and some very individual ones as well, in which they took pains to dissociate themselves from their fellow countrymen, as Goethe did in 1813–15, Hesse in 1914–18, and Mann in 1933–45. In regard to their literary development, a communalty of problems and motifs could be traced from *Peter Camenzind* and *Werther* through *Der Steppenwolf* and *Faust* to *Das Glasperlenspiel* and *Wilhelm Meisters Wanderjahre*, which would surely bring out the truth of Hesse's own assertion that 'among all German authors, it is Goethe to whom I owe most: he has pre-empted my attention, oppressed and encouraged me, and forced me to follow or gainsay him'.[1] There is, however, no need to rely on such speculations because the author himself has been quite specific in his remarks on Goethe, among other things in a crucial passage of his novel *Der Steppenwolf* and in an essay written in celebration of the centennial of 1932.

In what turns out to have been a last considered attempt to maintain contact with the middle-class sphere to which he once belonged, Harry Haller, the Wolf of the Steppes, accepts a dinner invitation. On being led into his host's living room, his eye falls on

a small picture in a frame that stood on the round table leaning back on its paste-board support. It was an engraving and it represented the poet Goethe as an old man full of character, with a finely chiselled face and a genius's mane. Neither the renowned fire of his eyes nor the lonely and tragic expression beneath the courtly whitewash was lacking. . . . No doubt this portrait was no worse than others of its description. It was much the same as all those representations by careful craftsmen of saviours, apostles, heroes, thinkers, and statesmen.

The picture, at any rate, so irritates Haller that he feels constrained to remark 'Let us hope that Goethe did not really look like this. This conceited air of nobility, the great man ogling the distinguished company, and beneath the manly exterior what a world of charming sentimentality! Certainly, there is much to be said against him. I have a good deal against his venerable pomposity myself. But to represent him like this—no, that is going too far.'[2] Hesse attached a pivotal significance to this episode: Haller's rejection of the falsified image of Goethe is not only a token but the immediate occasion of his final break with the normal world. The symbol of the adulterated Goethe is further stressed in the nightmare which Haller suffers after his first meeting with Hermine, who, Mephisto-like, is to lead him out of the morass of introspectiveness into which he had sunk.

According to Hesse's own account, the Goethe who engaged

---

[1] 'Dank an Goethe' (*Neue Rundschau*, April 1932), p. 522.
[2] *Der Steppenwolf*, cited from the English edition (New York, 1929) tr. by B. Creighton.

his attention throughout his life was no immutable quantity. It was the nature poet and author of *Werther* who first fascinated him and has not ceased to hold him in his grasp. Later he discovered the literary man and humanist who had dedicated himself to the noblest aim of all: that of establishing 'a life governed by the mind, not only for himself but for his people and period'. Goethe's great synthesis, to be sure, had not altogether been successful; life and the mind, Antonio and Tasso, had lived on as separate entities. But a part of Goethe's greatness actually lay in the fact that he formulated ideas which remained incapable of fulfilment, and that he did this in such a way that no German writer of any stature could afford to disregard either his achievements or his failures. The War of 1914–18 drew Hesse still closer to Goethe, for example when Romain Rolland designated the pacifism of his friend as 'Goethean', a term which had almost become insulting in that period when the patriotic propagandists had relegated the poet to the sidelines and resuscitated instead other figures from the past, such as Hegel and Nietzsche. Hesse's final vision of Goethe is that of a man who has 'achieved wisdom, and stripped off . . . the temporal and personal'.[1]

It is proper that this outline of the literary image of Goethe should close with another account couched in personal terms, written by a man who is only secondarily a man of letters. It is proper because not only the account itself but the personality and achievement of its author represent the most impressive contemporary emanation of that Janus-like aspect of Goethe which has repeatedly been touched upon in these pages: his literary impact on later writers, and his ethical impact on a distinguished company for whom he has been a guide through life. If these men represent a minority, it is of the kind that makes the world go round. Few will dispute Albert Schweitzer's place in that minority.

As a student of Windelband's in Strassburg, young Schweitzer was struck by the fact that Goethe had paid so little attention to the great thought structures which Kant, Fichte, and Hegel had erected during his lifetime. It took him aback to realize that along with such 'eruptions' of speculative philosophy there had existed, ever since the days of the Greek Stoa,

[1] 'Dank an Goethe', p. 528.

another road to an understanding of the universe and of our place in it: the path of nature philosophy along which Goethe had humbly walked while his contemporaries had been held spellbound by the great systematic thinkers. Long before he went to Africa, Schweitzer himself turned to this type of philosophy which takes the world not as construction but as given reality and interprets it on *its* terms. At the same time, he 'learned to love Goethe' and to tell himself, whenever he was engaged in some humanitarian task, that 'this is [your] *Harzreise im Winter*':[1] because he had seen the incongruousness, when re-reading Goethe's poem of that title, of the supposedly unconcerned privy councillor braving the winter storms in order to bring aid and solace to the melancholy Friedrich Plessing who had opened his heart to him. Schweitzer realized, however, that such charitable deeds were only one expression of Goethe's belief that mental effort and concern must be complemented by practical activity, and that the poet had not only lived his own life in accordance with that precept but let Faust and Wilhelm Meister end their days working, as colonizer and surgeon respectively, on behalf of their fellow man. A very similar inner need had guided Schweitzer himself to Lambaréné, where he found that the example of Goethe, 'full of smiling consolation and understanding', was beside him in the jungle—for example during the grim winter of 1925, when the threat of famine made him realize that helping one's neighbour is not restricted to medicine or poetry or whatever one does best, but can also entail 'tormenting [oneself] with recalcitrant labourers in order to wrest fertile land from the primeval forest'.

He had already discovered in earlier years, at medical school, how wrong it was to regret the fact that Goethe had let himself become absorbed by scientific interests at a time when he 'should have' husbanded his strength in order to give definitive shape to the teeming thoughts and projects in his mind. Schweitzer saw that far from losing, Goethe had actually found himself in these studies, which forced him to come to terms with facts and conditions which existed not because he had thought them out but simply because they were there. In much the same

[1] 'Ansprache bei der Verleihung des Goethepreises der Stadt Frankfurt am 28. August 1928', in *Goethe. Vier Reden von Albert Schweitzer* (3rd ed., München, 1950), p. 12.

manner, Schweitzer on his part derived from his medical studies a salutary clarification of his thinking, which benefited from being no longer allowed to remain abstract but having to 'pass through reality'. And when war broke out and the extremer forms of nationalism and socialism threatened to triumph at the expense of the individual, Schweitzer once more turned to Goethe. In his search for an antidote to the ideologies which put Might before Right, he was led to reflect on Goethe's love of justice, and on his wisdom in interpolating, into the *Faust* story, the retarding episode of Philemon and Baucis, as a warning that even the best-intentioned of actions carry within them the seeds of crime if they do not respect the sanctity of the individual.

These few examples could be multiplied from other accounts which Schweitzer has given, in more than twenty years, of his preoccupation with the Poet, Scientist, Thinker, and Man.[1] They may be considered as an extraordinary testimonial to Goethe from the pen of one of the greatest of living men, or they may be dismissed, shrugged off (precisely because the testimonial is so extraordinary and the man who gave it so great) with the thought that this is all very well for a Schweitzer, but that it has little relevance for the ordinary mortal toiling away at his daily work. Schweitzer himself has acknowledged, again with specific reference to Goethe, how very fortunate he has been in being able to serve mankind as a free agent. This has not kept him from sharing, 'with an intensity reaching down to the fibres of my being', the problems which beset those who are chained to humdrum tasks and yet have a spiritual life and a receptivity for ideals. He has pointed out that there is a way in which all of us, each in his own life and job, can help solve these problems:

There are three tasks which we have to face in a Goethean spirit. We have to fight against circumstances, so that the men and women who are imprisoned and consumed by these circumstances may yet retain the opportunity for a life of the mind. We have to fight against people, so that they may still find . . . the road toward the realization of their own individualities in our age which constantly distracts us by externals. And we have to fight ourselves . . . so that we may remain faithful, in a period of perplexing and anti-humanitarian

[1] It was from these aspects that Schweitzer examined his topic in the address *Goethe—The Man and the Work*, given at Aspen, Colorado, on the occasion of the Bicentennial of 1949.

programs, to the great humanistic ideals of the 18th century, and translate and realize them in their contemporary form.[1]

As one reads these lines one becomes aware that Goethe's function as mentor and guide has overshadowed not only all other images of this particular poet, but all other such images drawn from the world of letters as a whole. Just as if conditions had not changed at all in the last hundred years, each of the men here discussed has found in Goethe, as Hebbel had done a century before, an answer to the most pressing problems of existence. Hofmannsthal, and to an extent even Rilke, saw in him one who had overcome the fragmentation of the modern individual; Mann, a prototype of the artist and of the German; Hesse, a companion on the lonely road to self-preservation in a collective society. Schweitzer has called on Goethe for aid not for himself but for mankind, and in the figure of the clergyman's son from a small village near the Franco-German border whose life has come to symbolize to untold millions the realization of Man's highest aspirations, the image of Goethe, too, has transcended the limitations of time and place and encompassed the world.

[1] 'Ansprache bei der Verleihung', &c., p. 17.

VII

THE SCHOLARLY IMAGE

ERMAN GRIMM, who was as much at home in Society as in academic circles, once wrote that 'men of high position who take up learned matters, demean and at the same time raise themselves'.[1] The Goethe renascence of the 1870's and 1880's was, in part, the work of just such men of high position who were amateurs in the best sense of the word: hard-working enthusiasts without much formal training. They collected Goetheana, wrote on Goethe, helped to edit and publish his works. Thus they spread his fame, without 'demeaning' themselves, or the poet, by compiling facile generalities for the delectation of young debutantes or begging the critics' indulgence because Goethe was for them only a hobby. These men are significant not only on account of their scholarly work but because they sprang from certain segments of German society to which Goethe had hitherto been little more than a name: business and financial circles, the higher echelons of the civil service, the more articulate among the landed gentry. They were not motivated by any wish to make Goethe fashionable in the sense of transitory social acceptance. He is no poet for the dashing young man-about-town. Nor was there any need to 'raise' the dead Goethe socially, as the living Rousseau and Schiller once had to be raised. Goethe had spent much of his life among the Thuringian nobility, and been the intimate of many a person of exalted rank. Yet in belonging to, and helping to create a public for Goethe within, what might be termed the 'power *élite*' of Wilhelmian Germany, these men have materially affected the twentieth-century image of Goethe. Without the support of many of Germany's social and financial leaders, the Goethe Society could not have carried out its programme. With the wrong kind of support Goethe might have ended, as Rilke threatened to end until partially rescued by men like Simenauer

---

[1] *Goethe. Vorlesungen gehalten an der Kgl. Universität zu Berlin* (8th ed., Berlin and Stuttgart, 1903, 2 vols.), ii. 297.

and Graff, as the pet of titled ladies with literary pretensions.

Foremost among these men was G. von Loeper, the financial and legal adviser of the Hohenzollern dynasty. Loeper had two hobbies which were unusual for the Prussian Junker he was and very much felt himself to be: the piano (especially Bach, whose works he played for Bismarck by the hour), and Goethe. He wrote excellent commentaries on *Faust* and *Dichtung und Wahrheit*, and over the years collected a valuable Goethe library. Similarly his friend W. von Biedermann in his working hours managed the railways of Saxony, and in his spare time wrote a number of monographs on Goethe's connexion with various Saxon localities: *Goethe und Leipzig, Goethe und Dresden*. In the latter city, where his administrative duties compelled him to reside for many years, von Biedermann joined forces with K. von Beaulieu-Marconnay, himself a witness of Weimar's great days, and the author of contributions to the history of eighteenth-century dynasties. Eventually a whole cluster of Goethe enthusiasts collected around these two Saxon noblemen, similar to the groups which E. von Simson, presiding judge of Germany's highest tribunal, had informally gathered in Leipzig, and Grimm and von Loeper in Berlin. After his retirement von Biedermann edited *Goethes Gespräche*, which was later brought up to date by his son Flodoard and remains to this day an indispensable tool for the scholar.

On an entirely different plane, and far more important in the long run than the work of these inspired amateurs, was that of the first generation of professional German scholars who devoted the bulk of their academic research and teaching to Goethe. It was a fortunate coincidence that German literature became established as an academic discipline precisely at the time when a number of gifted young scholars had decided to make the study of Goethe their life's work. Germanic philology had just won its long fight for recognition as an academic subject distinct from classical philology. This had no sooner taken place, around the middle of the nineteenth century, than teachers of German literature on their part began to assert their independence both of the philologists and of the professors of philosophy and aesthetics, to whose suffrance they had hitherto owed their modest place in the curriculum. The first chair for modern (i.e.

post-Middle High German) literature at a major university was established at Munich in 1873. Its incumbent, M. Bernays, introduced into the study of German literature the quasi-scientific methods of textual criticism which the classical philologists had recently perfected. This was the more necessary as the precise determination of what Goethe had actually written formed the first great task of Goethe scholarship. Before anyone could hazard a definitive exegesis or interpretation, he had to make sure that the basic text was as sound as modern philology could make it; through the comparison of variants, the elimination of misprints and later additions by other hands, whenever possible by reference to the poet's own manuscript. Goethe had been an indifferent proofreader, and had so quickly lost interest in his own books, once they were published, that he occasionally had to buy a copy himself when he wanted to re-read some early work of his. He had dictated the major part of his production, to secretaries who were occasionally negligent. There had been no effective copyright in his day; entire editions had been pirated, printed not only without his consent but without his prior knowledge. When a copyright legislation was finally drawn up, toward the end of Goethe's life, the publishing firm of Cotta was confirmed in its exclusive right to print the last edition which the poet himself had arranged. However, Cotta did not bother to revise a text on whose publication he held a monopoly. When this copyright expired in 1867, no less than six publishing houses turned out editions of various works. (The first volume ever published in Reclam's famous Universalbibliothek was Goethe's *Faust*.) The demand for a critical edition soon became overwhelming, especially since other classics had already been revised and definitively edited (Lessing by Lachmann, Schiller by Goedeke). Bernays's *Über Kritik und Geschichte des Goetheschen Textes* (1866) brought to light some of the corruptions which Himburg and other pirating publishers had allowed to slip into the text, especially that of *Werther*. This investigation set off a staggering amount of philological emendation, until by 1919, when the final volume of the authoritative *Weimarausgabe* was published, the text had been restored as closely as humanly possible to its original wording.

When the great Goethe expert Wilhelm Scherer as a young student burst into the office of his teacher Müllenhoff with the words 'I have come from Vienna in order to learn the method', he was merely dramatizing a fact which the older man would have told him in any case: that in the Goethe scholarship of the period, 'the method' ruled supreme. The empirical procedures used in the natural sciences were transplanted in their entirety to research in literary criticism and even in aesthetics. (Before long, this approach to the study of literature had spread all over the world because it prevailed in German universities at a time when these institutions were imitated in various lands.) In the field of Goethe studies this method soon threatened to eliminate altogether the imaginative element in literary creation: imagination, and especially poetic inspiration, could not be measured even with the finest instruments borrowed from the natural scientists. Thus there began that search for 'models' which as early as 1877 prompted Wilhelm Dilthey to protest, in the essay *Goethe und die dichterische Phantasie*, against the compulsion to detect, behind every character fashioned by Goethe, some person, living or dead, who 'must have' furnished the poet with the raw material out of which he shaped the respective poetic image. The story of Goethe's life was also examined with a fine comb, not only in order to determine its true course but to glean from it such elements as might conceivably have found a poetic reflection in one work or another. The relationship between personal experience and poetic expression—'Erlebnis' and 'Dichtung' in Dilthey's frame of reference—was too often far-fetched, and conclusions were sometimes not so much drawn from as wrung out of arbitrarily assembled pieces of evidence. However, the work of textual criticism had to be done, and the positivistic scholars did it superlatively well; so well that the word 'Literaturwissenschaft', or the 'science' of literary research, conveys to German ears none of the absurdity inherent in the English term. Moreover, this work was in large part done by scholars who combined sound erudition with a mastery of written and spoken German and with a truly apostolic zeal. In the years when Bielschowsky and the other popular Goethe biographers of his generation were preparing their accounts of the poet's life and work, others were spreading the gospel of Goethe to academic audiences: Grimm lectured on him at the University of Berlin, Bernays in München, Fischer in Heidelberg, Scherer in Strassburg, Hehn in far-away Dorpat. By the end of the century,

the positivistic image of the 'Olympian' was complete in all
details. This image, however, was no sooner drawn than it began
to be questioned by a number of brilliant new scholars.

Houston Stewart Chamberlain occupied a position all of his
own among the stormy petrels of pre-1914 Germany. With
Naumann, Langbehn, and Nietzsche he shared the conviction
that much of what so spectacularly shone in the Wilhelmian
period was not gold but dross, and that the Germans should
not let their material and political accomplishments blind them
to the sterility of their art and literature, the shallowness of their
philosophy, and the Byzantinism of their public life. But if
Nietzsche was a revolutionary critic in prophesying a New Man,
and Langbehn a Romanticist one in advocating a return to the
pristine virtues he saw exemplified in Rembrandt, Chamberlain was a conservative critic who found himself deeply involved
in the affairs of his time. He viewed contemporary society not
from without but from within, as an aristocratic British admiral's son who had early settled in Germany, become an ardent
Wagnerian (and the master's son-in-law), and gained the
friendship of many powerful men. Among these was Wilhelm II
himself, whom Chamberlain encouraged in his pretentious and
portentous posture as the tool chosen by Providence for great
deeds. The performing of great deeds, furthermore, and especially
the creation of cultural values, was thought to be the preserve
of the Indo-european race. Such, in part, was Chamberlain's
message in *Die Grundlagen des 19. Jahrhunderts* (1899), a confused
but not ineffective work which has been said to contain 'nothing
that is quite right, and nothing that is quite wrong'. But its
author also wrote a much better book, the monograph *Goethe*
(1912), which contains a great deal that is right, and much that
was unquestionably new.

Chamberlain saw no virtue in knowing as much as possible
about Goethe unless that knowledge turned out to be of use in
determining what kind of a man the poet actually was. Precisely because his approach was 'relentlessly subjective',[1] it
allowed him to disregard a great many unimportant dates and
facts—such as the external story of Goethe's life, which he
quickly disposed of in a biographical outline—in order to con-

[1] *Goethe* (München, 1912), p. 3.

centrate on delving as deeply as possible into Goethe's personality. What he discovered (or rediscovered, because the poet himself had never laid claim to the preternatural calm so often imputed to him) was the true nature of Goethe's inner equilibrium. In a number of well-chosen examples Chamberlain illustrated the principle of polarity which is so important in Goethe's work, and which was here for the first time interpreted as the motive force of his personality as well. This personality was characterized by its ability to bridge a number of antinomies (between action and reflection, intellectual universality and purposeful self-limitation, reasoning powers and creativity based on sensual perception, and others) any one of which would have torn a lesser man asunder. As had already been suspected by Carlyle, Goethe had survived all these onslaughts of existence not because of his inner constitution but despite that constitution, which time and again threatened to be swamped by despair, frustration, and an excess of sensitivity.[1] His harmony was not inborn but the precarious result of instinct, of painfully gained wisdom, above all, of willpower. With this fundamental discovery, which was not made by Chamberlain alone but which he raised to the status of a dogma, the notion of Goethe's God-given harmony began to be discredited.

In probing deeply into specific aspects of Goethe's life and work, Chamberlain arrived at a number of novel findings. Thus he did away with the idea, comforting in its apparent simplicity but actually based on a superficial reading of the famous passage in *Dichtung und Wahrheit*, that all of Goethe's works were simply 'confessions'. He explained instead the poet's particular way of transforming that which he perceived with his senses into an impression, which was then poured, as it were, into a concrete poetic mould of universal appeal. In the section devoted to the 'Inquirer into Nature'—der Naturerforscher, to set Goethe apart from the empirical natural scientist—Chamberlain likewise concentrated on elaborating not the extent but the characteristic feature of the poet's investigations; his interest in determining the behaviour of organic and inorganic matter. Even

---

[1] On 9 Dec. 1840 Carlyle had written to Emerson that a day would come when 'you will find that this sunny-looking, courtly Goethe held veiled in him a Prophetic sorrow deep as Dante's,—all the nobler to me and to you, that he *could* so hold it. I believe this; no man can *see* as he sees, that has not suffered and striven as man seldom did'.

when dealing with details which had long been established, Chamberlain managed to illustrate his opinions with unusual sidelights. Instead of following tradition in considering Frau von Stein primarily as the woman who calmed Goethe's inner turmoil, he stressed her role as his social guide and sponsor: it was she who introduced the Frankfurt commoner into the intricacies of court life, and when she had fulfilled that function the relationship began to cool. (Goethe's introduction to the *haut monde* is more frequently attributed to Jeannette Luise von Werthern.) In much the same way Chamberlain was no less interested in what made Goethe return to Weimar than in what had made him go to Italy in the first place. Among the poet's friends, again, it is not Eckermann or Riemer or Zelter on whom this biographer dwells with particular affection, but the art expert Meyer. In each case the novel accentuation is convincingly documented. This is most notable where Chamberlain opened up ground which at the time had been almost untouched, as in his treatment of the scientific work and in the chapter on 'Goethe as Practical Man of Affairs'. It is characteristic of Chamberlain that he was not satisfied with listing Goethe's varied administrative accomplishments, such as the reorganization of the Jena University Library or the establishment of the (new) *Literaturzeitung*, but laid bare instead the qualities which enabled the poet to excel in an executive function: his power of decision, his willingness to rely on experts in fields where he had little formal competence (e.g. mathematics and chemistry), his readiness to delegate responsibility, and other gifts of the kind. Revolutionary at the time because of its newness, but in the long run perhaps less valuable than his more concrete findings, was Chamberlain's final chapter on 'The Sage'. It was no doubt suggested to him by his Kantian background and his preference for the late Goethe, which altogether tends to obscure the instinct-driven, demonic youth of the Storm and Stress. But the reader who is not thoroughly at home in German idealistic philosophy is more likely to be frightened than enlightened by this formidable introduction to Goethe's wisdom.

In the manner of many a convert, Chamberlain was prone to exaggerate the articles of his new faith. His espousal of everything German led him to range far and wide over the quicksands of national psychology (and to attack the land of his birth in so disgraceful an exhibition of Anglophobia that even some Germans were moved to protest against his *Kriegsaufsätze* of 1914–18). His belief in the superiority of the Indo-european and especially the German race culminated in the conviction that racial origin is, indeed, the chief determining factor of a person's worth. From these muddied sources spring his assertions that Frau von Stein's coolness of mind and heart were 'typically Scotch', through her mother, an Irving of Drum, and that Goethe feared and hated the Jews (in some ways he was what would now be called antisemitic, just as he might be called philosemitic in others). Chamberlain's great achievement, however, stands out clearly in his discovery of the coexistence, in Goethe, of many diametrically opposed instincts, interests, and abilities: it was the presence of these forces, which were daily conquered anew and thus rendered fruitful rather than destructive, which marks the poet's life as both tragic and heroic. If we add that Chamberlain's stress on the scientific and administrative accomplishments must be understood in the light of his search for the core of Goethe's personality, we arrive at the real problem opened up in this book: what degree of importance should be assigned to these non-literary emanations in the 'ideal' Goethe biography of the future? It is obvious that this genius cannot properly be understood without deep and detailed reference to his work in other fields, work in which he not only excelled but without which he would not have become the poet we treasure. But is it not the poet we treasure above all, rather than the inspired scientist or the capable minister? This problem hardly existed for the positivistic biographers, who enumerated, in a sequence and with a degree of thoroughness dictated by the respective author's own evaluation, the many strands woven into Goethe's work and personality. Beginning with Simmel, however, biographers have turned to re-creating the totality of Goethe rather than describing single aspects of him, and the structure of their works is no longer a straight line to which any number of segments may be added at will, but a circle centred on whatever the individual writer considered the motive force of the phenomenon of Goethe.[1] In his enthusiastic discovery of

[1] It is no coincidence that Simmel's, Chamberlain's, and Gundolf's books all bore the little *Goethe*, while most earlier and later biographies have antithetically formulated titles or subtitles (e.g. Lewes's *The Life and Works of Goethe*, Baumgartner's *Göthe. Sein Leben und seine Werke*, Engel's *Goethe. Der Mann und das Werk*).

the 'real' Goethe, Chamberlain so lost track of the poetic works that he insisted that Goethe would have been a great creator in any case, and became a poet only by the accident of birth and the conditions of life. This particular error was soon rectified by Gundolf. Other misjudgements of Chamberlain's, however, were perpetuated because he had the misfortune of being taken up, after his death, by the Nazis, who in some astounding feats of intellectual sculduggery twisted his views, on Goethe as on other subjects, to conform to their own doctrines. It is a fate which he shared with both Nietzsche and George.

Much time must still elapse before Stefan George's exact place in German letters can be determined. In the years before 1914 he bade fair to become one of the century's greatest lyric poets. He does not seem to have fulfilled this promise, but his influence has nonetheless been profound. In a period of growing conformity and collectivization, George, like Nietzsche, passionately defended the role of the autonomous creative individual as prophet and leader. He felt only distaste for the materialism of the age, and attempted to counteract it by stressing not only the prerogatives but the obligations of the supremely endowed artist. The poet, especially, was for him above all a master of disciplined form: a strong-willed and deliberate moulder of timeless beauty. Unlike Nietzsche, however, George was blessed (in some eyes, cursed) with a number of personal idiosyncracies which set him, and his disciples in the 'circle' or 'state', yet farther apart from his prosaic age. Not the least of these peculiarities was his barely concealed conviction—not groundless, nor yet altogether justified, and therefore perhaps doubly offensive—that he was a great poet himself, a keeper of the faith and presager of things to come, a *vates* in the manner of Dante. Also unlike Nietzsche, he was not only prophet, but in part Messiah. As such, his attitude to Goethe was characterized not by academic knowledge, which he affected to despise, but by a feeling of creative kinship.

How much his views were at variance with the opinions prevailing at the time became clear in 1899, when he published his poem *Goethe-Tag* as well as an anthology of German poetry (the latter with Karl Wolfskehl). The subtitle of the third and last volume of this work, 'Das Jahrhundert Goethes', indicates

George's estimate of his predecessor: Goethe had given his name to a century of German literary history, but new writers, such as George himself, had now come to the fore and would leave their mark on the century that was about to dawn. In an age when comprehensiveness was often reckoned a virtue in itself, George and Wolfskehl restricted their selections to the works of only twelve authors. They left out the popular Uhland, and put in the long-neglected Hölderlin; they censured Schiller as too rhetorical and Heine as too facile; and they reproduced from Goethe not the Storm and Stress poems which had so delighted the Naturalists, but the accomplished works of the form-conscious old poet: not *Der König in Thule* or *An Schwager Kronos,* but *Trilogie der Leidenschaft* and parts of *Der westöstliche Divan.* Similarly, George underscored the unfashionable nature of his private view of Goethe in the poem he wrote on the occasion of the 150th aniversary of the poet's birth. Its final stanza proclaims George's aristocratic aloofness and his claim to a deeper understanding of the poet than that vouchsafed to the multitude:

> Ihr nennt ihn euer und ihr dankt und jauchzt —
> Ihr freilich voll von allen seinen trieben
> Nur in den untren lagen wie des tiers —
> Und heute bellt allein des volkes räude ...
> Doch ahnt ihr nicht daß er der staub geworden
> Seit solcher frist noch viel für euch verschließt
> Und daß an ihm dem strahlenden schon viel
> Verblichen ist was ihr noch ewig nennt.[1]

In a later poem, *Goethes letzte Nacht in Italien* (1908), George took the final step and for all practical purposes proclaimed himself as Goethe's successor, or at least as the man who has realized Goethe's dream of a synthesis of Germany and Greece.

George's views on Goethe might not have had much perman-

---

[1] You claim him as your own, and thank, and cheer,
You who, indeed, are filled with all his urges,
Only on lower levels, like a beast's.
Today the nation's mongrels do the barking.
But you will never guess how many secrets
He who has long been dust, still guards from you,
And that in him, the radiant, even now
Much that you will think will always last, has paled.
(Tr. O. Marx and E. Morwitz.)

ent effect on Germany if his favourite disciple, Friedrich Gundolf, had not been under their spell when he wrote his *Goethe* (1916). Taking his cue from Dilthey, he saw in Goethe a sovereign creative spirit for whom writing was not an occupation or even a channel of self-release but the very essence of his *Gestalt* or inner nature. There is no dichotomy, or even distinction in this book between the poet's life and his works. They form a unit, and Gundolf's purpose in describing this unit was not that of 'mastering' Goethe by categorizing him, History-of-Literature fashion, and neatly tucking him away under some label or other; it was, rather, that of impressing on the reader his own, personal view of the poet. The latter's works are no longer seen as milestones in a chronological line of development, or even as a circle centred on the essence of Goethe. They are, in Gundolf's own image, emanations of a sphere whose centre will always remain hidden from the viewer. He thus offers little information of a specifically biographical nature, little by way of details, titles, or quotations referring to the poet's life. Even Goethe's own characterization of his ancestral endowment, the famous lines:

> Vom Vater hab ich die Statur,
> Des Lebens ernstes Führen,
> Vom Mütterchen die Frohnatur
> Und Lust zu fabulieren.

have fallen by the wayside as by now 'commonplace'. Gundolf's approach is biocentric rather than biographical in that it is concerned with Goethe's specific inner structure as revealed in the works. This structure Gundolf sees as modified by a number of 'Urerlebnisse' ('shocks to which a man is exposed by virtue of his inner constitution') such as the religious, titanic, and erotic experiences, and by certain 'Bildungserlebnisse' ('intellectual [and] historical influences... views handed down from the world of art, science, religion') like the discovery of the German past, of Shakespeare, or of Italy. Disregarding as irrelevant the traditional divisions of lyric, dramatic, and epic writing, Gundolf devised other categories into which he separated Goethe's works according to the degree of immediacy with which they reflect his inner structure. These three zones of Goethe's poetry are the lyric, the symbolic, and the allegorical. (They do not, of course, coincide with the concepts they replace; the lyric zone, in which Goethe's inner life found its most immediate expression, includes both the epic *Werther* and the dramatic 'Urfaust'.)

In thus raising Goethe above the system of co-ordinates by reference to which literary figures are usually defined, Gundolf has purposely created a myth, not in the sense of falsification but by presenting Goethe as symbol of Man's poetic endowment. Along with E. Bertram's Nietzsche legend and other such stylizations, Gundolf's Goethe 'myth' was an expression of the George Circle's desire to re-enthrone certain great symbolic figures of the past, in a period of disillusionment when many such figures were being divested of their distinction, and their achievements explained on the basis of neurotic traumas, social background, economic pressures, racial origin, and other such factors suggested by the latest fads in science, literature, and politics. Gundolf's particular merit lay in putting together again all the bricks into which the great structure of Goethe had been dismantled, and of breathing life into the reassembled totality until it became an image, both concrete and symbolic, of poetry in the flesh.

Despite his sweeping view, Gundolf was not a writer easily carried away by abstractions. It is unlikely that his account of the rejuvenation of the German language through Goethe will ever be surpassed either in its over-all formulation or in the acuteness of its detailed observations on such points as synaesthesia (both as expression of inner form and as stylistic device) or the use of the present participle as independent adjective, rather than as an encapsuled subordinate clause. Gundolf gives a very clear account also of the reasons for, and results of, Goethe's Italian journey, and elucidates a number of other points in a new fashion. An example will show the aptness of his remarks and the cogency with which they are expressed. In Gundolf's view Goethe's political beliefs sprang from the fact that

it was disorder, not injustice, which he found unbearable, as a man who perceived the world through his senses and eyes; for disorder is seen, but injustice can only be imagined: it is the invisible result of reflections made on an ethical postulate. As a matter of principle, Goethe was neither a democrat nor an advocate of aristocratic rule; he knew no such principles, and acknowledged only perceptions and sensations. He admired the democratic revolution when he met it face to face, not as vague bungling but as personified in the genius of Mirabeau and Napoleon: for there, it had legitimized itself as ability, as order.[1]

It was in no small measure due to this book, and to Oswald Spengler's almost contemporaneous *Der Untergang des Abendlandes* with its acknowledgement of Goethe's spiritual ancestry, that our poet was not affected by the collapse of German Idealism which followed the defeat of 1918, when a disenchanted people re-examined many of its great men—Kant, Schiller, Wagner, and others—and, rightly or wrongly, found them wanting in terms of its own needs. Probably no other major work on Goethe has evoked such admiration, and such hostility, as Gundolf's biography. At its best, it represents the modern tendency toward intellectual synthesis, as applied to a phenomenon which has all too often been fragmentarily treated; an almost poetic account of a great poet; a unique combination of 'Literaturwissenschaft' and inspired writing; a perfect blending of content and style. Georg Simmel, himself the author of a profound interpretation of Goethe, hailed Gundolf's book as a break-through toward a not uncritical, but positive and vital Goethe image; the competent Adolf von Grolman, a 'Germanist' of the old school, damned it with very faint praise; and Benedetto Croce lost no time in protesting against the 'mystic union' of life and works which it postulates.

There is no doubt that Gundolf's *Goethe* has weaknesses; but they are potential rather than real. Its methodological skeleton is as restrictive as it is original. It is not readily transferable to any other subject, even to the biography of another great author: if Goethe was altogether a law unto himself, then we surely cannot hope to understand other writers through methods of investigation which were specifically designed to do justice to him. And if Gundolf, too, (implicitly) claims to be a law unto himself, other and lesser biographers will fail where he succeeded. In an author of this calibre, the reader will not object to the many oddities of diction and punctuation which make this book unique in Goethe studies: the wealth of adjectives, the almost total absence of commas, the arbitrary word formations like

---

[1] 13th ed., Berlin, 1930, p. 402. The juxtaposition of disorder and injustice is, of course, Goethe's own (*Die Belagerung von Mainz*).

umglühn (to transmute, to 'transforge' prose into verse) or *betochtern* (to 'daughter' someone, analogous to 'mothering'), or to the highly personal views on such topics as politics or marriage. These peculiarities in large measure go back to Stefan George, and what is occasionally sublime in him and Gundolf can easily become ridiculous in others. What has been called Gundolf's 'Mephistophelian smile' at the minute emendations made by the professional Goethe scholars can also be forgiven in this work of a man who despite his cavalier attitude was very much at home in his subject. With anyone less expert, the almost complete lack of footnotes, references to the works of others, exegetic and bibliographic apparatus, and sources of quotations would be thought arrogant. It is, in fact, curious to observe that for all their differences in method and aims, Grimm and Gundolf, the authors of what may well be the two most important Goethe biographies of all, were praised and damned for much the same reasons. They had in common a sovereign knowledge of their subject, and complete indifference toward their fellow-toilers in the vineyard; a contempt for all learned scaffolding (which they carefully removed from the finished structure of their work) and great rigour in eliminating anything they did not consider germane to the topic at hand. This includes a number of figures so important in the poet's life that they ineviably occur in more orthodox treatments.[1]

Gundolf's was not only the most original, it was for some time also the last of the biographies which interpreted Goethe as a phenomenon *sui generis*, an honourable tradition which had begun, some three-quarters of a century before, with Carus. In the period which followed the First World War, a new viewpoint came to dominate German Goethe studies: that of the History of Ideas. Perhaps the most important single work of this type was H. A. Korff's *Geist der Goethezeit* (1923–53), whose main theses were also elaborated in a number of supplementary studies. Instead of stressing their differences, Korff endeavoured to define the common denominators of Storm and Stress, Classicism, and Romanticism. In his view, these three movements were

---

[1] The most notable omission in both works is that of Count Thorane, to whom Goethe had devoted an entire chapter in *Dichtung und Wahrheit*. Nor is there any mention, in the 700-odd pages of Gundolf's book, of Beaumarchais.

separate but parallel reactions to Rationalism, literary complements to the great flowering of German idealistic philosophy from Kant to Schopenhauer, and, above all, quasi-religious expressions of a golden age characterized by a far greater idea-content than were the classical periods of other literatures. In this cultural panorama which extended from 1770 to 1830, Goethe was but a *primus inter pares*. Furthermore he was, in this view, primarily a thinker: a poet, to be sure, and a great one, but a poet whose main function lay in giving symbolic expression to the problems which dominated the thinking of his time. This tendency to see in Goethe not the literary giant beholden to few if any men, but the greatest representative of what since Dilthey has increasingly come to be called the German Movement, has had two immediate results. It has led both to an investigation of certain aspects of Goethe which had hitherto been neglected but now became topical, and to a general reappraisal of many of the leading ideas of German Classicism. Even before Korff, the philosopher E. Cassirer had re-examined the problem of *Freiheit und Form* in German thought from Leibnitz to Hegel (1916). In the 1920's and 1930's this was followed by Franz Schultz's *Klassik und Romantik der Deutschen*, a reinterpretation, in the light of Nietzsche's views, of the Greek ideal treasured by Goethe and his contemporaries from Winckelmann to the Schlegels, as well as by many other works dealing with pivotal concepts of the age of Goethe.[1]

Side by side with such fundamental studies in intellectual history went many investigations of a more restricted nature. For example, it is not surprising that the sociological aspects of Goethe's works should have been examined often in that period of rapid and radical social change. These contributions range

---

[1] It is undesirable (and impossible) even to list many of these works here. A fairly complete such list is found in H. Kindermann, *Das Goethebild des XX. Jahrhunderts* (Wien and Stuttgart, 1952). However, it is well to differentiate between two divergent approaches within the History of Ideas method: that to the 'Urerlebnisse' and that to the 'Bildungserlebnisse' of the Goethe period. Books in the former group tend to focus on the period's attitude toward fundamental questions of human existence (e.g. P. Kluckhohn's *Die Auffassung der Liebe in der Literatur des 18. Jahrhunderts und in der deutschen Romantik*, 1922); those in the latter group deal with cultural problems endemic with or highly significant for that age (e.g. O. Walzel's *Das Prometheus-Symbol von Shaftesbury zu Goethe*, 1912).

The *mystique* of the History of Ideas movement is presented by W. Mahrholz in *Literargeschichte und Literarwissenschaft* (2nd ed., Leipzig, 1922).

from the detailed studies of F. List and G. Keferstein to evaluations in essay form such as Thomas Mann's *Goethe als Repräsentant
des bürgerlichen Zeitalters* (1932)—that is, of the historical period,
beginning with the Renaissance and ending in our own day,
when the *bourgeoisie* was the guiding force in the social, political,
and intellectual life of Western Europe. This line of investigation derived in part from a new sub-discipline which came into
its own in the years after 1918: that of literary anthropology, a
field of inquiry originally charted by Dilthey and Unger, whose
concern is the adaptation to literary research of the typological
and characterological concepts developed by Kretschmer,
Klages, and Jung. A representative attempt to make use of these
procedures was G. Reitz's work on *Die Gestalt des Mittler in
Goethes Dichtung* (1932), where the recurrent figure of the Media-
tor (e.g. the 'Mittler' of *Die Wahlverwandtschaften*) was examined
from several viewpoints: that of literary history, as offshoot of the
gracioso of the Spanish theatre; that of dramatic theory, as means
by which the tragic conflict can be bridged or headed off; and
characterologically, because 'mediation' rather than tragic
intransigence was not only a technical device with Goethe but
the expression of a profound psychological need. However, the
most important 'type' created by Goethe, or at least raised by
him to symbolic dimensions, was that of Faust—more precisely,
its modification as Faustian Man which was popularized by
Spengler and contrasted, in *Der Untergang des Abendlandes*, with the
Apollinian and Magian types. Spengler's loose definition and
usage of the term has brought about some reassessments of the
characterological peculiarities of Goethe's hero; W. Schultz's
article on *Wilhelm von Humboldt und der Faustische Mensch* (1930),
for example, represents a regular defence of Goethe's Faust
against the perversions to which he has been subjected.[1] In con-
ducting this defence, Schultz has based himself on the text of the
tragedy and redefined the term 'Faustian' within this frame of
reference. From a more generic viewpoint, much the same
problem was tackled by J. Obenauer, H. Kindermann, and
others. Probably the most revolutionary work of this kind is
W. Böhm's *Faust, der Nichtfaustische*, originally published 1933 and
later reissued, in the form of a scene-by-scene commentary, as
Goethes Faust in neuer Deutung. Instead of seeing in Faust Goethe's

[1] *Jahrbuch der Goethe-Gesellschaft*, xvi, 1930.

alter ego, Böhm endeavours to show the distance which separates the poet from his hero. The latter is, in this view, a self-intoxicated adventurer described in a drama which, far from being a glorification of Man's eternal striving, is really a satire against a weakling ruled by preconceived notions and bedevilled by a manic-depressive temperament. Faust is not let down by the disciplines he had studied, but incapable of drawing sustenance from philosophy, law, medicine, and theology; not a hero to be looked up to, but the victim of his own shortcomings. Not unlike Werther, he represents the warning example of a man sick unto death.

It would, perhaps, have been too much to hope that the reluctance shown by the great pioneers of the psychoanalytical movement in the wholesale application of their theories should also have been observed by their popularizers. Here, more than in any other approach to Goethe except that based on political doctrines, a distinction must be drawn between responsible and sensational works. The former category is exemplified by such authors as Freud himself, Adler, Jung, and the literary historian W. Muschg. The doubts which these men harboured about the feasibility of arriving at conclusive evidence in regard either to the psychological structure of a given work, or to the psychology of its creator, are epitomized in Jung's warning that 'the present state of psychological science—which is, incidentally, the youngest of all sciences—does not by any means permit us to establish in this field incontrovertible causative connexions . . .'.[1] In the few instances where these experts did postulate such connexions, they proceeded with a maximum of caution. A case in point is Freud's analysis of *Eine Kindheitserinnerung aus 'Dichtung und Wahrheit'* (1917), where Goethe's smashing of crockery, described at the very beginning of the autobiography, is diagnosed as evidence of suppressed sibling rivalry. Freud, of course, knew his Goethe well, and was careful to restrict his speculations to this particular explanation for this particular incident in the poet's life. At the opposite pole stand such authors as W. Stekel, who delivered himself of a number of pseudo-scientific potboilers and was later disowned by Freud, and F. Theilhaber, who saw in Goethe's literary production the compensatory

---

[1] C. G. Jung, 'Psychologie und Dichtung' (in *Philosophie der Literaturwissenschaft*, Berlin, 1930), p. 315.

release of feelings of sexual inadequacy. The impression of Goethe which results from this thesis is, of course, a somewhat dismal one, and this particular attempt to explain the inexplicable by means of the irrelevant is further vitiated by the author's lack of familiarity with some of the works.[1] In common with other psychoanalytical researchers, Theilhaber makes much of two biographical details which are usually relegated far to the background of Goethe's life: his ancestry, and the supposedly pathological attachment to his sister Cornelia.

The psychoanalytical approach to Goethe has inspired what was, perhaps, the most 'successful' of all biographies, at least in the number of copies sold and the frequency of reprints, of which there were twenty-three in the first ten years. Emil Ludwig's ↶ *Goethe* (1920) is a smoothly written case study which aims at divesting the poet of his twin haloes as youthful Apollo and ancient Olympian. The book does, indeed, divest Goethe of most of the qualities which have made him unique. It is a novelistic exposé of the 'real' Goethe who was unhappily torn between the free exercise of his great gifts and the demonic undercurrents of his instinctual nature. The artfully simple subtitle, 'Story of a Man', gives the reader little warning that he is going to be shown a Goethe whose main characteristics were a mastery of all the tricks of a promoter, along with a propensity for shocking the good citizens of Frankfurt, Wetzlar, and Weimar. There is no evidence in this book that the poet's life was ruled by anything more than blind chance (hence, in part, Ludwig's great dependence on letters and conversations), and no hint of any guiding principle of a moral, historical, artistic, or otherwise organic kind. There are, however, many statements and innuendoes of a sensational nature, such as the assertion that Charlotte von Stein was Goethe's mistress, and that the poet tried, 'as a diplomat', to hold on to both Charlotte and Christiane by cleverly disparaging one in the eyes of the other, until he was forced to throw off Charlotte when she had become too old for him. Nevertheless, Ludwig's central argument is not without merit: that Goethe's whole life was a struggle against the destructive forces

---

[1] As sample of the 'Urfaust's' forceful language, Theilhaber cites Valentin's lines: 'Ich sag dirs im Vertrauen nur:/Du bist doch nun einmal eine Hur;/So seis auch eben recht!'—which were first published in *Faust I* (pointed out by H. Kindermann, op. cit., p. 300).

within him, and that his significance for us lies not only in the half-dozen well-known dramas and novels, but in what might be called the 'applied philosophy of life' of his old age, as expressed in letters, conversations, diaries, and aphorisms.

On the whole, the adaptation of psychoanalytical techniques to literary research has tended to be concentrated not on the acknowledged masterpieces but on works which fall short of perfection: fragments, imitations, very early works. This is natural because the psychoanalytical approach is much more rewarding in the investigation of the genesis of a work, and of the dynamics of the creative process itself, than in dealing with a finished literary product. (It will be remembered that Freud's own decision to study medicine was influenced by an unfinished essay, the *Fragment über die Natur* attributed to Goethe, and that the first classic psychoanalytical treatment of a literary work was his interpretation of a quite insignificant story, Jensen's *Gradiva*.) Such influence as this type of investigation has had on the Goethe image at large has been in the direction of humanizing the great symbolic personality shaped by Gundolf and Simmel. The method has, perhaps, been most fruitful in the hands of literary scholars who have used it in their own way: not as a magic key with which to unlock doors which should perhaps not be unlocked at all, but as a discreetly wielded tool for the interpretation of individual works. Böhm used it thus in his abovementioned *Faust* commentary, and H. Pyritz in his excellent study *Goethe und Marianne von Willemer* (1941).

Mention must be made of one other field of studies which particularly flourished in the period after 1918: Goethe's religious views now came to be seen in a new light. Aside from determining the various stages and expressions of his religious development, many studies dealing with this subject had the secondary purpose of pointing out to a generation severely shaken in its faith the example of Goethe's religiousness, as profound as it was unorthodox. This therapeutic element is apparent in the dedication 'To Those Who Search'—den Suchenden— of K. Obenauer's book on *Goethe in seinem Verhältnis zur Religion* (1921), and in the very title of such works as *Goethe als Erzieher* by R. Zilchert or *Die Rettung des Abendlandes durch den Geist der Goethezeit* (1932). The author of the last-named work, Friedrich Muckle, takes issue with Spengler's view that the flowering of every national *Kultur* is followed by a phase of *Zivilisation*, such as that which marked the decline of the Roman Empire and now seems to have overtaken the Western world as a whole. In Muckle's opinion, such a period of *Zivilisation*—which is technological in nature, anti-individualistic, atheistic, with a highly diversified economic structure and an atrophied cultural life—is in turn replaced by yet another stage, that of *Spätkultur*: a cultural renaissance of which we have examples in the Babylon of Hammurabi, the China of K'ung Fu-tse and Lao-tse, the India of Gautama Buddha, the Greece of Plato and the Stoics, and the period in European history which began with Shaftesbury and culminated in Goethe. The main reason for the disintegration of the values created in that period lies in our disregard of an historical law according to which '. . . Man, as soon as he forgets that there exists a God who commands him to act in accordance with a moral ideal—der das Hohe gebietet—is struck down by hard blows, and all that which pious ancestors have built up, collapses'.[1] Yet a return to established religions, with their dogmatic framework, is out of the question. What is far more likely to save us, in Muckle's view, is a return to Goethe, whose outlook on life represents the only system of ethics possible in the twentieth century; among other reasons because it is based, as a modern religion must be, on that spirit of free scientific inquiry which, once gained, we cannot give up. The first two of the projected eight volumes of this unfinished work accordingly define Goethe's religious beliefs. These chapters are directed, as indeed the whole work was to have been, against what the author calls the 'Godforsaken brotherhood of sceptics': those who believe, with Spengler, that the higher forms of Western cultural life are about to disappear from the earth.

Muckle, like Korff, no doubt went too far in crediting Goethe and the other leading spirits of his time with a kind of crypto-Christianity which could replace the traditional religious concepts which they considered outworn. However, the tendency is indicative of the degree to which Goethe was felt to be a living influence. It need hardly be pointed out that this figure of the healer and consoler was derived not from that of the harmonious

---

[1] *Die Rettung des Abendlandes durch den Geist der Goethezeit* (Leipzig, 1932, 2 vols.), i. 28. The concept of faith as a prerequisite for a healthy society is based on Goethe's introduction to *Der westöstliche Divan* ('Israel in der Wüste').

Prince of Poets, but from the image of the wise councillor we find
in Kühnemann's biography: the man whose own mental health
was the result and reward of much inner strife and much conscious resignation. It was, in fact, in the religious and philosophical sphere, in the works of H. Leisegang, E. Spranger, and
others, that a recent change in the German view of Goethe first
became apparent. Although it is a generalization, it may still
be said that until about 1918 the German people tried to learn
about Goethe, and that since that time they have tried to learn
from him.[1] This is borne out also by two works which may be
said to mark the end of the period characterized by the History
of Ideas approach to Goethe, much as the first volume of Korff's
work can be taken to symbolize its beginning. E. Kühnemann's
Goethe (1930) is a biography *à thèse*, predicated on the argument
that the poet's development ran parallel to that of the *Faust*
tragedy. Each of its chapters consists of two sections, one dealing
with a given period in the poet's life, the other with the corresponding stage in the genesis of the drama. Since Goethe worked
on *Faust* all his adult life and put so much of himself into the
play, this arrangement seems reasonable enough at first sight.
In practice, however, it has proved to be a methodological
straightjacket which has atrophied the biographer's ability to
do justice to those aspects of Goethe which have not found an
expression in *Faust*. Kühnemann had planned the book as a
companion volume to his earlier studies on Herder, Kant, and
Schiller; in assigning to Goethe his proper place alongside
these men, however, and therewith completing his history of the
German Movement, he has made the poet into a somewhat
bloodless repertory of ideas. The work, in fact, exemplifies the
advantages and drawbacks of this entire method of literary
investigation—its capacity to correlate seemingly disjointed
aesthetic and intellectual phenomena as well as its reliance on
what is, in the final instance, speculation.

No less philosophically grounded, but much clearer in outline
and detail, is Friedrich Muckermann's *Goethe* (1931). This
author, too, equates the poet with Faust; and in the belief that
the History of Ideas is best suited to arrive at a balanced view
of Goethe's significance in German life, he even enlarges the

[1] The formulation is R. Buchwald's (*Goethezeit und Gegenwart*, Stuttgart, 1949),
p. 326.

basis from which the period 1775–1830 is usually examined. His approach is that of a modern Jesuit convinced that Roman Catholics must come to positive terms with the fact that the Age of Goethe was essentially rooted in Protestant thought. From this starting position, Muckermann ranges far and wide over the intellectual history of Europe, comparing Goethe with Dostoevsky no less than with Albertus Magnus and Dante, and emphasizing, beyond the traditionally acknowledged kinship of monad to entelechy, Goethe's indebtedness to Leibnitz. In dealing not so much with external biography as with specific elements of the poet's outlook on life, Muckermann has made some fine, original observations. While commenting, for example, on Goethe's health and impressive bearing, he points out a significant difference between the poet and us: 'Goethe, a visitor tells us, could spend half an hour at a time in his garden, standing before a plant and observing its structure. Goethe had that much time, he who accomplished so much!'[1] A concrete image of the poet's active yet unhurried existence, of his contemplative way of studying the morphological side of Nature, and also of the way of life of this man who never sacrificed the essential to the ephemeral. According to Muckermann, the believing Roman Catholic will find in Goethe a kindred spirit, a great human being and writer who somehow never came in close enough contact with Catholic beliefs and practices:

If one reads these paragraphs [about the sacraments, in *Dichtung und Wahrheit*], one painfully wonders why this young man, recalling in later years the days of his childhood, had to come up against ... religious instructors who were unable to familiarize [him] with the views which we find amply represented in the works of St. Augustine, St. Bonaventure, and the great teachers of sacred doctrine. They would have been indelibly imprinted upon an imagination nourished by the Old and New Testaments. All his life Goethe showed the greatest understanding of Christianity, when he encountered it in a form germane to his nature.[2]

The form germane to Goethe, we are clearly given to understand, was that of Roman Catholicism. As an authoritative evaluation of the poet from that quarter, Muckermann's monograph has replaced Baumgartner's biography, which by 1911 had gone through three editions. With this book, which is based

---

[1] *Goethe* (Bonn, 1931), p. 71.   [2] Ibid. 41.

on the belief that the essence of all religious sentiment is humility before a Higher Power and that Goethe, who had a great deal of such humility, should thus be acceptable to Catholics, the century-old schism was finally healed which had kept so many German Catholics from a full appreciation of the poet.

In literary scholarship, as in literature itself, there exist few if any clear-cut temporal divisions at which one trend or movement stops and another begins. In the 1920's and 1930's the History of Ideas dominated but by no means monopolized German work on Goethe. Among the other roads to Goethe which continued to be taken in that period was that of fact-finding positivistic research, particularly in problems of textual purity and in the genesis and interpretation of individual works. At the same time M. Kommerell, P. Hankamer, and F. Wolters continued to clarify the George Circle's own, rather stylized version of Goethe as leader and literary law-giver. Much work was also done on Goethe's scientific studies and on his influence abroad; contributions to the latter topic were usually based on the concept of a world literature which the poet had established in his old age, and which was now elaborated and given wide currency, especially by Fritz Strich. Other fields, to be sure, only began to be opened up in those years: for example the stage history of the dramas, and the effect which certain works have had on posterity. Some works which had earlier been regarded as peripheral in terms of Goethe's total achievement were now re-examined and, as it were, 'upgraded' by enthusiastic specialists (*Der westöstliche Divan* by K. Burdach, *Römische Elegien* by R. Petsch); for the analysis of others new hypotheses were advanced—such as G. Roethe's 'splinter theory' in regard to the origin of *Faust*—which led to a radical revision of opinions.

The year 1932 represents a turning-point in the German image of Goethe. The centennial of his death was observed throughout the country and celebrated by the publication of a quite extraordinary number of books, brochures, articles, and speeches. Some of these utterances, which were almost universally reverent in tone, were hastily written and spoken; they seem to have sprung more from a sense of the solemnity of the occasion than from any deep conviction that Goethe was a topical author. Yet the year also brought forth many fine scholarly contributions,

as well as avowals on the part of Thomas Mann, Gerhart Haupt-
mann, Albert Schweitzer, Hans Carossa, and other eminent
Germans of what Goethe meant to them individually. Some
peripatetic scholars embarked on lecture tours abroad (E.
Kühnemann to the United States, K. Vossler to Spain and
South America), and foreign men of letters on their part joined
in paying homage to the poet: Gide and Valéry in France, Croce
in Italy, Madariaga and Ortega y Gasset in the Hispanic lands,
Masaryk and Čapec in Czechoslovakia, John Buchan in
England. From far-away India came a message which well
expressed the sentiments of the day, in the form of a telegram
from Rabindranath Tagore to President Hindenburg to the
effect that 'the Bengal Goethe Society, celebrating the centennial of the poet's death, takes the liberty of sending its greetings
to the German people'. A common denominator of these declar-
ations was the stress on the supranational dimension of this poet
who since the War of 1914–18 had come to exemplify in the eyes
of the world at large all that was best, and fondly believed to be
most enduring, in the German character. He was extolled as an
author who had expressed his indebtedness to the writings of
other countries, and later evened the account by instituting, in
theory and practice, a type of universal literature which among
other things tended to counter the divisive forces of nationalism.
As it turned out, the expectation that Goethe's example would
help alleviate the political tensions of the day was soon proved
futile. Less than a year after the great ceremonies of 22 March
1932 the Nazis came to power in Goethe's own land, and a new
phase opened not only in German but in world history.

It is too early to give more than a fragmentary account of the
work done on Goethe during that phase. Too many of the problems, literary as well as political and social, which have arisen
within the past quarter-century are still waiting to be solved,
and too many recent books on Goethe were written from viewpoints whose place in literary criticism and history has yet to be
established. For all that can now be said, there may even be
another Carus or Dilthey among contemporary scholars, whose
findings, presently familiar to only a small circle of experts, will
in due course outweigh those made by better-known men. We
shall accordingly limit ourselves here to a very brief survey of
those developments in contemporary Goethe research whose

ultimate value cannot now be assessed, but whose relevance for the problems of the mid-twentieth century is beyond dispute.

For better or worse, the practice of looking at Goethe from the standpoint of a political ideology is likely to be with us for a long time to come. In the recent past this approach has led to some startling distortions of the Goethe image. During the National-Socialist period, for instance, the poet's cosmopolitanism formed a dangerous hurdle for the Goethe lovers and scholars who wanted to integrate him ideologically—gleichschalten—with the tenets of the official faith. They cleared this hurdle in a variety of ungainly postures: Goethe cannot really by any stretch of the imagination be said to have been a precursor of the Nazis, to the more fervent and honest of whom he remained a 'dubious character' to the end.[1] Some who knew better presented to the public a carefully trimmed and expurgated Goethe of strongly nationalistic tendencies, in the hope of thus assuring his survival in what was to have been the 1,000-year-*Reich*. Others, who also knew better, attempted to show that his relative indifference to political questions was a legend nurtured by biographers who had mistakenly believed that he had been more interested in the concept of humanity than in that of *Vaterland*; some scholars now pretended to see in the imputation of cosmopolitanism to Goethe 'one of the worst misinterpretations of the recent past'.[2] A third group—among men who, it must in fairness be remembered, were more or less forced to find a synthesis between German Classicism and the Third *Reich*—altogether threw scholarly caution to the winds and claimed Goethe as prophet of a mighty German Empire and as a poet whose true significance becomes clear only if we see his work 'in its proper place in the development of the German mind and *Reich*, and interpret his conscious and subconscious intentions accordingly'.[3] It would seem that yet another group exhibited both valour and discretion in subtly elaborating such aspects of Goethe as would tend to

[1] J. Goebbels, *Das eherne Herz* (München, 1943), p. 233.
[2] H. Kindermann, 'Persönlichkeit und Gemeinschaft in Goethes dichterischem Werk', *Goethe* (Viermonatsschrift der Goethe-Gesellschaft), iii, 1938, p. 59. How unrelenting the pressure for 'Gleichschaltung' was in those days has been nicely documented by G. Mathieu, 'A Nazi Propaganda Directive on Goethe' (*Publications of the English Goethe Society*, xxii, 1952–).
[3] K. Hildebrandt, *Goethe. Seine Weltweisheit im Gesamtwerk* (Leipzig, 1941), p. 566.

counterbalance particularly destructive articles of the Nazi philosophy. Thus Goethe's concept of personality and human dignity was often and pointedly contrasted in that period with the party's insistence on the submergence of the individual in the mass of the *Volk*.

Far more portentous than these views are those which the modern Marxists have expressed on the subject of Goethe. They are perhaps most clearly formulated in the various studies by G. von Lukács, who along with E. Fischer, J. Becher, A. Zweig, and A. Kantorowicz, sees in Goethe's attitude to his environment a sort of adaptation syndrome which grew out of his 'continuous struggle against his own epoch'. Far from being a free agent as had been claimed, the poet had in reality been 'chained to a hostile environment, repeatedly rebuffed in the efforts dearest to his heart, bowed down . . . morosely silent . . . resigned and ironical'.[1] If this were true, the traditional picture of his life and work would have to be radically revised. In Lukács's own revision, Goethe's achievement in writing *Götz von Berlichingen* is no longer indicative of a desire to reform the German theatre, or to rescue from oblivion the figure of a robber knight whom Lassalle was to call, in the famous Sickingen Debate, 'a thoroughly retrograde wretch'. It lies, rather, in having demonstrated, in the course of the play, the historical and economic inevitability of the downfall of a decadent social class. In the same spirit, the famous lines

> Noch hab' ich mich ins Freie nicht gekämpft:
> Könnt' ich Magie von meinem Pfad entfernen,
> Die Zaubersprüche ganz und gar verlernen,
> Stünd' ich, Natur, vor dir ein Mann allein,
> Da wär's der Mühe wert, ein Mensch zu sein!

do not indicate Faust's attempt to free himself from the bonds of magic so much as his surfeit with the 'inhuman living and working conditions of capitalism'. Similarly the reasons for Goethe's Italian journey were not those advanced by bourgeois historians—for example, the critical stage reached in the relationship with Frau von Stein, or an overwhelming desire to see the locale of so much of classical antiquity—but primarily a sense of disappointment at having failed to make the Duchy of Weimar into a truly enlightened state and to align it against that bugbear of

---

[1] G. von Lukács, *Goethe und seine Zeit* (Berlin, 1950), p. 339.

Marxist historians, the Prussia of Frederick the Great. It is no exaggeration to say that Goethe is here considered as forerunner of Marx and Engels, and even of Lenin and Stalin: for, as the 'more than thirty years of Socialist practice in the Soviet Union prove, every man now "stands on free soil among a free people", [because] the Great October [Revolution] has chased Mephistopheles with his magic off the stage of history'.[1]

Although Lukács shares with Hildebrandt and other Nazi scholars a certain turgidity of expression, he differs from them both in the value of his findings and in the method by which he arrives at them. The above interpretation of Goethe's 'message' is in essence no more than a reiteration of statements originally advanced by Engels and Mehring. Its grotesque character must not be allowed to obscure Lukács's accomplishment in disposing of the notion, so reassuringly presented by the bulk of liberal scholars from Scherer to Gundolf, that Goethe had been quite unconcerned with what went on around him politically, or perhaps even been a *laudator temporis acti*. The truth is that we have much evidence that Goethe considered that his time was out of joint, but very little to suggest that he ever felt that he was born to set it right. What he did advocate, of course, was not the Marxist State but a social order to whose demands men would submit voluntarily and even proudly, because their rulers would ask of them nothing that was incompatible with their own dignity as individuals; this dignity, in turn, was not a free gift but an endowment of which every member of society had to show himself worthy by constantly working to perfect his talents. It must also be granted that Lukács's non-political comments are often profound and valid, as in the observation that Goethe, in availing himself of any traditional literary form, has always re-created that form in using it: for all their differences, Shakespeare's dramas are variants of a basic dramatic type, while Goethe has re-created the genre in every work from *Götz* to *Faust*.

However, Lukács is primarily an expert practitioner of the Marxist method of re-adapting the past to the changing ideological demands of the present. The Nazis, in one gigantic act of cosmetic surgery, had drawn up their private version of the literary past by subjecting certain established authors merely to

[1] G. von Lukács, op. cit., 363.

discreet face-lifting (Schiller, Hölderlin). Others, like Lessing and Hauptmann, had to be remade rather more stringently, and a third group seems to have escaped the knife altogether (Nietzsche, Jünger, George). Once operated upon, however, the patients were subjected to little if any further treatment, and those who had survived (among them, the amputated Goethe) were left to recover as best they could. The practitioners of Marxist literary surgery, on the other hand, are forced to perform a never-ending series of minor operations. The dialectic nature of their belief, their high average level of technical knowledge, and the great flexibility of their modes of thought make them far more concerned than the Nazis had been with their predecessors in Goethe biography and exegesis. Marxist literary scholarship accordingly abounds in ghoulish discussions of the work of long-deceased scholars: not only of those who had helped draw the bourgeois image of Goethe, but even of fellow Marxists whom death or deviationist depravity had kept from bringing their views up-to-date. This is characteristic of Marx and Engels themselves, who had sharpened their wits not so much on Goethe as on the opinions which Pustkuchen, Grün, Lassalle, and others had expressed on him; it likewise applies to S. Lublinski, F. Mehring, and as recent a practitioner as P. Rilla. The argumentative strain in their scholarship, and indeed the whole sorry spectacle of Goethe in the tug-of-war of contemporary politics, came to a head on the occasion of the Bicentennial of 1949, where, in marked contrast to the almost studiously 'neutral' celebrations of 1932, it became clear that 'all the participants [could and did] claim him as their champion; he was at once the progenitor of Marxism, the apostle of Western Humanism, and a shining example of the "Real", the "Other", or the "Good" Germany'.[1]

When the philosopher Karl Jaspers said that we find in Goethe 'solace and encouragement, but no relief from the burden we must carry', he gave one possible answer to another question which was much discussed in the years after 1945: what meaning can Goethe still have to us? The question was suggested by the experience of existential anxiety suffered by a people who

---

[1] C. P. Magill, 'Goethe Literature in England', *Publications of the English Goethe Society*, new series, xx, 1951, p. 166.

had lived through the worst war in history and a barrage of propaganda from the most diverse sources, as well as the destruction of their economic and political structure of life, the relativization of public and private morals, and an almost total disillusionment with the traditions of the past. To the German people, among whose traditions had also been a habit of 'stepping up to Goethe with any and all of life's problems, and asking what he thought... of them',[1] the question of how the poet would have reacted to the conditions of life in the mid-twentieth century (and, conversely, what revelance his hypothetical answer would have for us) outweighed in emotional immediacy all other Goethe problems. It was asked by scholars, and among other things led to a renewed interest in Goethe's connexion with an earlier period of eschatological anguish, the Baroque. It was asked by men and women to whom Goethe had hitherto been but a name and who now wondered, in the rubble-strewn streets of German cities, whether life held any promise for them at all. It was in this terminal situation, for example, that an anonymous young woman came to admire Goethe and draw comfort from him, simply because one of her teachers, realizing that 'a large part of our generation had gone out to seek the grail not as result of their schooling or aesthetic development, but [driven by] the miseries of our national life and daily existence', had emphasized in his lectures 'all those junctures in Goethe's life ... where he had like no one else experienced, and overcome, the human condition as threatened in its very existence and shaken to its very roots'.[2] The question was also asked by those who had been on the other side, by men who had tried to hold on to reason, and life itself, in the concentration camps, during the grim winter of 1944–5 when corpses were stacked like cordwood outside the barracks. It was then that two men began to wonder how Goethe would have fared if he, too, had been a prisoner of the Nazis. He would have been very prominent among the inmates, they concluded, and 'in dealing with the SS, very courteous and diplomatic, but in such a manner that we [i.e. his fellow prisoners] would have no reason to object. And he would, of course, have received special permission to let his hair grow.'[3]

[1] G. Radbruch, 'Wilhelm Meisters sozialistische Sendung' (in *Gestalten und Gedanken*, 2nd ed., Leipzig, 1948).

[2] W. Stutz, *Goethe in unserem Leben* (Willsbach, 1947), p. 149.

[3] N. Rost, *Goethe in Dachau* (Berlin, 1948), p. 180.

Many similar comments could be culled from the pages of recent and contemporary German books. They all express an impatience—more than that: an indifference bordering on surfeit—with the traditional views of Goethe, whether these stressed the great poet or the divinatory scientist, the young Prometheus or the old Olympian, the minister or the thinker, the favourite of Fortune or the frustrated reformer. Common to them is also a surfeit with all attempts to postulate aesthetic or literary lines of communication between the Germany of Goethe's time and that of the present; Jaspers's contention, that Goethe is in some ways closer to Homer than to us, turns up in many modifications.[1] The point of departure of many such private and public examinations of Goethe in the spirit of existentialist lostness-in-life is a curiously paradoxical one: a belief that the poet is infinitely far removed from us because he represents all that we are not, and very close to us at the same time because he stands for so much of what we once were and would again like to be. ('The poet' should perhaps be amended to read 'the wise old man—who could so well express what he felt because he happened to be a poet—whose faith in the future was not lessened by war, revolution, the destruction of an old order of society, and the loss of wife and son'.) This outlook on Goethe was shared by many Germans who claim no literary or philosophical competence, and it would be pretentious if we were to construct from its varied expressions any general definition of what Goethe means to the contemporary German in terms of a guide through life. It is, however, instructive to enter for a moment into the thought of a man who has weighed this question as earnestly as anyone. In his speech of acceptance of the Goethe Prize of the City of Frankfurt, Jaspers urged his audience to realize that they must look at the poet from the other bank, across the chasm of anxiety through which they had passed and through which Kierkegaard insisted we must all pass on the road to God and the real life. The fact that we have left Goethe behind on the other bank constitutes his greatest limitation for us, along with his attitude to women (which Jaspers

---

[1] K. Jaspers, *Unsere Zukunft und Goethe* (Zürich, 1948), p. 15. H. E. Holthusen asked outright whether 'the word of a poet who among other things was also the greatest representative of the bourgeois era [can] still strike a responsive chord in us' ('Goethe als Dichter der Schöpfung', in *Der unbehauste Mensch* [München, 1951], p. 198).

characterizes as irresponsibly selfish) and his views on experimental science (which Goethe abhorred because he feared the creation of a technology abstracted from natural man, without, in Jaspers's view, admitting its inevitability and our obligation to learn to live with it). The traditional objections raised against the poet disappear on closer examination: he was assuredly no fawning servant of the high and mighty, no self-satisfied *bon vivant*, no arch-conservative. His denial of the tragic basis of existence, however, is the more regrettable because it proceeded not from ignorance but from circumspect avoidance, and from his willingness to 'venerate calmly the inscrutable' instead of endeavouring to break through the limits of human cognition and experience. What remains, then, is a Goethe who still represents a standard of human values, who can teach us to forgo illusions and speculations about the future and to concentrate on the essential.

It is quite possible that Jaspers himself was taken aback by the storm of protest evoked by this address, which was soon countered with far more optimistic appraisals of Goethe's meaning for our age, by E. R. Curtius and many others. At any rate he modified his views somewhat in a later essay, *Goethes Menschlichkeit*, in which he discovered an exemplary quality in Goethe's constant dissatisfaction with himself and his propensity for losing, seeking, and remaking his personality. While reiterating his conviction that we are 'infinitely far removed from his age', Jaspers praised Goethe's stress on activity: not uncontrolled exertion like Faust's, whose undertakings fail without exception, but purposeful action accompanied by reflection and rewarded by positive consequences. With this revised evaluation, Jaspers arrived at a position very close to that of some writers whose views have here been examined.

In the field of methodology rather than interpretation, the greatest advance in the Goethe research of the recent past lies in the introduction and perfection of literary morphology. According to Goethe himself, who did not invent the term but first gave it wide currency in his scientific writing, morphology as such is 'the investigation of the *Gestalt*, formation, and metamorphosis of organic bodies'.[1] Unable to make much of issues or

---

[1] 'Betrachtung über Morphologie überhaupt', in *Vorarbeiten zu einer Physiologie der Pflanzen* (*Gedenkausgabe*, xvii. 115).

concepts which he could not transpose in his mind into organic forms, Goethe postulated his idea of *Gestalt* ('pattern' or 'shape', as modified below) to underline his aprioristic conviction of the unity of all living things. His entire scientific work was devoted to the search for such a law (or such laws) which determine the elements that make up the *Gestalt*, not only genetic, but structural and functional, of any given phenomenon. His concept of *Gestalt* is an expression of the inner law of all things, of the basic type which embraces all possible types. Much like the Platonic 'idea', this law is both visible, in the 'type', and an ideal postulate. In characteristic fashion Goethe arrived at this concept not by speculation but inductively, by minute observation of natural objects in osteology, mineralogy, meteorology, and other fields.

In transplanting this procedure from Goethe's very individualistic phenomenology of Nature to fields other than biology, the morphologists have endeavoured to follow the poet in tracing those basic forms of a given phenomenon which can be taken as laws. With the exception of such pioneers as Dilthey and Wundt, the literary scholars were rather late in doing so. Quite apart from the psychological term *Gestalt* or its sociological applications, which had been outlined by von Ehrenfels as early as 1890, L. Frobenius had drawn up a system of cultural and anthropological morphology in his *Paideuma* (1921). At about the same time Spengler finished *Der Untergang des Abendlandes*, an 'Outline of a Morphology of World History' where civilizations are considered as individualized social units which show well-defined similarities and parallelisms in the structure of their development. In saying 'I owe the philosophy of this book to Goethe's philosophical views', Spengler was one of the first to acknowledge Goethe's parentage of modern morphology.[1] Somewhat later W. Troll published Goethe's morphological writings in a separate edition, and since then F. Weinhandl, E. Spranger, G. Müller, H. Pyritz, as well as many others have proceeded, with varying success, to experiment with literary adaptations of the morphological approach. In their attempts to determine the particular *Gestalt* of literary works they have simply

[1] O. Spengler, *Der Untergang des Abendlandes* (48–52nd ed., München, 1923, 2 vols.), i. 67, and elsewhere. Spengler's adaptation of the Goethean method has not gone unchallenged: J. Bab (*Goethe und der Aufgang des Abendlandes*, 1928), Thomas Mann (*Über die Lehre Spenglers*, 1924), and others have expressly denied his right to claim Goethe, even implicitly, as authority for his own dismal visions.

applied Goethe's views on the investigation of natural phenomena:

> When we observe natural objects, especially living beings, to the
> degree of wanting to gain an insight into the context of their essence
> and function, we think we can best acquire such knowledge by
> dividing [the whole] into [its] component parts. . . . Yet these
> endeavours to subdivide further and further also have some dis-
> advantages. To be sure, what is living is divided into its elements; but
> we cannot put it together again from these, and make it live again.
> . . . Hence the urge, present in scientific man in all periods, to
> understand living structures as such, to grasp their outward visible
> and tangible parts in their context, to view them as indications of
> what is inside, and thus, as it were, to master the entire unit by
> observing it. There is, surely, no need to dwell in detail on the very
> close connexion between this scientific urge and the artistic and
> imaginative drive. . . . The German has a word for the complex of
> the existence of a concrete phenomenon: *Gestalt*.[1]

From the viewpoint of non-biological morphology, the
pivotal sentences are the first and the penultimate: the concept
of *Gestalt* as primarily a living structure, and the implied existence of one set of laws for natural and man-made or artistic
objects. In practice this has meant that the literary morphologist
has been less interested in the finished product than in its genetic
structure. He has been concerned not with the biographical connotations of its genesis which so fascinated the positivist, but with
the latent, dynamic connexion both between individual segments: word sequence, imagery, sequence of paragraphs, &c.,
and between each part and the entire work. (The concept of the
parts as determined by their relationship to the whole is, of
course, a basic one in the idea of *Gestalt*, in psychology and other
fields as well as in literature.) The method is particularly rewarding in dealing with autobiographies, which are by definition characterized by an intimate connexion between author and
work. Thus another morphologist, H. Oppel, has shown that
Goethe was bound, by the law of his inner structure, to describe
Frankfurt as he did in the beginning of *Dichtung und Wahrheit*.
It is the consistency with which he followed that law which
makes his account of his native city more convincing than the

---

[1] 'Die Absicht eingeleitet' (*Gedenkausgabe*, loc. cit., 13).

many similar descriptions left by other autobiographers, who, in imitating Goethe, violated their own *Gestalt*.

In helping us grasp the essence of a work of art, morphology comes close to accounting for the undefinable 'personal touch' inherent in all great art. Neither the enumeration of facts nor an impressionistic or aestheticist 'sympathy', nor yet the definition of the idea-content of a work explains how we just 'know' that this scene 'must be' by Shakespeare, and that movement by Beethoven. The individual elements of plot, motif, characterization, or orchestration do not tell us that; but the *Gestalt* of the whole work often will, if we but train our eye and ear to perceive it. For the present it is hard to tell where this line of investigation will lead. It is, however, safe to say that the concept of morphology represents the most recent if not necessarily the last major emanation of Goethe that has come to life for us. It is an extension of his scientific procedure which was glimpsed by Schiller, Carus, and a handful of other contemporaries; it has then lain dormant, except with some natural scientists, and was only recently rediscovered. Like the psychoanalytical approach, it is only beginning to be applied to literary research; unlike some practitioners of the former, its advocates are practically unanimous in insisting that it can at best form an aid for the solution of critical and exegetic questions. It resembles the psychoanalytical approach also in that it tends to suspend the system of valuation—historical, aesthetic, moralistic, or other—which has been built up in the past: if all individual works are variations of a basic theme conditioned by the *Gestalt* of an author, then the fact that some are good and others bad is almost immaterial. In the long run, the most promising feature of this procedure may turn out to be its universalist tendency, because it is based on the postulation of laws which transcend the gulf between 'Geistes-' and 'Naturwissenschaften'. Ever since it became clear that the universe is composed of more than indivisible particles or atoms, the physical sciences, too, have begun to lean heavily on the concept of *Gestalt* (as opposed, or complementary, to matter).

These and several other viewpoints from which Goethe has been examined in recent years have found a reflection in some contemporary biographies. One of these is an outstanding recapitulation of the advances made since the History of Ideas era, while two others have opened up new ground and may eventually bring about a thorough revision of the Goethe image. Karl Viëtor's _Goethe_ (1949) is a splendid account of the poet's work and personality which conscientiously avoids one-sided judgements, especially in regard to those aspects of Goethe which tend to be exaggerated in the heat of present-day literary and political discussion. Those, for example, who like to underscore their despairing views about the future of Western civilization with quotations from Goethe, will find in the final section of the book many statements which would seem to bear out their contention that Goethe, too, was beset by forebodings of doom. Those of more faith, like Viëtor himself, will find in the same chapter a great many expressions of the poet's belief in the future of Mankind.[1] Viëtor has incorporated into this work the results of a life-long concern with Goethe, and supports his opinions with documentation which is not only thorough but often taken from other sources than the standard references found in biographies.

Barker Fairley's _A Study of Goethe_ (1947, German version 1953), on the other hand, is a highly original reinterpretation of the poet's growth to maturity. Fairley believes that past biographers have, on the whole, 'been so much more at pains to bring out the range and many-sidedness of his genius, his so-called universality, than to arrive at the specific character of the man . . . that they have robbed him of his character and made him hollow and unreal, an inflated Goethe, reminding us of the bogus elephant that the poodle turned into before Faust finished exorcising it'.[2] The point is well taken. No doubt we do tend to consider Goethe's early tribulations as mere by-products of youthful exuberance in a man who—as he himself believed in retrospect, and made us believe in _Dichtung und Wahrheit_—knew his characterological and creative endowment and the destination to which it would lead him. No doubt his biographers have been too inclined to read into the unfolding of his life an inappropriate _post hoc, ergo propter hoc_. They have disregarded his near-identification with the storm-tossed Werther, which is assiduously empha-

---

[1] Another recent biographer, E. Staiger, is even more anxious than Viëtor to refute any possible identification of his view of Goethe with the 'mythical, depth-psychological, sociological, existentialist Goethe images' which are currently being established (_Goethe_, Zürich and Freiburg, 1952–9, 3 vols.), i. 7.

[2] p. 262.

sized by Fairley in favour of such rational interpretations of his life as that which he himself provided in the famous letter to Lavater of September 1780, where he likened the structure of his existence to that of a well-planned Tower of Babel. Fairley's special contention, however, is that Goethe's 'specific character' in his youth was marked by a painful disproportion between a highly developed imagination and slowly maturing reasoning powers. The key to the young man's inner nature is his volatility or 'sudden incalculableness', which the biographer has nicely traced in such manifestations as the chameleon-*motif* in the early writings. Goethe's abnormal slowness in maturing as a person has led Fairley to emphasize the poet's growth at the expense of the maturity of later years; in this respect, his book complements that of an earlier author who also aimed at an 'inner biography', H. S. Chamberlain (who, however, had seen in Goethe only the finished personality). Another novel accentuation, if not a regular discovery, lies in Fairley's description of the static character of the relationship with Frau von Stein, which in fact seems to have kept Goethe in a state of suspended animation from which he broke loose, or recovered, only with the trip to Italy. It was only at that time, when he was approaching his fortieth year, that Goethe became one personality after so long being divided into a poetic and a scientific half.

In his general outlook on the subject, Fairley stands half-way between the overwhelming majority of German biographers and a scholar whose work shall be the last one here considered: Heinrich Meyer. His *Goethe. Das Leben im Werk* (1951) bids fair to usher in a new type of biography. From Carus to Kühnemann many great biographers have entered the inner sanctum of Goethe research in a spirit of monastic unconcern for the realities of their own times. They have been inclined, in Fairley's phrase, to 'carry him off by himself' and to turn him into another Homunculus, a disembodied spirit roving about the realms of abstract thought. In their search for the higher meaning of his every idea and action, they have arrived at a number of interpretations which are often valid and sometimes brilliant, but almost invariably incomplete because they interpose between Goethe and us a kind of soundproof wall which effectively cuts off the noise of the market-place. Perhaps an example or two will bear this out.

It is with some astonishment that we read, in Meyer's work, that Goethe was a shade over 5 ft. 9 in. tall (according to his passport), that he was slightly shortsighted, and that his rather stubby, working-man's hands were just right for a man who liked to 'putter around' at home, gardening, looking after his collections, examining rocks, glueing albums. We read this with astonishment because we have not seen Goethe's hands so described before: as the Queen of Spain has no legs, Goethe, in most accounts, has no hands. He does, to be sure, have eyes, and his biographers have been unanimous in pronouncing them— on good evidence, to be sure—'magnificent', or 'superb', or 'glorious'. That they were also shortsighted is a detail that is usually left out; an unfortunate omission, it would seem, because Goethe's notorious dislike of glasses, microscopes, and other such aids may well have had two reasons: not only a reluctance to pry open the secrets of Nature with the aid of mechanical devices, but the well-known scorn with which shortsighted men regard glasses. It is with astonishment that we read in Fairley's book, on a somewhat higher but no less vital level, that this poet, among whose time-honoured epithets had been that of *Kinderfreund* or child-lover, was in reality 'not especially well qualified by experience to write about children. At no time in his life did he live in daily contact with them, though in earlier years he liked to play with them occasionally and ... remained fond of them in his rather tutorial way.'[1] It is with astonishment also that we gather from Meyer's work that this poet whom Chamberlain and countless others had depicted as, among other things, the epitome of a 'jolly good fellow', was actually devoid of a sense of humour, often incapable of anticipating even the most predictable human reactions (for example, in expecting Frau von Stein to countenance if not bless the affair with Christiane), and annoyingly fond of lecturing those he considered his intellectual inferiors (e.g. his sister Cornelia). Lest it be thought that these evaluations are necessarily of a negative nature, we might add another statement, of a literary rather than characterological nature, in which Fairley gives a classic and, one is tempted to believe, final definition of what sets Goethe apart from all other authors:

The difference between Goethe's writings and those of most other

[1] *A Study of Goethe*, p. 50.

men of letters, using the word broadly to cover all who use the literary medium, is that wherever we touch him, in a lyric, or an epigram, or a novel, or a drama, or an essay, or a review, or a scientific monograph, or even in a letter, we cannot, unless we are indifferent to him, leave it at that, but are gradually, insensibly, involved, led on, started on a journey; and the journey, we find, though not a day's or a year's journey, but rather that of a lifetime, always points or leads to the common centre of experience in his mind and person, from which the whole of his immense production seems to radiate. It is this reference to a centre which gives Goethe's works their peculiar, their specifically Goethean, character.[1]

One reads these and many similar sentences with astonishment and surprise because they deal with such basic aspects of Goethe from physical appearance to literary significance, that one wonders why more than a century had to elapse before they were written down. After all, none of these details detract one iota from Goethe's stature as a poet and even as a man. The great men of history are seldom distinguished by such traits as a sense of humour or an overpowering love of little children, and the thought that Leonardo da Vinci, Milton, or Napoleon should have been so endowed is little less than ludicrous.

Another decade or two will have to pass before this outline of a Goethe resurrected for our time can supersede the stereotype images of the past. Yet it may be well to hazard, in conclusion, a reasonable estimate of some of the salient features of the Goethe biography, and image, of the future. It seems clear that the days are gone when any evaluation of Goethe could be motivated by a feeling of kinship with him, such as the conviction which still animated authors like Gundolf and Kühnemann: that no matter how imperfectly and unworthily, we, his posterity, still walk in his steps and dream his dreams. The Goethe biographies to come will probably be actuated by considerations not of kinship but of contrast. They will spring from a desire to keep him before our eyes as part of 'the store of lost and forgotten, but still viable possibilities of existence',[2] or from the realization that we are 'no longer capable of facing up to Goethe's word',[3] or even from impatience that Goethe did not advance as far on the

[1] Ibid. 164. [2] E. Staiger, op. cit. i. 7.
[3] H. E. Holthusen, op. cit., p. 197.

road toward socialism or technocracy or whatever as we have meanwhile done. Many of his works, although not necessarily the same ones in every case, will inevitably fall by the wayside: not so much regarded as of slight value, as certain ones always have been regarded, but dismissed as outlived and meaningless in all but an antiquarian sense. Statements to this effect may be circumspect, like Viëtor's remark that the once so admired metric form of *Hermann und Dorothea* seems freakish in our day and age, or outspoken like Meyer's observation that it is 'quite impossible' that everyone can find *Iphigenie* and *Tasso* as wonderful as they say, and that *Werther* strikes young Americans as ridiculous. Irreverent or not, such judgements will continue to be passed even on works as central as the above, which may remain alive for the modern reader because they express an ideal that lives in many of us, but not because they are by Goethe.

Nor can there be much doubt that the Goethe we will continue to read, and read about in the biographies of the future, will be the nervous poet who was 'exposed' to life and in the end survived against all the odds of a fragile personality and an indifferent environment. This Goethe, however, is not only truer and more meaningful than the Olympian once was; he is also much more difficult to draw. There will be no more neat divisions between poet and minister, youth and old man, life and works. Meyer knew this when he announced in his foreword that he intended to describe Goethe's life 'in as complicated a fashion as it was lived', and then proceeded to make use in his work of the most recent techniques of cultural anthropology, depth psychology, comparative morphology, and half a dozen other tools of contemporary literary research.

'The majority of Goethe biographies in existence', Ortega y Gasset once observed, 'have been written by university professors, and some of them—let it be noticed that I say *some*—know very little of life, because their own life is likely to be an academic one and the academic life is almost no life at all: it is an aseptic life.'[1] Be that as it may, we have seen that too many biographies have been written by men (not necessarily professors; many were clergymen and writers) who have considered their subject within a frame of reference restricted to Goethe alone. In this

[1] 'Concerning a Bicentennial Goethe', in *Goethe and the Modern Age* (Chicago, 1949), p. 356.

respect, also, some recent works have taken new roads, and it is
amusing as well as instructive to see how one author in a few
words illustrates the distance which separates Goethe's vision of
Greece as the home of the καλὸν καὶ ἀγαθὸν from our own concept of that civilization: Goethe, it seems, had shared Winckelmann's

romantic notion that the Greeks were noble figures of classical
antiquity, gifted with a marvellous feeling for art and an admiration of
eternal, timeless beauty. They appeared ideal not because they were
so, but because he wanted them that way and therefore idealized
them. [He] failed to recognize in their mannered marble statues—
for which one would nowadays find prettier models on any beach,
but which seemed incomparable in the period before sports became a
part of life—a glorification of the spectator-sporting instincts of the
Athenian rich, who were able to bring about a shortlived decadent
flowering of the arts by engaging in their aristocratic and occasionally
pederastic cult of youth and thus providing work for sculptors and
brass-founders. Instead, [he] imagined the Greeks as so many Phid-
iases and Platos, or at least as marble statues come to life, replete with
'noble simplicity and quiet grandeur'. Goethe laboured under this
illusion all his life, and thus helped establish it as part and parcel of
German education and misinformation.[1]

Harsh words, perhaps, to be said in a characterization of
Iphigenie; but fruitful words because they deal with the play in a
modern frame of reference: from Marx, Nietzsche, and Freud
to the sports stadium and the beach. And that, for better or worse,
is the world we live in.
  It is not by accident that these sentences, which so coolly
dismiss two centuries of German infatuation with Greece, were
written by an author who resides outside Germany. For a
number of reasons—the establishment of a true world literature
in Goethe's sense, the break with the past which is so acutely felt
in Germany, the growing internationalization of all cultural life,
last but not least the universal appeal which Goethe exerts even
(and especially) now—the development of a characteristically
'German' image of Goethe has come to an end. This became
clear in 1949 when the Goethe Celebrations in Aspen, Colorado,
as well as those in Paris and London, far outshone in the stature
of guest speakers and the originality of scholarly offerings the

[1] H. Meyer, *Goethe. Das Leben im Werk* (Hamburg, 1949), pp. 322–3.

festivities held in Frankfurt and Weimar. With this process, perhaps the most recent which has achieved a sufficiently clear outline to be included in this brief account, Goethe seems to have attained, some 125 years after his death, the final and most exclusive quality of a great classical writer: from now on he seems destined to be homeless as well as timeless, no more restricted to Germany than Homer is to Greece or Shakespeare to England.

INDEX

A. GOETHE'S WORKS AND GOETHE EDITIONS

B. PERSONS AND SUBJECTS